Economic Networks

Economy and Society

Markets, Patrik Aspers
Economy and State, Nina Bandelj and Elizabeth Sowers
Money and Credit, Bruce G. Carruthers and Laura Ariovich
Global Capitalism, Miguel A. Centeno and Joseph Nathan Cohen
Institutions and the Economy, Francesco Duina
Economic Networks, David Knoke

Economic Networks

David Knoke

polity

First published in 2012 by Polity Press

Polity Press
65 Bridge Street
Cambridge CB2 1UR, UK

Polity Press
350 Main Street
Malden, MA 02148, USA

ISBN-13: 978-0-7456-4997-9
ISBN-13: 978-0-7456-4998-6(pb)

A catalogue record for this book is available from the British Library.

Typeset in 11 on 13 pt Sabon
by Servis Filmsetting Ltd, Stockport, Cheshire
Printed and bound in Great Britain by the MPG Books Group

For further information on Polity, visit our website: www.politybooks.com

For Felix, grandson extraordinaire

> But the truth, even more, is that life is perpetually weaving fresh threads which link one individual and one event to another, and that these threads are crossed and recrossed, doubled and redoubled to thicken the web, so that between any slightest point of our past and all the others a rich network of memories gives us an almost infinite variety of communicating paths to choose from.
>
> Marcel Proust
> *Time Regained* (1927)

Contents

List of Figures

Preface

Economic network analysis grew almost exponentially over the past three decades, spurred by the revival of economic sociology and belated interest in networks by some mainstream economists. It benefited from general improvements in network data collection and methods for analyzing them. Most importantly, the quality of explanation and understanding of economic action as both cause and consequence of relations among social actors greatly advanced. This book assesses and interprets diverse economic behaviors from a network perspective. It blends theoretical explanations about structural relations among economic actors – persons and organizations – with empirical evidence from network research on domestic and international economies. Its central themes are: economic actions are embedded in, and are explained by, the social connections among actors; an actor's social capital consists of others' resources that can be accessed by the actor; and benefits and costs within economic systems are jointly determined and constrained by the network ties among participants.

The six chapters examine economic networks spanning levels of analysis from individuals, to teams and firms, to markets and interorganizational systems, to the global economy. I strive to explicate core network concepts, measures, and analysis methods in nontechnical terms. Several network diagrams convey visual insights into complex structural patterns. The primary audiences are undergraduate and graduate students taking courses in economic sociology, organizational studies, and social network analysis. The book draws heavily from my experiences in teaching those courses during the past quarter century at the University of Minnesota. I thank the many students from diverse disciplines who participated enthusiastically and contributed in numerous ways that helped me to become a better teacher and scholar. I also thank two anonymous reviewers, Jonathan Skerrett, and Lauren Mulholland at Polity for their invaluable assistance in bringing the project to fruition.

David Knoke
Minneapolis, Minnesota
January 18, 2012

1

Economics and Social Networks

On April 20, 2010, the Deepwater Horizon – a gigantic rig leased by BP plc to drill its exploratory Macondo Prospect oil well 50 miles off the coast of Louisiana – exploded, killing 11 workers and injuring 17 others before sinking a mile deep into the Gulf of Mexico. As much as five million gallons of oil spewed from the borehole before two relief wells plugged it four months later. The spill contaminated coastal marshes and beaches, killed untold numbers of birds and sea turtles, wreaked havoc on four state economies, and further eroded President Barack Obama's public support. Even before a presidential commission finished investigating the nation's worst environmental disaster, evidence quickly surfaced about a tangled web of incompetence, criminality, and collective delusions by BP and the regulatory agency charged with overseeing the oil and gas industry. The Bush Administration had allowed the industry to write its own regulatory rules, scrapped environmental impact reviews, and fast-tracked drilling permits. The Interior Department's Minerals Management Service (MMS) had a structural conflict of interest: it collected royalty payments from the very companies it was supposed to regulate. MMS let oil firms regulate themselves; for example, BP employees penciled in report forms for inspectors to trace over in ink and sign. In 2008, MMS granted BP, a corporation implicated in all major oil disasters beginning with the 1989 *Exxon Valdez* spill, an exemption from submitting an emergency plan for deepwater blowouts. Instead, BP submitted a "regional plan" to deal with general spills anywhere in the Gulf.

Despite the Obama Administration's reform rhetoric, business continued as usual under the new Interior Secretary, Ken Salazar, who failed to remove many long-serving MMS bureaucrats. Just two months after he took office, MMS approved BP's Deepwater Horizon well application, which consisted of boilerplate apparently copied from an Arctic drilling plan (it mentioned walruses and other cold-water sea mammals). The plan contained neither discussions of potential deepwater blowouts, nor any site-specific plans to respond to a spill (Dickinson 2010). BP cut many safety corners at Deepwater Horizon, most notoriously in deploying a blowout preventer without a remote-control trigger. When a series of human and technological errors culminated in the April explosion, BP had neither effective means to shut off the flow nor to mop up its impact.

Behind this farce turned tragedy lay a social network explanation, the cozy connections between regulatory agents and corporate employees that skirted ethics and violated laws. Just weeks before Deepwater Horizon exploded, the US Interior Department's Office of Inspector General completed a report on MMS corruption between 2005 and 2007. It found a flourishing culture of corruption and criminality. Employees watched porn, used coke and crystal meth, accepted gifts, travel, and sports tickets from oil and gas companies. "When agency staffers weren't joining industry employees for coke parties or trips to corporate ski chalets, they were having sex with oil-company officials" (Dickinson 2010). One MMS employee "conducted four inspections on drilling platforms when he was also negotiating a job with the drilling company" (Urbina 2010). Bureaucrats at the Lake Charles MMS office repeatedly went on hunting and fishing trips with employees of the Island Operating Company, whose Gulf drilling platforms they regulated. When investigators showed Lake Charles District Manager Larry Williamson photos of two inspectors at a 2005 Peach Bowl game tailgate party paid for by Island Operating, he explained:

> Obviously, we're all oil industry. We're all from the same part of the country. Almost all our inspectors have worked for oil companies out of these same platforms. They grew up in the same towns. Some

> of these people, they've been friends with all their life. They've been with these people since they were kids. They've hunted together. They fish together. They skeet shoot together ... They do this all the time. (Office of Inspector General 2010: 3)

A revolving-door phenomenon, also known as regulatory agency capture, emerged as early as the nineteenth century in the canal and railroad industries (Levine and Florence 1990). The failure of agencies to act on behalf of the public interest, but instead serving special interests, is prevalent in the federal and state governments. One common capture mechanism, exemplified by MMS negligence preceding the Gulf oil spill, is the web of interpersonal ties spun among personnel routinely flowing between agencies and corporations. Also relevant is "cognitive capture," a consensual taken-for-granted mindset emerging among people who share numerous formative experiences, which can blinker them to looming dangers and alternative solutions.

This introductory chapter provides brief and broad sketches of mainstream and heterodox economics, economic sociology, and social network theories that set the contexts for more detailed examinations of economic networks in subsequent chapters. Readers interested in learning more about broader debates within economics and economic sociology should consult the huge primary literatures of those disciplines. The Appendix lists sources for instruction, software programs, and datasets for further self-study. Economic networks operate at multiple levels of analysis, including individuals (consumers, employees), groups (households, work teams), organizations (firms, interest groups), and populations (industries, markets), as well as across these levels. An important goal for this book is to develop concepts and principles useful for understanding complex economic relations.

Mainstream and Alternative Economic Theories

This section summarizes the core assumptions and principles of mainstream economic theory and its application to actors and markets. A discipline's mainstream "consists of the ideas that are held by those individuals who are dominant in the leading academic institutions, organizations, and journals at any given time, especially the leading graduate research institutions. Mainstream economics consists of the ideas that the elite in the profession finds acceptable, where by 'elite' we mean the leading economists in the top graduate schools" (Colander et al. 2004: 490). After describing the neoclassical synthesis that dominates mainstream economics, I briefly review some critiques and describe some alternative theories proposed by heterodox economists seeking to diversify the dominant paradigm. These developments prepare the stage for the economic sociology and social network approaches discussed in subsequent sections.

Mainstream Economic Theory

The dominant paradigm of mainstream economists originated in the neoclassical theories of late nineteenth-century economists, who built on the ideas of such classical founders as Adam Smith, David Ricardo, and John Stuart Mill. Among the key contributions of neoclassical economists – including William Stanley Jevons, Carl Menger, Léon Walras, and Alfred Marshall – were general equilibrium, marginal analysis, and price theory. By the middle of the twentieth century, a neoclassical synthesis, combining neoclassical microeconomics with the macroeconomic approach of John Maynard Keynes, became the mainstream economic theory presently taught to generations of countless undergraduates in introductory economics courses. Mainstream economic theory encompasses decision making at both micro- (individuals, firms) and macro- (markets, industries, whole economies) levels of analysis to explain the production, exchange, and consumption of economic goods and services. Key components include rational actors, independence of decision making, and utility maximization. In simplified terms, the core assumptions of mainstream economic theory are:

- Economic actors – whether individuals, households, or firms – are rational; that is, their preferences among a set of two or more alternatives, such as purchases of goods and services or investments in production machinery, are logically consistent (follow a transitive ordering).

- In deciding which alternative to choose, individuals always try to maximize personal utility (benefit, satisfaction), within the constraint of a limited budget. Similarly, firms seek to maximize profits on the goods or services they produce and sell. Choices occur on the budget line not below it, although actors may spend more than their current incomes by borrowing or spending savings.
- Atomization, or methodological individualism, prevails in economic decisions. One actor's preferences and choices are not influenced by the behaviors of others and all pursue their self-interests.
- Decision making applies the law of diminishing marginal utility. Utility decreases with each incremental amount of a good, and the maximum utility for two alternative goods occurs at that point on an actor's budget line where the marginal utilities of both goods are equal.
- All economic actors possess perfect information: complete and up-to-date knowledge about the prices of all commodities and services available in an economy. Information is free, that is, available without cost in time or money (Knight 1985 [1921]: 76–9).
- Markets, consisting of sets of buyers and sellers who may exchange with one another, are perfectly competitive. Because buyers and sellers are numerous and small (control few resources), no individual's actions can influence market prices; thus, all actors are price-takers not price-makers.
- Price, the amount of money a buyer pays a seller for a specific good or service, is determined at market equilibrium by the intersection of demand and supply curves, which are aggregations across all buyers and sellers in a market. No quality of a good or service except its price is relevant to market exchanges. The demand–supply intersection also determines the aggregate quantity sold at the particular market price. The price mechanism enables exchanges to occur smoothly

and efficiently with minimal transaction costs (e.g., acquiring information; negotiating and haggling).

- The point where supply and demand curves intersect, and thereby determine market prices and quantities, may shift through diverse exogenous factors, such as population changes, wealth increases, government regulation and price supports, catastrophic weather. The capitalist market remains the most efficient mechanism for allocating private resources in a free economy. With few exceptions – e.g., instances of market failures, such as the underproduction of public goods (roads, harbors, national defense) – governments should not intervene in the market process.

Mainstream economic theory's simplifying assumptions enable modern economists to apply powerful deductive methods to its axioms, specify elegant systems of mathematical equations, and apply sophisticated statistical procedures to empirical data to generate precise predictions and forecasts about economic activity. Consequently, economists have become highly influential in shaping a wide range of public policies affecting individuals, families, firms, and industries. However, hosts of critics inside and outside the discipline raised doubts about the realism, validity, and accuracy of mainstream economic theory as both explanation of economic action and guide to policymakers.

Criticism and Rebuttal

A persistent criticism, voiced principally by economists themselves, is that the core assumptions of the neoclassical synthesis vastly oversimplify economic reality, and hence provide a shaky foundation on which to construct accurate theoretical explanations of empirical observations (e.g., Rappaport 1996). For example, Geoffrey Hodgson argued that mainstream theory "is steeped in the metaphors and presuppositions of classical physics," creating "an artificial world where time is reversible, where individuals are self-contained, atomistic units, and where both extreme complexity and chronic problems of information and knowledge are excluded. The idea of rational, maximizing actors interacting and reaching an equilibrium is modeled precisely in these mechanistic terms" (Hodgson 1992: 757). Similarly, Steve Keen (2001) cataloged numerous instances where mainstream theoretical premises are either inconsistent or lack empirical evidence. For example, Keen and Standish (2006) argued that Alfred Marshall's assumption that firms in a perfectly competitive industry do not react strategically to one another's actions is demonstrably false. "As a consequence, the Marshallian model of atomistic behavior leads to industry output being independent of the number of firms in it, in contradiction of standard neoclassical pedagogy and belief" (p. 82). Other critics complained that mainstream economists grew too reliant on simplifying assumptions because they permit tractable estimates of complex mathematical models.

Milton Friedman, in his famous 1953 essay, "The Methodology of Positive Economics," defended the epistemological bases of mainstream economic theory against the complaint of unrealism. Mainstream theory is an ideal type that isolates crucial features of a particular economic problem, and is not intended to be descriptively accurate. Whether businessmen really make their decisions by rationally calculating marginal costs and revenues, and seek to maximize utility in every economic transaction, is irrelevant. Instead, Friedman argued, the theory hypothesizes only that, over a wide range of economic situations, people and firms behave

> *as if* they were seeking rationally to maximize their expected returns (generally if misleadingly called "profits") and had full knowledge of the data needed to succeed in this attempt; *as if*, that is, they knew the relevant cost and demand functions, calculated marginal cost and marginal revenue from all actions open to them, and pushed each line of action to the point at which the relevant marginal cost and marginal revenue were equal. (Friedman 1970: 21–22)

The ultimate criterion for judging a theory's usefulness lies, not in the realism of its untestable assumptions, but in its simplicity in making precise predictions about observable economic phenomena of broad scope. Friedman concluded that mainstream theory makes demonstrably superior economic predictions, in comparison to alternative theories which all produce inferior predictions.

If predictive accuracy is the criterion for judging theory, then mainstream economic theory did a very poor job of anticipating and explaining recent speculative bubbles and busts, particularly the high-tech or dot.com bubble of 1998–2000 and the Global Financial Crisis of 2007–9. Mainstream finance economists proposed an efficient markets hypothesis: because stock prices and other financial assets reflect complete economic information, investors always have realistic expectations about future prices and hence will act rationally. Irrational beliefs and actions, such as betting on continually rising stock and housing prices, could never occur because financial markets are self-regulating, and, thus, require no interference or constraints by government. But, by excluding bankers and investment institutions from their simplified economic model, mainstream economists ignored the possibility that both lenders and consumers could lack complete information and might inaccurately assess the high risks of buying and selling the complex securitized mortgage bundles which inflated an enormous subprime-mortgage bubble. Mainstream economists "turned a blind eye to the limitations of human rationality that often lead to bubbles and busts; to the problems of institutions that run amok; to the imperfections of markets – especially financial markets – that can cause the economy's operating system to undergo sudden, unpredictable crashes; and to the dangers created when regulators don't believe in regulation" (Krugman 2009: 2). Chapter 5 examines the social relations that exacerbated the 2007–9 Global Financial Crisis.

Alternative Economic Theories

Challenges to mainstream economic theory arose throughout the discipline's development. Nonmainstream, or heterodox, theories make diverse assumptions that are incompatible with mainstream conceptualizations of economic actors and markets (Colander et al. 2004). In rough order of their historical emergence:

- An early alternative, grounded in the nineteenth-century writings of Karl Marx, was based on a labor theory of value rejected by mainstream economists. Marx adapted an assumption of classical economists, notably David Ricardo, that the value of a commodity is determined, not by its sales price at the market's supply and demand intersection, but by the "average socially necessary labor time" necessary to create it (Marx 1981: 375). Capitalists, as owners of the means of production, pay wages below the full labor value embedded in commodities produced by their employees. In extracting this surplus value, and thus exploiting workers by not fully compensating their labor, capitalists expropriate economic value in the form of rents, interest, and profits. Marx predicted that relentlessly competitive capitalist economies, increasingly reliant on technological innovations to increase labor productivity and capital accumulation, will push workers' wages toward subsistence levels while the long-term average rate of profit inexorably falls. The eventual outcome of steadily worsening economic crises will be a proletarian revolution abolishing the capitalist mode of production. Socialist economies will emerge to distribute wealth according to the full labor value embedded in commodities. Although that utopia seemed ever-more remote after the collapse of twentieth-century communism, contemporary Marxist economists continued to defend and refine Marx's labor value theory (e.g., Kliman 2007).
- The Austrian School flourished in Vienna from the late nineteenth into the early twentieth century, but its present-day adherents are spread across the world. Although some of its founders contributed to the neoclassical theory of marginal utility, the School split from the mainstream in rejecting statistical modeling and experiments as methodologies for testing economic hypotheses. Its preferred approach was logical deduction from axiomatic assumptions. For example, the opportunity costs of production factors and reservation demand define economic values; economic choice involves uncertainty rather than complete information; and markets should be analyzed from "a dynamic perspective, by defining

competition as a disequilibrium *process* rather than a *state of affair*" (Gloria-Palermo and Palermo 2005: 65). In early 1929, Friedrich Hayek applied Austrian business cycle theory to warn of a looming financial crisis – later known as the Great Depression – due to an unsustainable expansion of the money supply.

- The "old institutional economics" (OIE) – developed in the early twentieth century by Wesley Mitchell, Thorstein Veblen, Clarence Ayers, and John R. Commons – emphasized how social, political, legal, and financial institutions jointly shape economic markets. Institutions are systems of rules and regulations, including customs and habits, that facilitate and impede social actions. Laws, court decisions, collective bargaining agreements, governmental regulations, and ethical norms are all examples of institutions influencing economic transactions. Commons' economic institutionalism "provides a theoretical framework for an integration of the economic and social dimensions of human behaviour" (Kaufman 2007: 6). Commons accepted but modified some key neoclassical assumptions. For example, he qualified the utility-maximization principle by arguing that individuals' preferences are often interdependent and affected by emotions such as envy and status-seeking (Veblen's "conspicuous consumption"). The "new institutional economics" of the late twentieth century, rooted in Ronald Coase's transaction cost theory, is usually considered more compatible with mainstream economics than was the OIE.
- Evolutionary economics drew inspiration from Darwinian biological evolution to posit that economies, rather than functioning in the static general equilibrium of mainstream theory, experience dynamic structural transformations. Evolutionary economic theory assumes uncertainty, "cumulative causation, path-dependency, and irreversibility" (Hodgson 1992: 758). Evolutionary processes involve variation, selection, and retention or inheritance, with market competition as the primary environmental mechanism for choosing the fittest economic actors and institutions. Equivalent to genetic inheritance in

biological evolution is the organizational routine, a recurrent pattern of thought and action that enables a firm to gain competitive advantages over its rivals in the struggle for economic survival (Nelson and Winter 1982). Through innovation, organizational learning, and knowledge transfers, firms can acquire new routines that improve their chances for success. By fostering technological innovation, entrepreneurs launch "gales of creative destruction" that shake apart an old macroeconomic order and propel it in radically unpredictable directions (Schumpeter 1942). Economic evolution involves not gradual transformations but discontinuities similar to biologists' punctuated equilibria model: "What we are about to consider is that kind of change arising from within the system which so displaces its equilibrium point that the new one cannot be reached from the old one by infinitesimal steps. Add successively as many mail coaches as you please, you will never get a railway thereby" (Schumpeter 1934 [1912]: 64).

- Behavioral economics imported insights from psychological theories and empirical research on cognition and emotion to explain seemingly nonrational decisions by consumers, investors, firms, and other economic actors. Challenging the assumption that rational actors make utility-maximizing calculations based on complete information, behavioral economists argued that a more realistic decision-making assumption is bounded rationality (Simon 1957). Faced with limited time and incomplete information, people typically follow a satisficing strategy to choose actions perceived as achieving a satisfactory outcome, but not necessarily a maximal result. For example, rather than trying to maximize profits, firm managers aspire only to profit levels that will satisfy share owners and other stakeholders, so that management can pursue its own interests (Cyert and March 1963). Prospect theory (Kahneman and Tversky 1979) provided another empirically grounded, psychologically realistic alternative to the utility-maximization assumption. People who face choices among risky alternatives with large rewards, such as investments in financial markets, tend to be risk-averse, and thus give greater weight to potential

losses than to prospective gains when making decisions. In an amusing application of prospect theory, the risky choices by contestants in a high-stakes TV game show, "Deal or No Deal," were better explained by their previous experiences in playing the game than by expected utility theory (Post et al. 2008).
- Recent additions to the lengthening list of heterodox theories include complexity economics, game theory, ecological economics, computer modeling and simulation, feminist economics, and neuroeconomics (Colander et al. 2004). The only commonality among these diverse perspectives is rejection of the neoclassical synthesis within which the majority mainstream economists continue to work.

The preceding summaries of mainstream economic theory and its heterodox challengers reveal substantial disagreement and intellectual ferment. Some observers perceived unprecedented opportunities for alternative approaches to move from the discipline's periphery toward the center where transcendent syntheses might occur (Colander et al. 2004). Others saw mainstream economics as deeply entrenched and resistant to change (Hodgson 2007). With no fully integrated alternative theory to the neoclassical synthesis yet at hand, the prospects for the radical transformation of mainstream economics appear dim. "None of these is at present strong enough or complete enough to declare itself a contender for the title of 'the' economic theory of the 21st century" (Keen 2001).

A few economists grew more receptive over the past two decades to using network ideas and methods to explain economic behaviors. Some challenged mainstream economics to develop network theories and methods to improve understanding of global economic interdependencies and reduce the risks of catastrophic failures: "We need, therefore, an approach that stresses the systemic complexity of economic networks and that can be used to revise and extend established paradigms in economic theory" (Schweitzer et al. 2009: 422). Matthew Jackson was possibly the earliest and most persistent advocate, exploring stylized models of network stability and efficiency (Jackson and Wolinsky 1996), network evolution (Jackson and Watts 2002), and labor markets (Calvó-Armengol and Jackson 2007). His methodological tome, *Social and Economic Networks* (Jackson 2008), drew heavily from sociology, game theory, computer science, and physics to illustrate analytic techniques and exemplify substantive research. Adalbert Mayer (2009) argued that economists take a distinctive approach to modeling social networks that emphasizes the role of choices under constraints, for example, in educational attainment and matching workers to jobs. Nevertheless, Nobel laureate Kenneth Arrow succinctly expressed the prevailing skepticism of many mainstream economists: "Network theory has been imported into economics as a tool, although it may not be all that useful or needed" (Arrow 2009: 14). The economic sociology perspective discussed in the next section can best be seen as yet another challenger to mainstream economic orthodoxy.

The Economic Sociology Perspective

This section sketches a history of economic sociology and summarizes some core principles of the new economic sociology that emerged over the past three decades. This overview provides the context for a more detailed examination of social network perspectives on economic activity in the following section.

A Brief History

Although an economist, William Jevons, first used the term "economic sociology" (Jevons 1965 [1879]: xvi; see Swedberg 2003: 5), it was quickly appropriated by several founders of classical sociology – including Max Weber, Émile Durkheim, and Georg Simmel – for their investigations of the great eighteenth- and nineteenth-century transformations from agrarian to industrial society, typified as the transition from community (*Gemeinschaft*) to association (*Gesellschaft*). Weber's distinctly sociological understanding of the economy still provokes lively debate a century later, with some scholars viewing him as increasingly relevant today (e.g., Swedberg 1998; Parsons 2006), while others are skeptical that he truly transcended neoclassical conceptualizations of rationality and utility maximization (e.g., Peukert 2004). Ironically, Weber never held a professorship in sociology, but was an economics professor in the 1890s at Freiberg and Heidelberg universities before mental problems forced him to become a private scholar. However, he briefly headed a new institute of sociology at the University of Munich shortly before his death in 1920. Weber's typology of action, as applied to economic behavior, is explicated below among the core principles of contemporary economic sociology. Durkheim's main contribution to classical economic sociology, in *The Division of Labor in Society*, was a functionalist argument: strong collective consciousness norms are necessary to overcome tendencies toward economic anomie arising from the pursuit of self-interest in modern, highly differentiated societies. He advocated the creation of occupational corporations – associations of professions and crafts – where participants could thrive in "a warmth that quickens or gives fresh life to each individual, which makes him disposed to empathize, causing selfishness to melt away" (Durkheim 1984 [1893]: lii). Simmel, in *The Web of Group Affiliations* 1955 [1922], influenced the subsequent development of social network analysis through his investigations of dyadic and triadic forms of group structure (see chapter 3). Other contributors to classical economic sociology include heterodox economists Thorstein Veblen, Karl Marx, and Joseph Schumpeter, briefly discussed above, as well as Vilfredo Pareto who influenced the economic sociology of Talcott Parsons.

After its classical flowering, economic sociology experienced two notable developmental phases. Between the 1930s and 1960s, Parsons developed his general structural-functionalist "action theory" of society involving four subsystems, one of which is the adaptive subsystem or economy (A), which interchanges with the political (G), integrative (I), and cultural-motivational (L) subsystems to achieve overall societal development and coordination (Parsons 1951). In *Economy and Society* (1956), Parsons and Neil Smelser further developed the AGIL framework, theorized about the generalized media of exchange between each subsystem, and appealed for economists and sociologists to collaborate on a grand socioeconomic theoretical synthesis. Obviously, their call to action was ignored by both disciplines. In its most recent phase, beginning in the 1980s in the US, economic sociology revived through a convergence of neoinstitutionalism, cultural, and social network perspectives on economic phenomena (Convert and Heilbron 2007). Mark Granovetter's manifesto (1985) and later programmatic statements (1992, 2002, 2005a) challenged sociologists to supplant both the neoclassical synthesis in economics and the old economic sociology with a distinctively contemporary social action theory. Components for an ambitious imperialistic agenda include socially constructed economic institutions, economic action embedded in social relations, and integration of culture and economics. The next subsection explicates core principles of the new economic sociology.

Core Principles

A serviceable definition of the new economic sociology is the use of sociological ideas to analyze economic phenomena: "the application of frames of reference, variables, and explanatory models of sociology to that complex of activities which is concerned with the production, distribution, exchange, and consumption of scarce goods and services" (Smelser and Swedberg 2005: 3). Economic sociology morphed into a "strange other" that is dissimilar to both sociology and economics (Finch 2007: 124). In contrast to mainstream economics, the discipline of sociology never had a dominant theoretical tradition comparable to the neoclassical synthesis. Absent any sociological mainstream, economic sociologists eclectically borrowed and freely adapted the principles, concepts, and theories of diverse specialties, including organization studies, political sociology, sociology of work, culture, historical-comparative research, and social network analysis. Economic sociology maintains affinities to several heterodox economics theories discussed above, especially Marxist economics, old institutional economics, and the Austrian School (Mikl-Horke 2008).

Among these heterogeneous roots, a few core elements of the new economic sociology may be discerned:

- Economic actors are more broadly conceptualized than the mainstream economics idea of rational, utility-maximizing individuals and firms transacting in atomized markets. Following Karl Polanyi (1957 [1944]), economic sociologists emphasized that both persons and firms are *embedded* within complex social, political, cultural, and economic contexts that shape their beliefs and behaviors. "Actors do not behave or decide as atoms outside a social context, nor do they adhere slavishly to a script written for them by the particular intersection of social categories that they happen to occupy. Their attempts at purposive action are instead embedded in concrete, ongoing systems of social relations" (Granovetter 1985: 487). Economic actors are connected to one another, by multiple types of direct and indirect ties, and those enduring relations enable them to influence one another's thoughts and actions. Prevailing societal norms can constrain the legitimacy and desirability of economic activities, such as religious prohibitions against lending money at interest. Economic decision making may involve collective actions to achieve common ends; for example, by consumers forming cooperatives, employees forming unions, and firms forming business associations to influence prices, wages, and profits. Although some economic sociologists proposed jettisoning the neoclassical synthesis altogether and replacing it with a uniquely socioeconomic approach (e.g., Etzioni 1988; Granovetter 1992), others acknowledged that mainstream economic theory provides fairly accurate explanations when its core assumptions approximately hold. Such conditions occur where markets comprise many small buyers and sellers that are incapable of price-making during exchanges involving products of indistinguishable quality. Commodities markets for agricultural products (corn, wheat, cattle) and metals (gold, copper, steel) may approximate the market model prescribed in the neoclassical synthesis. But, economic sociologists argued, such conditions are more exceptional than typical. In markets dominated by a few large producers, corporate market power offers a better explanation of economic transactions (a situation acknowledged in mainstream economics theories of monopoly and oligopoly). Other interest groups, such as consumers and unions, similarly use power to influence governments to intervene in the marketplace. Hence, much about economic life remains poorly explained by mainstream economics and requires a more comprehensive perspective that takes into account the social, political, and cultural contexts within which economic actors are embedded.

- Economic action takes diverse forms, beyond the utility-maximizing calculus assumed by mainstream economists. Perhaps the most famous framework was Max Weber's typology of social action, based on his interpretive method of analyzing "human behavior when and to the extent that the agent or agents see it as subjectively meaningful" (Weber 1978 [1922c]: 7). As summarized in *Economy and Society*, his four ideal types of social action, classified by primary modes of actor orientation, are: instrumental or goal-rational (*zweckrational*), value-rational (*wertrational*), affectual, and traditional (Weber 1947 [1922b]: 115–18). The first type corresponds to the utility-maximizing actor of mainstream economics because it involves "the actor's own rationally chosen ends" (p. 115) and "the end, the means, and the secondary results are all rationally taken into account and weighed" (p. 117). In contrast, the value-rational type involves the pursuit of an ultimate end or absolute value for its own sake; for example, religious, spiritual, ethical, or artistic goals. Affectual actions are emotionally based, "determined by the specific affects and states of feeling of the actor" (p. 115), such as love for family, friends, and country. Traditionally oriented actions are customary behaviors that emerge "through the habituation of long practice" (p. 115). Empirical actions often combine these analytic types, depending on the subjective meanings to the actors, and may also include nonrational behaviors to which actors attach no subjective meaning. In his renowned application of the typology to explain economic behavior, *The Protestant Ethic and the Spirit of Capitalism* (1930 [1904]), Weber argued that the goal-rationality motivating Western capitalism originated in various Protestant Reformation sects' value-rational orientations toward nonreligious work as a "calling" in the service of God.

- Economies are social subsystems with multifaceted relations to the larger societies in which they operate. Some economic sociologists embraced the AGIL structural-functionalist framework of Parsons and Smelser (1956). Marxists preferred a base-superstructure imagery: "The totality of these relations of production constitutes the economic structure of society, the real foundation, on which arises a legal and political superstructure, and to which correspond definite forms of consciousness" (Marx 1989 [1859]: 521). Regardless of the specific relationship between economy and society, most economic sociologists regarded them as mutually influencing one another's development. Rejecting the mainstream economic assumption of a static equilibrium, and agreeing with heterodox economists' views on economic evolution as described above, many sociologists adopted historical-comparative perspectives in which economies and their societies constantly change. Nineteenth-century capitalism radically differed from its twenty-first-century descendants, taking distinctive forms in Europe, North America, East Asia, and elsewhere (Groenewegen 1997). Contemporary transitions from communist command economies toward market-based economies took alternative paths in Russia, Eastern Europe, and China (Hsu 2005). And the development of a global economy ebbed and flowed dramatically over the last half-millennium (Wallerstein 1979).
- Economic sociology's eclectic branches are rooted in three main theoretical perspectives: neoinstitutionalism, culture, and social network analysis (Granovetter 1985; Swedberg 2003: 32–52). Although each perspective emphasizes different important influences on economic behavior, their common theme is that "economic action is always shaped by institutions rooted

in history and by the structures of social relationships in which economic actors are embedded; with the consequence that the former cannot be explained without including the latter in the explanation" (Ballarino and Regini 2007: 338). Institutions, cultures, and networks influence the preferences and decisions of economic actors in ways much more complex than assumed by mainstream economic theory. Or, as James Duesenberry, himself an economist, only half-jokingly put it, "Economics is all about how people make choices. Sociology is all about how they don't have any choices to make" (Duesenberry 1960: 233).

- Neoinstitutional theories in sociology and organization studies, like the old institutional economics discussed above, reject the rational-actor model at the heart of mainstream economics. Neoinstitutionalism examines systems of rules and regulations that influence social action, stressing "an interest in institutions as independent variables, a turn toward cognitive and cultural explanations, and an interest in properties of supraindividual units of analysis that cannot be reduced to aggregations or direct consequences of individuals' attributes or motives" (DiMaggio and Powell 1991: 8). W. Richard Scott's typology classified variations among institutional theories under three major pillars – regulative, normative, and cultural-cognitive – which differ in their assumptions and principal dimensions, such as the bases of compliance, order, and legitimacy (Scott 2001: 52). For example, the regulative pillar involves "informal mores or formal rules and laws" (p. 53), which rest ultimately on coercive power of governments but usually achieve normative compliance through legally sanctioned bases of legitimacy. Given the broad diversity among neoinstitutional theories, their applications to economic phenomena span every level of analysis: job searches, employment contracts, workplace regulations, management practices, markets, industries, organization fields, and international trade and development (for overviews, see Fourcade 2007; Krippner and Alvarez 2007).
- Cultural theorists followed Weber's interpretative lead in paying attention to the subjective meanings that actors attach

to social objects and actions. Meanings are socially constructed frames arising through interactions as actors seek to make collective sense of events. Routines, customs, and habits become taken-for-granted beliefs and practices in organizations, scripts to be enacted reflexively rather than questioned and challenged (Meyer and Rowan 1977). As noted in the preceding paragraph, the cognitive-cultural pillar is also a mainstay of neoinstitutional theories. Pierre Bourdieu contributed two important cultural concepts to economic sociology: *habitus*, defined as dispositions that organize the economic practices of daily life (Bourdieu 1979), and *cultural capital*, reflecting families' investments in developing their offsprings' cultivated personalities (Bourdieu 1986). Drawing from anthropological views of culture as the entire way of life of a people, some sociologists examined the impacts of national cultures on economic beliefs and behaviors; for example, divergences among European, American, and East Asian managerial practices (Guillén 1994). Others revealed how cultural beliefs shape economic transactions in disparate commodity and services markets, including contemporary art (Velthuis 2005), life insurance and personal intimacy (Zelizer 1994, 2005), corporate law (Uzzi and Lancaster 2004), blood and human organs (Healy 2006). Peter Levin argued that economic sociologists have treated culture both as a "constitutive element of markets and as an externalized variable that affects markets" (Levin 2008: 127). The challenge for researchers is to combine both aspects simultaneously in a multidimensional fashion.

- Social network theories, a major tributary to economic sociology, are the topic of the next section and, of course, examined throughout the book.

Economic sociology is far less formalized and mathematical compared to mainstream economics' emphasis on the rigorous quantification of economic transactions. Consequently, economic sociology theory is less capable of generating precise testable hypotheses. Its analysts are more disposed toward discursive historical-comparative, ethnographic, and thick narrative description of socioeconomic phenomena. However, as discussed next, social network analysis applies a quite rigorous methodology to examine structural patterns in economic relations.

The Social Network Perspective

Social network analysis is a multidisciplinary perspective in which structural relations among social actors are core explanatory concepts and principles. The web of ties among actors in a social system comprises the larger contexts that affect the perceptions, beliefs, attitudes, and actions of individuals and groups. Social influence and collective action may be both facilitated and constrained by direct and indirect transactions among actors possessing diverse resources, such as information, money, authority, and power. Network analysts view social actors as highly interdependent decision makers whose preferences and behaviors mutually influence one another to varying degrees through their network connections. By engaging in micro-level dyadic and triadic transactions, whether exchanging economic services or bodily fluids, actors collectively generate the macro-level sociospatial contexts within which all are embedded. In turn, these network structures may impede or assist subsequent transactions. Furthermore, network structures are themselves the result of dynamic processes, changing continuously over time as actors form new relations or drop old ties, enter or leave the system. Social network analysts seek to identify specific mechanisms through which social influence transpires and social structure evolves. Used in conjunction with neoinstitutionalism and resource dependence theories, network analysis reveals how rules and regulations gain acceptance and legitimacy within a population; how conformity to social norms is enforced and deviant behaviors penalized; and how information, ideas, and innovations diffuse or dissipate. In short, social network analysis captures the complex interactions that collectively constitute ongoing social systems.

In emphasizing relations among actors as basic units of analysis, social network theory diverges sharply from predominant substantialist explanations, which treat an actor's attitudes and attributes, such as gender and race, as the basic units. Many sociologists depict "individuals as self-propelling, self-subsistent entities that pursue internalized norms given in advance and fixed for the duration of the action sequence under investigation" (Emirbayer 1997: 284). Other sociologists take a "variable-centered approach" in which fixed entities with attribute variables cause outcomes that are also measured as attributes (or, as the Nowhere Man pithily put it in *Yellow Submarine*, "causes of causal causation"). Similarly, in mainstream economics and game theory, the self-interested rational actor chooses the alternative that maximizes personal utility, independently of any other actor's choices. Social network analysts reject such atomized, noncontextual approaches in favor of structural-relational explanations that take into account the embeddedness of actors and their actions in concrete connections.

A seminal application of network analysis in the new economic sociology was Harrison White's model of markets as multiple networks among firms. White and his colleagues had previously developed rigorous research methods for identifying social roles as jointly occupied, structurally equivalent positions within network relations, for example, friendships and antagonisms among novice monks in a seminary (Lorrain and White 1971; White et al. 1976). In an article published in 1981, and expanded to book-length treatment two decades later, White applied network analytic concepts to identify three critical market roles played by firms – supplier, producer, and purchaser. "Markets are self-producing social structures among specific cliques of firms and other actors who evolve roles from observations of each other's behavior" (White 1981: 518). Rather than reacting to customer demands as mainstream economics assumes, firms continually search for signals and clues about what their rivals are doing, specifically the quantity and quality of goods they produce. Collectively, a few large producers socially construct the structure of an industry, comprising a status-ranked quality order among firms interconnected by upstream and downstream exchanges of goods and services. Chapter 2 examines White's model in greater detail.

As Mark Granovetter (1985) remarked, regarding the importance of trust and order in the economy, social network concepts and methods are indispensable for operationalizing embeddedness, a core concept of economic sociology. Contrary to assertions that institutional arrangements or generalized morality mitigate opportunism, fraud, and social disorder, "the embeddedness argument stresses instead the role of concrete personal relations and structures (or 'networks') of such relations in generating trust and discouraging malfeasance" (p. 490). This claim also reflected Granovetter's prior research on the differential impacts of strong and weak ties on job candidates' chances of success when seeking information in the labor market (Granovetter 1973, 1982). In a programmatic statement, he identified four "core principles" by which social structures and social networks affect economic outcomes such as "hiring, price, productivity and innovation" (2005a: 33): (1) norms and network density; (2) the strength of weak ties; (3) the importance of structural holes; and (4) the interpenetration of economic and noneconomic action. These principles, and many others, receive extensive treatment in this book.

In addition to its theoretical formulations, social network analysis also encompasses many stunning techniques for visually representing networks of relations among actors by sets of lines and points. A psychotherapist, Jacob Moreno (1934), pioneered "sociograms" to display children's likes and dislikes of classmates as directed graphs. An anthropologist, John Barnes, is usually credited as the first researcher to apply the term "total network" to refer to depictions of "the whole of social life" as "a set of points some of which are joined by lines" (Barnes 1954: 43). Network analysts subsequently developed rigorous methods, based on the finite mathematics of matrices and relational algebra, to measure diverse network structural properties and identify social positions and role relations in multiple networks. Because this book emphasizes substantive analyses of economic networks, it cannot explicate formal network methods in depth. (For basic primers, see Knoke and Yang [2008] and Scott [2000]; for more advanced treatments, see Wasserman and Faust [1994] and Jackson [2008].)

However, where appropriate, I describe network measures and methods in accessible terms.

Summary and Outline of the Book

The first chapter summarizes the intellectual disciplines whose theories and empirical research contribute to an understanding of economic networks: mainstream and heterodox economics, economic sociology, and social network analysis. These diverse approaches provide numerous concepts and definitions, assumptions and principles, methodologies and measures, propositions and hypotheses with which to investigate and test ideas about the origins, development, structures, and consequences of economic relationships at multiple levels of analysis and across time and space. Familiarity with details of the contents of this bulging toolkit, accumulated over the past two centuries and into which analysts are busily cramming ever-more sophisticated instruments, is vital to making sense of the myriad interwoven networks suffusing economic life. My hope is that this book provides a roadmap for the puzzled novice networker.

The following five chapters offer an orientation toward key historical and contemporary social network analyses of economic action. Each chapter highlights major theoretical ideas and empirical research results, with morsels of methodology and visual examples. Chapter 2 scrutinizes theories and research on networked markets ranging from labor markets, to consumer purchases, and producer markets. Chapter 3 looks at networks among employees and executives inside work organizations. Chapter 4 examines interorganizational networks, while Chapter 5 explores transnational networks and networks in the Global Financial Crisis of 2007–9. Chapter 6 looks forward to new directions for further development of theory and research on economic networks. The exponential explosion of economic network analysis in recent years precludes in-depth coverage of all these topics. Fortunately, the large primary literature is readily available for interested readers to pursue on their own.

(25-415)

2

Markets and Networks

In Thomas Hardy's 1886 pessimistic novel set in rural England, *The Mayor of Casterbridge*, Donald Farfrae, a self-described "struggling hay-and-corn merchant" from Scotland, visits Lucetta Templeman, a wealthy heiress. Through a window, they observe the village's annual hiring fair where laborers seek farm jobs. They overhear a farmer from a distant county refusing to take an old shepherd unless his robust son is part of the bargain. But, the son is reluctant to go because he would have to leave behind the girl he loves.

> Lucetta's eyes, full of tears, met Farfrae's. His, too, to her surprise, were moist at the scene. "It is very hard," she said with strong feelings. "Lovers ought not to be parted like that! O, if I had my wish, I'd let people live and love at their pleasure!"
>
> "Maybe I can manage that they'll not be parted," said Farfrae. "I want a young carter; and perhaps I'll take the old man too – yes; he'll not be very expensive, and doubtless he will answer my pairrpose somehow."

Farfrae goes outside and hires both son and father. Lucetta praises his kindness and vows "that all my servants shall have lovers if they want them! Do make the same resolve!" Apparently thinking he may have acted rashly, Farfrae replies, "I must be a little stricter than that," and concludes, "I try to be civil to a'folk – no more!" This fictional incident shows how emotion and sentiment disrupt rational bargaining in the Casterbridge labor market. The hiring process is embedded in social ties that may override pure cost-benefit calculations, as exemplified by the farmer's offer. Economic network analysis clarifies the impact of diverse social relationships on market dynamics.

A market is a transaction system in which sets of buyers and sellers exchange money for a good or service. The actions by members of both sets comprising the market for a specific product – whether potatoes at a local farmers' market or derivatives in an international financial market – jointly determine its equilibrium price. As discussed in chapter 1, the neoclassical model of perfect competition assumes the absence of market power: buyers and sellers are too numerous and too small for individual actions to affect prices. Instead, the intersection of all participants' aggregate supply and demand curves determines both the quantities and prices that "clear the market." This market model further assumes that information about prices is quickly available to all participants at negligible cost, hence neither opportunism nor strategic manipulation are possible. Because previous transactional histories are unrelated to current price-setting exchanges, markets are atomized institutions in which the social, political, religious, cultural, and other connections among participants are irrelevant. Free markets form the ideological bedrock of modern capitalist economies: if producers and consumers can freely pursue their self-interests, without government interference or constraint, they will collectively choose the most efficient allocation of scarce resources, thus maximizing the utilities of individuals and society. In *The Wealth of Nations* (1937 [1776]), Adam Smith encapsulated this principle in his famous Invisible Hand metaphor of a capitalist who "intends only his own gain, and he is in this, as in many other cases, led by an invisible hand to promote an end which was no part of his intention. Nor is it always the worse for the society that it was not part of it. By pursuing his own interest he frequently promotes that of the society more effectually than when he really intends to promote it" (Book IV, Chapter II, paragraph IX). The self-regulatory dynamics of unfettered markets allegedly create the best of all possible economic worlds.

Economic sociologists and social network analysts reject this Candidean imagery in favor of socially embedded perspectives on markets. Economic exchanges are not isolated from other societal systems, but are continually shaped, impeded, and distorted by social relations linking market participants to diverse societal institutions. Constant intermixing of economic and noneconomic activity results in the "embeddedness of economic action in social networks, culture, politics and religion" (Granovetter 2005a: 35). Social norms, habits, and customs – created and reinforced within kinship groups, friendship cliques, cultural circles, ethnic communities, religious organizations, and political parties – may affect market transactions under a variety of conditions. In contrast to the neoclassical market's free flow of information among the atomized actors, the networked market model assumes differential communication relations among and between buyers and sellers.

The sociograms in figure 2.1 sketch these contrasting market images, with letters representing buyers (B) and sellers (S) and lines representing their direct communication ties. In a neoclassical market, the buyers are unconnected to one another, as are the sellers. All price information flows between each set, either by direct communication or through open media such as stock-exchange tickers or Websites. In a networked market, buyers and sellers can communicate among themselves, and not everyone is privy to the same price information. Information may be impacted, targeted, disrupted, distorted, blocked, or accessible only through selected channels at substantial cost. Sellers and buyers may collude and coordinate to gain market power advantages. They may form coalitions to undertake collective actions to raise or lower prices for self-interested, even corrupt, purposes that could be detrimental to the larger community's well-being. Brokers may emerge who find, assemble, and selectively disseminate data to privileged clients for a fee. Market behavior cannot be explained just by rational, utility-maximizing calculations of unconnected buyers and sellers, but must take into account diverse social structures and their attendant psychological motives, such as imitation, persuasion, altruism, even "irrational exuberance" and "animal spirits" (Keynes 1936; Akerlof and Shiller 2009).

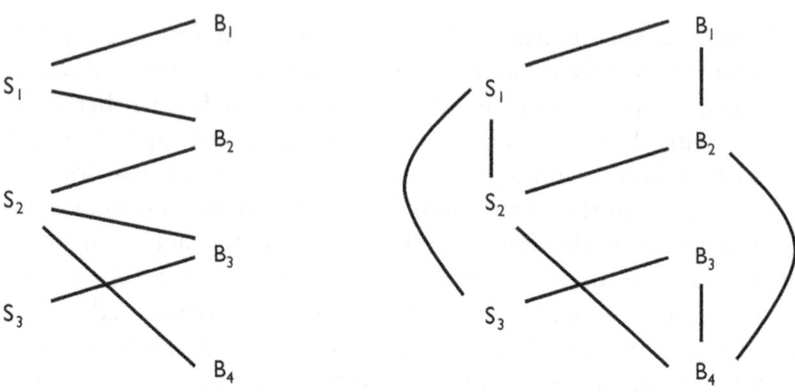

Figure 2.1 Neoclassical and networked markets

This chapter examines network structures and processes in three basic types of markets: labor, consumer, and production. A fundamental proposition on market networks is that the participants' demands for and supply of goods and services are influenced by their direct and indirect relations with one another and also by connections to social actors uninvolved in the market. Another pervasive theme is that the strength of ties among participants and nonparticipants vary in their consequences, with weak ties sometimes more valuable, while under other conditions strong ties can be more important.

Labor Markets

Along with capital and land, labor is one of three traditional inputs to economic production. A labor market is a market where workers (suppliers of labor services) compete for jobs and employers (demanders of labor) compete for employees. The price of labor is wage compensation, typically paid either as an hourly wage rate or as earnings in the form of a monthly or annual salary (piece rate is a rarer third form of payment). Compensation packages may include both direct monetary pay and nonwage ("fringe") benefits, such as housing, medical care, pensions, and keys to the executive washroom. In contrast to commodity markets, and despite Marx's critique of "labor commodification," the price of labor is not strictly determined by the equilibrium intersection of labor supply and demand curves. Unlike iron ore, cabbages, and widgets, additional workers cannot be mined, grown, or manufactured when employer demands for more labor increase. As biological and social beings, employees have limited hours that they're capable and willing to supply as more labor in exchange for higher compensation. As members of families and voluntary associations, they have distinct preferences for leisure activities versus additional income-generating work. When firms demand more labor, and hence offer higher pay, employees become less willing to supply additional labor (e.g., by working overtime). Instead, they prefer to substitute greater leisure for more work, a tradeoff labeled the "backward-bending labor supply curve" by mainstream economists. This relationship implies that workers' embeddedness in social networks and family norms shape their preferences about a suitable mixture of work and leisure activities.

For some purposes, labor markets could be treated as homogeneous; that is, all workers are assumed to have roughly equivalent skills and to compete for all job openings in the economy. In such undifferentiated labor markets, relations among workers and firms tend to be diffuse and random, carrying predominantly low-quality information about available job opportunities. However, for other analytic purposes, labor markets should be conceptualized as segmented, or differentiated, by types of labor supplied. Job-seekers possess real differences in skills and experiences that make them more or less valuable to certain employers. On the supply side, prospective employees who lack high-level "human capital" – measured by innate abilities, formal schooling, skills training, experience, and other credentials – are effectively barred from many professional, managerial, and crafts jobs. On the demand side, employers may stipulate minimum education or experience to be considered for jobs, such as high-school diplomas for janitors, even if those qualifications have little bearing on actual work performance. The numbers of workers in a specific labor market segment can be further restricted by institutionalized public policies regulating access, such as certification, licensing, or union bargaining agreements. Barbers and cosmetologists, for example, are required to graduate from a state-approved school and pass a state licensing examination. Discriminatory racial, ethnic, gender, or religious preferences and practices of employers can erect additional barriers to labor market entry. In complexly segmented labor markets, highly differentiated both by firm and employee characteristics, network relations should have greater impacts on the hiring process. Professional and crafts community networks tend to be smaller and socially structured, hence valuable employment information flows more quickly to better-connected job searchers.

The following two subsections examine network theory and research on the effects of interpersonal relations in labor markets. Specifically, they examine how the strength of network ties influences job searches in two societies: in the United States, where weak ties are often important, and in China, where strong ties are usually more valuable. These divergent results imply that network impacts are contingent, or conditional, on the cultural contexts of labor markets.

Finding a Job through Weak Ties

In a 1973 article that became a citation classic, Mark Granovetter introduced a conceptual conundrum, "The Strength of Weak Ties." A naïve belief about how social relations produce benefits is that people rely heavily on their kin and close friends to look out for their best interests by providing information, resources, and emotional support. In turn, the general reciprocity norm obligates a receiver to provide assistance of comparable value when needed. The resulting web of affiliations builds group cohesion, strong and enduring social bonds that enable small groups to survive and prosper. Granovetter's insight was to point out that, for some purposes, strong social ties could be less useful than weak-tie relations. He defined *tie strength* as "a (probably linear) combination of the amount of time, the emotional intensity, the intimacy (mutual confiding), and the reciprocal services which characterize the tie" (1973: 1361). Kin and close friends are instances of strong-tie relations, while acquaintances exemplify weak-tie connections. Granovetter argued that weak ties are superior for diffusing information and ideas if they serve as *local bridges* that bring socially distant people closer together, in the sense of fewer intermediaries between any pair (dyad). Strong ties seldom function as bridges because they typically create a tightly knit subgroup whose network consists of many direct ties and short path lengths (the smallest number of links that connect a dyad). Strong ties enable subgroup members to become intimately familiar with one another and quickly share information. However, members require longer paths to connect to people outside the subgroup, to whom they are linked mainly by weak ties. Yet, the main route for new information and ideas to diffuse into a strong-tie subgroup is across such weak-tie bridges. "The significance of weak ties, then, would be that those which are local bridges create more, and shorter, paths" (p. 1365). Granovetter's principle weak-tie proposition was that "whatever is to be diffused can reach a larger number of people, and traverse greater social distance (i.e., path length), when passed through weak ties rather than strong" (p. 1366). A major implication for labor market processes is that job-seekers who use their weak-tie connections will obtain better and timelier information about employment opportunities, and consequently should secure superior jobs compared to searchers who rely on their strong ties.

The sociogram in figure 2.2 illustrates these tie-strength principles using a stylized example of Ann, an engineer looking for another job after being laid off by her employer. Ann's egocentric network consists of her direct ties with four alters: three close friends from her former firm (Bob, Cora, Dee), whose strong ties are shown as solid lines; and an acquaintance (Erin), whom she met at an engineering conference, whose weak tie to Ann is shown as a dashed line. Although Ann's three close friends may be highly motivated to help her find a new job, they've probably already shared with her, and with one another, all relevant employment information that subgroup possesses. While Cora and Bob don't yet know one another, given they have two close friends

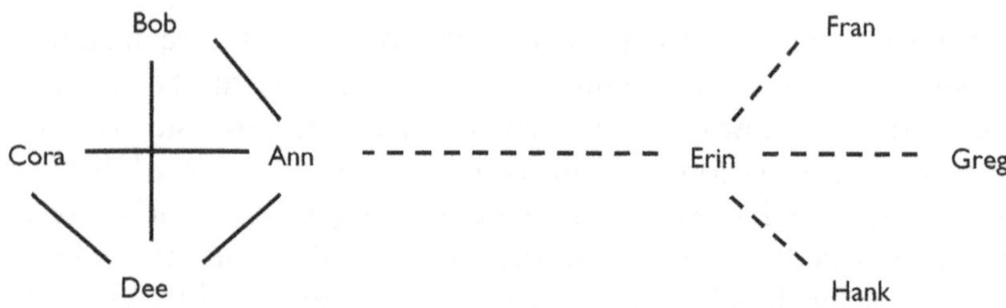

Figure 2.2 Ann's egocentric job search network

in common, they're soon likely to become friends, thus forming a four-person clique in which information is severely impacted. This clique will doubtless give Ann much emotional support, but its redundant knowledge seems unlikely to offer her any useful new intelligence about job vacancies. In contrast, Erin's egocentric network has four alters who are engineers, but none know one another and hence cannot directly share job information. Erin occupies the center of a hub-and-spokes, or star-shaped, egocentric network. Fran, Greg, and Hank presumably have access to diverse sources of job data through *their* egocentric ties (not shown). According to the strength-of-weak-ties argument, Ann's best employment opportunities should come across her weak-tie bridge to Erin, which is the only connection between the left and right sides of the sociogram. Erin could either pass information to Ann about job openings that she hears from her alters (a two-step path length), or she might broker new direct ties by introducing Ann to some of her alters. Erin's weak-tie alters are neither highly motivated to offer Ann emotional support nor to recommend her for a job, but they might casually pass along any knowledge they acquire about engineering openings at their own firms or elsewhere.

Among numerous examples of weak-tie dynamics, Granovetter (1973) cited his own labor market study, which he later expanded to book-length treatment (Granovetter 1974). He investigated how professional, technical and managerial job changers in a Boston suburb found jobs through bridging weak-tie contacts. He measured tie strength as "how often they *saw* the contact around the time he passed on job info to them," in other words, frequency of contact rather than emotional intimacy. He found that 83 percent of the job changers saw their contact only occasionally or rarely (less than twice a week); that the initial source of job information obtained through a contact traveled over a long path (62 percent of changers had one or more intermediaries between himself and the eventual employer); and that the contacts typically provided only information without attempting to influence the hiring decision. The job search results were consistent with Granovetter's weak-tie proposition that "those to whom we are weakly tied are likely to move in circles different from our own and will thus have access to information different from that which we receive" (1973: 1371). Not only are weak ties important at the level of individuals seeking new jobs, but they are vital generators of macro-level social cohesion for occupational communities:

> Especially within professional and technical specialties which are well defined and limited in size, this mobility sets up elaborate structures of bridging weak ties between the more coherent clusters that constitute operative networks in particular locations. Information and ideas thus flow more easily through the specialty, giving it some "sense of community," activated at meetings and conventions. Maintenance of weak ties may well be the most important consequence of such meetings. (Granovetter 1973: 1373)

The strength-of-weak-ties hypothesis yielded mixed empirical results across diverse substantive settings. Taking stock of a decade of investigations testing his argument, Granovetter concluded, "The results of these studies are very encouraging, but not conclusive" (1983: 228). Sociologists examined how an ego's *social capital*, the influential resources controlled by its alters, affected labor market outcomes. (See chapter 3 for more detail on social capital inside organizations.) For example, men in the Albany, New York, area were more likely to obtain higher-status jobs only when they could use weak ties, such as acquaintances or friends-of-friends, to connect themselves to people higher in the occupational structure (Lin et al. 1981). However, many men lacked upward status connections and thus were limited to strong ties of friends and relatives. Other analysts found no relation between network tie strength and wages after controlling for worker characteristics (Bridges and Villemez 1986; Marsden and Hurlbert 1988). A model of the status attainment process (Lai et al. 1998) differentiated between two types of social capital resources: network resources (alters' socioeconomic characteristics) and contact resources (socioeconomic characteristics of a successfully activated tie). Reanalysis of the Albany men found that both factors affected a job searcher's status outcome, with resource-rich networks operating through weak-tie connections to boost a man's contact resources, which in turn increased his chance of landing a high-status job. More recent research on job searches and hirings gave qualified support to the strength-of-weak-ties hypothesis for Scottish rural, small-town, and "peri-urban" labor markets (Lindsay et al. 2005); a post-Soviet Russian city (Yakubovich 2005); and in prosperous Canadian cities and stressed rural areas (Matthews et al. 2009). For example, rural Canadians, especially long-time inhabitants, used both weak and strong ties to find jobs, but city-dwellers more often relied on formal mechanisms such as help-wanted advertisements or recruitment agencies. Moreover, rural residents who used weak-tie paths obtained significantly lower incomes, possibly because rural labor markets are more constrained than urban markets and "rural networks tend to be smaller, denser, and contain more strong ties to family and longstanding friends than found in the cities" (Matthews et al. 2009: 309). Other sociologists cautioned that the apparent causal effect of alters' social capital on ego's labor market outcomes may be biased by *homophily*, the tendency of similar people to prefer one another as friends (Mouw 2006).

Labor economists also studied informal job search methods, such as referrals by friends and relatives (e.g., Holzer 1988), and increasingly incorporated social network indicators in their formal models of labor market processes and outcomes. An early economic model of job searches combined Granovetter's and Lin's hypotheses about informal weak- and strong-tie relations with formal search methods, such as newspaper ads and placement services (Montgomery 1992). "Individuals with large networks and/or a large proportion of weak ties in their networks will set relatively high reservation wages," that is, the minimum acceptable wages below which they reject job offers (p. 592). Other labor economists modeled how growing isolation from job networks explain high unemployment rates among African-Americans (Krauth 2004); how networks sustain racial differences in dropping out of the labor market and persistent income inequality (Calvó-Armengol and Jackson 2007); and how intergenerational occupational mobility is limited in poor neighborhoods where personal networks contain few skilled workers possessing information about scarce job opportunities (Anderberg and Andersson 2007). Elegant predictions were derived from highly stylized assumptions about job-seeker networks but seldom tested using empirical data.

Most theorizing and research on labor market networks emphasized the demand side (job-seekers' ties), but network processes are also highly relevant on the supply side of the equation (firm staffing practices). Employer recruitment strategies often involve formal mechanisms, such as Internet advertisements and job-placement agencies, that widely broadcast information about job openings which are, in principle, accessible to all potential employees (Marsden 1996). However, if employers rely heavily on informal networks to search for prospective applicants, such as requiring referrals from a current employee, they are less likely to reach diverse pools. Candidates who have limited access to social networks containing high-status contacts – racial minorities, low-income women, welfare recipients, and the long-term unemployed – are disadvantaged or excluded from superior labor market opportunities (Kmec 2007; Kmec and Trimble 2009). Jacobs and Cornwell (2007) combined a typology of organizational positions with Granovetter's network tie-strength hypothesis to model the conditions under which employers have incentives to use strong or weak ties to recruit employees. For example, when "stellar employee performances can help but serious harm is unlikely" (e.g., retail cashiers and custodians), organizations will use weak-tie connections to fill those positions (pp. 49–50). In contrast, if a poor job performance can be extremely destructive to an organization – accident-prone airline pilots and butter-fingered brain surgeons – firms have huge incentives to screen out unreliable candidates. In such circumstances, "strong ties are beneficial to employers due to their ability to generate information that is more accurate" (p. 52). Like other formal labor market network models, these hypotheses await empirical testing. The crucial theoretical insight is that the types of networks which firms use to recruit workers are contingent on the perceived risks of obtaining faulty information about job candidates.

Technological innovations enabling people to network across long physical distances are also altering how firms assess potential employees. Firms increasingly scan computer-based social networking sites – Facebook, Friendster, MySpace, Twitter, LinkedIn, Aardvark – to perform background checks on intern applicants and job candidates (Clark 2006). Popular peer-communication media proliferated on college campuses over the past decade, eventually spilling over into the work world. Many students network with their online friends by posting personal information and photos of risqué partying, underage drinking, and illegal drug use. Many seem oblivious or unconcerned that prospective employers can easily gain access to those images, although students who seek to portray a "hardworking" image are less likely to post inappropriate information than those trying to project a "sexually appealing, wild, or offensive" image to their peers (Peluchette and Karl 2010). Scattered evidence suggests that youthful indiscretions can haunt and harm college graduates when they enter the labor market. One nonrandom survey of managers and human resource personnel found that 35 percent had decided not to offer a job based on inappropriate content uncovered at a candidate's social networking site (Wortham 2009). A Microsoft survey of US, UK, French, and German hiring managers found that 79 percent had used the Internet to assess applicants and 70 percent had rejected job candidates based on online information (Goldberg 2010). Social networking data were so recent and evolving so rapidly that few researchers investigated them from a labor market perspective. In the meantime, students are well-advised to self-censor their online content and set high security barriers for accessing their pages.

Guanxi: Finding a Job through Strong Ties

A major consequence of China's transition from a centralized state command economy toward a market economy, starting in 1978, was a transformed labor market in which increasing numbers of private-sector firms competed against state-owned enterprises for workers. As Chinese and Western scholars conducted research on both traditional and transitional economies, they uncovered complex webs of *guanxi* flourishing in the job market. In dyadic form, *guanxi* refers to a strong-tie relation, involving trust and reciprocal obligations, through which one person can prevail on another to provide a favor or perform service. Blood-based *guanxi* relations include family members and distant relatives, while socially based relations arise at school, work, or neighborhood. Obligations to one's family or friends carry strong emotional and moral overtones, while failure to reciprocate risks the loss of face. More broadly, *guanxi* can also refer to networks of interpersonal ties through which people seek favors and intervene on behalf of others. Although using *guanxi* for economic purposes long predated the Chinese transitional economy, it grew increasingly important "as an appropriate response to the uncertainties posed by China's cumbersome bureaucracy" (Yi and Ellis 2000: 25). By relying on personal connections for information and influence in business affairs, *guanxi* networks can reduce transaction costs, mistrust, and deceitful opportunism in a society with an inadequately institutionalized legal system. To the extent it facilitated more efficient economic exchanges, *guanxi* enabled China to lubricate its transition to the market economy.

Guanxi networks are distinguished by "an emphasis on fulfilling role obligations rather than pursuing self-interest, a never-in-balance personal ledger of debits and credits rather than prompt repayment of outstanding debts, and the Confucian deterrent of shared shame, which contrasts with the Judeo-Christian concept of subjective guilt" (Yi and Ellis 2000: 25). *Guanxi* networks are sustained by perpetual disparities between favors given and obligations incurred among people with different hierarchical statuses. They "entail reciprocity, obligations, and indebtedness among actors, as well as the aesthetic protocol that comes from cultivating these relationships" (Vanhonacker 2004: 49). *Guanxi* networks bear some resemblance to the patronage, or clientelistic, systems prevalent in many Mediterranean, Eastern European, Latin American, and East Asian societies (Wank 1996). Clientelism flourishes in cultures with predominantly collectivist and hierarchical conceptions of social organization, such as Catholic or Confucian ethics. "Patron-client systems combine strong emotional, particularistic ties with simultaneous but unequal exchanges of different types of resources. ... Clients exchange personal loyalty, deference, and awe for the protection, understanding, and material benefits provided by their patrons" (Knoke 1990: 142). Long-term entourages and dependent cliques surrounding a patron are modeled after patriarchal clans and extended families. Kinship forms an inner hub, grounded in familial intimacy and trust. The spokes are friends and factotums who perform brokerage services with outsiders, manipulating others' resources for their own profit. The result is a hierarchical status structure created and sustained by exchanging favors and deference between higher and lower strata. Patron-client systems are susceptible to such corrupt practices as bribery, embezzlement, fraud, malfeasance, and discrimination. For example, in the Soviet Union, *blat* was the petty "use of personal networks and contacts to obtain goods and services in short supply and to skirt formal procedures" of the inefficient command economy (Ledeneva 2008: 120). After the collapse of the Soviet Union, Russian government officials colluded in the wholesale illegal transfer of public resources into the hands of private-sector oligarchs and criminal mafias, enriching those corrupt elements at the expense of the larger society's welfare. Although some analysts asserted that *guanxi* relations are inherently corrupt (e.g., Fan 2002), other researchers argued that they necessitate ethical conduct. Whereas Westerners tend to view using network connections for self-benefit as immoral, Chinese culture conceives of *guanxi* exchanges as incurring the obligation to reciprocate:

> As long as you eventually fulfill that obligation, you are considered ethical. It is the ethical dimension that sets a *guanxi* relationship

> apart from money-based or commodified transactions. *Guanxi* is not the same as corruption because *guanxi* is relation-focused whereas corruption is transaction-focused. And the relational ethic of *guanxi* implies that it cannot be bought. (Vanhonacker 2004: 50)

The precise mixture of high ethical standards and corrupt practices may be impossible to disentangle. Both academic research and business practitioner interest in the role of *guanxi* in the Chinese labor market has proliferated over the past two decades.

As strong-tie relations, *guanxi* networks shaped job searches and hirings in the Chinese labor market before and during the transition economy. Yanjie Bian (1997) investigated traditional institutions for assigning jobs in state-owned enterprises or collective work units, such as banking and manufacturing, during the initial phase of marketization (1980–92). Job-seekers did not use their *guanxi* connections to gather information about job openings in state firms, because they could not apply for those positions. The job-assigning authorities ("control agents") secretly and illegally gave jobs as favors to people who were directly or indirectly connected to them. Consequently, job-seekers tried to use their *guanxi* relations to contact and informally influence those agents. But, because few Chinese job-seekers had direct contacts with high-level authorities, "many must use indirect ties to gain influence" (Bian 1997: 367). In this early-reform institution, successful job searches required activating strong-tie bridges to connect a job-seeker to a control agent. Strong ties were indispensable to successful influence because a control agent would feel obligated to perform favors for someone with whom he or she had a strong *guanxi* connection. Furthermore, given the illegality of the transaction, both parties "must necessarily know and trust each other so as to eliminate concerns about potential risks," such as denial of employment opportunities and loss of official positions (p. 371). In a 1988 survey of Tianjin, China's third largest city, Bian found that 45 percent of the respondents obtained their first urban job through substantial assistance from an "ultimate helper" (i.e., control agent). About 55 percent found their ultimate helper through a direct tie, which consisted mainly of strong connections such as relatives and close friends. The 45 percent who found their helpers via indirect ties (through an intermediary) tended to use weaker ties, such as acquaintances and coworkers. Overall, job-seekers and ultimate helpers were indirectly connected through intermediaries to whom both had strong ties. Job-seekers who used indirect ties tended to obtain higher-status jobs than seekers who relied on direct ties. Contrary to Granovetter's weak-tie hypothesis, "strong ties prove to be necessary to bridge the Chinese *guanxi* networks used to obtain influence, because mutual third parties offer trust and obligation that ultimately connect job-seekers to job-control agents" (Bian 1997: 382). In a 1993 survey of Singapore, Bian and Ang (1997) again found that respondents obtained jobs through strong ties, and that job changers and ultimate helpers "tend to be bridged through intermediaries to whom both are strongly rather than weakly tied" (p. 981).

In later stages of China's transition economy, when expanding private-sector employment eclipsed the state-owned sector and the labor market grew increasingly meritocratic, the role of *guanxi* connections in finding a job changed. For example, in-depth interviews with 65 job searchers revealed that *guanxi* networks remained influential within the shrinking state-owned sector, particularly for highly desired and soft-skill jobs, and where job performance was difficult to measure and monitor (Huang 2008a). But, *guanxi* influence was undermined when a private-sector employer "adopts an open and standardized recruiting procedure to carry out its merit-based policy, and when such goals and procedures are safeguarded by hiring authorities with high professional integrity and commitment to procedural rationality" (p. 481; see also Huang 2008b). Other evidence pointed to a shifting locus of *guanxi* influence. A study of 150 Tianjin workers laid off from state-owned textile mills found that their eventual fates were contingent on the composition of their personal networks (Johnston and Alvarez 2008). Laid-off employees with a government administrator as a helper were more likely to be reemployed and to enjoy higher wages than were workers connected only to officials of state-owned enterprises. The researchers concluded that "officials in government agencies maintain their capacity to influence labor market outcomes by virtue of their increasing regulatory power, but officials in state-owned enterprises suffer a decline in their influence because their power has been curtailed with withering of the system of redistribution" (p. 492). Thus, during China's market transition, *guanxi* ties to influential government officials developed into economic assets, but ties to the impotent state-enterprise sector increasingly became liabilities.

The American and Chinese labor markets exhibit divergent personal network structures used to find jobs. In the US, job-seekers appear more likely to obtain useful information about job openings through their weak-tie and bridging connections, who typically have little interest in influencing the outcome of the hiring process. In China's labor market, especially in traditional state-owned enterprises, job-seekers more often rely on strong ties to forge connections to helpers who could influence firm hiring decisions. An intriguing question for future research is whether China, as it continues the transition toward a fully institutionalized market system embedded in the global economy, will experience convergence toward the American model or will the importance of *guanxi* networks persist?

Consumer Markets

Consumer markets are socioeconomic institutions where end-users (consumers) purchase goods and services. They contrast with production markets, considered in the next section, where businesses exchange intermediate goods and services for further use in production activities. Although manufacturing firms and governmental agencies buy numerous final-use products (e.g., letterhead stationery, lawn-mowing services), research on consumer markets primarily concentrates on the purchasing behaviors of individuals, families, and households. In contrast to voluminous theorizing and empirical research on labor markets, the social structure of consumer markets "has been largely ignored" (DiMaggio and Louch 1998: 619), and network analyses of consumer markets are even rarer. This section examines the network hypothesis that the structure of social relations among consumers influences their consumption behaviors. The following subsections examine three applications: the classic two-step flow of communication, the diffusion of innovative consumer products, and socially embedded consumption.

The Classic Two-Step Flow of Communication

Social network analysis of mass communication originated in research on the flow of information, opinions, and influence in election campaigns (Lazarsfeld et al. 1948; Katz and Lazarsfeld 1955). On the left in figure 2.3, an antecedent model conjectured that mass media (radio, newspapers, magazines, eventually television) directly broadcast information about political parties and the opinions of political elites to an atomized mass-public audience. People passively absorb it and decide individually for which candidates to vote. Finding substantial evidence of interpersonal influences on opinion-formation, Lazarsfeld, Katz and their colleagues proposed the alternative two-step flow of mass communications model, shown on the right in figure 2.3. In the first step, messages broadcast by the mass media reach a handful of opinion leaders (OL) in local communities, who then integrate and interpret what they read and hear. In the second step, these leaders disseminate their views to less-attentive and less-informed followers, the people who look to them for political guidance and influence. Thus, the two-step flow model implies that the egocentric networks of centrally positioned opinion leaders mediate between the macro-level of mass media organizations and the micro-level of individuals.

An obvious implication of the two-step model for political markets is that election and public education campaigns should identify and mobilize opinion leaders, those local activists who would persuade their friends and neighbors to support a candidate or policy. Peer opinion leaders can be identified, recruited, and trained to perform effectively in community-based health education and promotion activities; for example, programs to increase mammography screening, tobacco prevention in schools, and

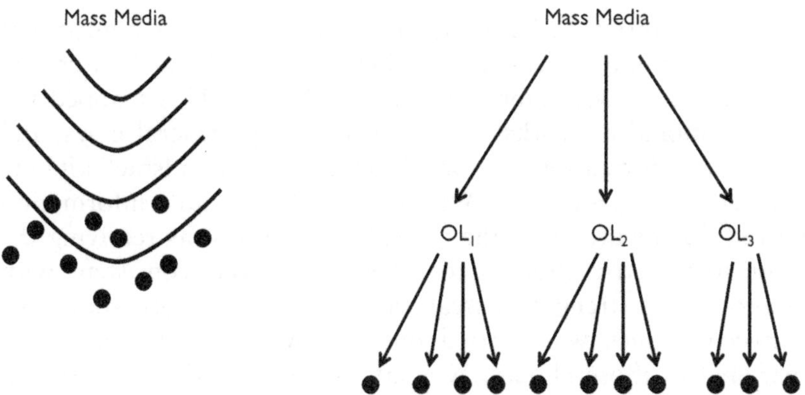

Figure 2.3 Broadcast and two-step flow models of opinion formation

HIV/STD risk reduction (Valente and Pumpuang 2007). An implication for consumer markets is that advertisers and marketers should target messages about goods and services toward opinion leaders, who will relay and validate those messages to their face-to-face contacts. Numerous research studies over the past half century generally supported the two-step model's implications about the social mediation of mass communication in political, public health, and consumer markets (Rogers and Shoemaker 1971). For example, a study of two Canadian social activity clubs showed that opinion leadership was positively correlated with centrality in friendship networks, and with a multi-item measure of consumer susceptibility to interpersonal influence (Lee et al. 2010). But, contrary to the hierarchical flow model, members in highly central positions were also the most susceptible to influence, possibly because "they have the responsibility of balancing their flow of influence from different parts of the network" (p. 75).

Some critics suggested two-step model refinements. Analysis of the 1968 presidential electorate disclosed more complex patterns of opinion-giving and opinion-receiving than posited in the classical model's downward hierarchical flow (Robinson 1976). Some voters' choices were directly influenced by mass media, especially by newspapers, while other interpersonal political discussions occurred without media influence. Other researchers argued that not only opinion leaders but marginal actors could mediate crucial information flows. Gabriel Weimann (1982, 1983) mapped the conversational networks – comprising gossip, general news, and consumer information – among 270 members of an Israeli kibbutz and identified 16 cliques. Within each clique, most information flowed downward from the central actors (persons receiving the most sociometric choices) to others. However, consistent with Granovetter's strength-of-weak-ties hypothesis, information flow between cliques was carried out mainly by actors who were marginal to those cliques. Weimann concluded that the original two-step model of vertical communication should be modified to include horizontal, "marginal-to-marginal" intergroup bridges:

> The findings highlight the potential of social network analysis as a bridge between micro-level interaction and macro-level patterns including diffusion of innovation, formation of public opinion and social solidarity. Weak ties serve as the crucial paths between groups, thus providing the means by which individual behavior and ideas, originating in small face-to-face groups, are routinized and agglomerated into large-scale patterns. (Weimann 1983: 245)

Ronald Burt (1999: 37) reached a different conclusion about social actors who carry information across boundaries between social groups: "They are not people at the top of things so much as people at the edge of things." He argued that the two-step flow of communication is actually a compound of two distinct network mechanisms: (1) "contagion by cohesion" via opinion leaders who bring new information into a group; and (2) "contagion by structural equivalence," which facilitates adoptions within the group. In Burt's perspective, opinion leaders are information brokers who closely resemble network entrepreneurs in social capital theory. Chapter 3 examines brokerage inside formal organizations.

The rise of new digital media and information technologies in the 1980s and 1990s – Internet, email, teleconferencing, Web-based social networking sites – stimulated rethinking by academic theorists about relationships between mass media and interpersonal communications. In contrast to older one-way mass communication channels carrying centrally produced content, the new media technologies fostered multi-way exchanges of locally produced information. Communication technologies and social structures were reframed as "mutually implicated and co-determining phenomena, and encouraged a turn to diffusion theories, social network analysis, and a networked, relational perspective on the communication process itself" (Lievrouw 2009: 315). Indeed, the Internet may have supplanted the classic two-step flow process as the go-to information source for many consumers. For example, a Kentucky survey asked 882 adults to mention three sources of information on genetic testing for inherited cancers. The overwhelming first choice was the Internet (46.5 percent), then healthcare opinion leaders (medical doctors; 18.4 percent) and family members (10.6 percent), while traditional mass media such as newspapers and TV accounted for just one percent (Case et al. 2004). Arguably, many Internet sources of information on genetic testing are neither reliable nor accessible to laypeople (p. 664). Research on online viral marketing (word-of-mouth) processes found that people with moderate-size personal networks were as likely as highly connected elites to disseminate consumer product information to their network alters, casting further doubt on the validity of the two-step flow model for new media (Smith et al. 2007). Future theory construction and research on consumer choices must take a multidimensional approach to identifying media and social network influences on opinion formation about consumer products.

Diffusion of Innovative Consumer Products

In the nineteenth century, French sociologist Gabriel Tarde (1969) proposed "laws of imitation" to explain how innovations diffuse among a population of potential adopters. Tarde argued that an invention involves the recombination of existing imitations; that acceptance or resistance depends on its compatibility with other imitations; and that diffusion is a stratified process, with social inferiors imitating their superiors. Bryce Ryan and Neal Gross (1943) conducted pioneering research on technological innovation diffusion, the adoption of hybrid seed corn by farmers in two Iowa counties. Anticipating the two-step model, they concluded that the adoption of an innovation depends on both interpersonal ties and exposure to mass communication. The rate of adoption over time followed an S-shaped curve, beginning with just a few early adopters, followed by accelerating numbers, then leveling off as a ceiling of saturation approaches. However, Ryan and Gross did not specify details of the interpersonal influence mechanisms. Research on the diffusion of a new antibiotic, tetracycline, among 125 physicians in four Illinois towns, collected data from pharmacy records about the dates of first prescriptions and from the doctors about their advice, discussion, and friendship networks (Coleman et al. 1957, 1966). The more sociometric choices a doctor received, the earlier he wrote his first prescription. But the three networks did not behave identically: "the networks of doctor-to-doctor contacts operated most powerfully in the first 5 months after the release of the new drug. . . . The discussion network and the advisor network showed most pair-simultaneity at the very beginning and then progressively declined. The friendship network . . . appears to reach its maximum effectiveness later" (Coleman et al. 1957: 266). Over the next half century, four reanalyses of the tetracycline data applied differing methodologies to draw conflicting conclusions about network and mass media effects (see the overview by Kilduff and Oh [2006], who called "for greater embeddedness of data in context"; p. 452).

Influenced by Tarde's ideas about imitation, Everett Rogers (1962) synthesized more than 500 empirical research projects on the diffusion of innovations to specify a stage typology. It classified adopters of new technologies or ideas according to their temporal position on a standardized normal distribution (bell-shaped curve). When the cumulative proportions in successive stages – innovators, early adopters, early majority, late majority, and laggards – are graphed, they produce the familiar S-shaped curve observed by Ryan and Gross and numerous others. Individuals proceed through a decision sequence (awareness, interest, evaluation, trial, and adoption), at each stage of which an innovation might be rejected or accepted. If enough people adopt an innovation (critical mass), the adoption becomes self-sustaining. Whether an innovation reaches sufficient critical mass depends both on intrinsic characteristics, such as its complexity and compatibility with existing innovations, and on social features, for example, whether high-status members adopt or resist it. Drawing from Rogers' stage typology, Frank Bass (1969) created a simple diffusion model, aggregated to the market level of analysis, which was widely used by marketing and management scientists to forecast the adoption of new consumer products and technologies and to compare the life cycles of specific products across countries. The Bass model uses time series data to estimate and extrapolate trends with just three parameters – market size (the ultimate number of adopters), innovation (the individual conversion rate absent any adopters' influence), and imitation (the effect of adopters on non-adopters). Notably absent from the equation are effects of social networks connecting adopters and imitators.

As a curve-fitting technique, the Bass model and similar prediction equations closely approximate the empirically observed S-shape curves for the cumulative adoption of numerous consumer products from their introduction until saturation (typically around 40–60 percent, but much lower for innovations failing to reach their potential customers). Historical examples include the telephone, radio, television, telex and fax, personal and laptop computers, VCRs and DVDs, video games, compact discs, cell phones, cable and Internet (Boswijk and Franses 2005). Economists identified a salient feature of several markets for high-tech products, particularly where devices enable customers to interact directly with one another, as *network effects* or *network externalities* (Katz and Shapiro 1985; DiMaggio and Cohen 2005). A network effect occurs when the utility of a product to a consumer increases if many consumers also use that product. Hence, a consumer's adoption decision partly depends on what she expects other consumers will do. The old joke about the first customer to buy a telephone, but had no one to call, illustrates a network effect. A challenging research question is "whether consumers only care about overall network size when choosing a product or whether they are more interested who is in a particular network" (Birke 2009: 789). Some researchers proposed network effects models that explicitly incorporate structural relations among consumers. For example, to simulate the frequent under-adoption of telecommunication services, investigators applied a small-world network model to examine two contrasting structures (Choi et al. 2010; for more about small worlds, see chapter 4). In random networks with many bridge-building activities, such as conferences and Internet chatrooms, initial diffusion is slow and innovations are likely to be under-adopted. However, "once the diffusion goes beyond critical mass, the diffusion tends to be precipitously accelerated with more random bridges" (p. 175). In a highly cliquish network, where all pairs of customers are likely to share acquaintances, "such an acceleration is almost absent . . ., thereby causing slower diffusion after the early stage." These divergent dynamics imply that firms should implement marketing strategies suitable to the network structures of their consumer markets.

Structural diffusion models hypothesize that local and global network properties influence adoption rates. For example, more centralized networks favor the rapid diffusion of nonrisky innovations but slow the adoption of innovations seen as risky or irrelevant (Valente 1995). Threshold models explain diffusion as a function of the number or proportion of others that an actor must see adopting an innovation before she will adopt (Granovetter and Soong 1983). Thomas Valente proposed a threshold diffusion model of how adopters influence nonadopter decisions, which could be measured at either the system level or the egocentric network level. His approach assumed that influence occurs by "behavioral contagion through direct network ties" (1996: 85), which he used to calculate exposure scores for individuals. Ego's adoption threshold is its exposure at the time-of-adoption, measured by composition of the egocentric network. Ego's degree of exposure varies over time with changes in the proportion of alters who adopt the innovation. To illustrate, figure 2.4 tracks the changes in the exposure of Doctor #20 from Peoria, a participant in the tetracycline diffusion study. His egocentric network consisted of five alter-physicians (two friends, two discussion partners, and one advice partner). At the first interval, no alters had prescribed the drug so Doctor #20's exposure was 0 percent. Over the next eight months, the number of adopting alters increased until his exposure was 100 percent at which time Doctor #20 wrote his first tetracycline prescription. Valente applied the threshold model to three datasets: adoption of tetracycline by Illinois doctors, hybrid corn by Brazilian farmers, and family planning methods by South Korean women. He examined the consistency between social system and personal network thresholds; extent of external influence; and opinion leadership, as measured by number of network nominations received. Persons adopting the innovation when their system and network exposures are similar were most likely to be opinion leaders. However, the diffusion patterns varied across systems, which Valente attributed to unique sources of external influence. The medical data supported a two-step flow mode "in which external influence [measured by medical journal subscriptions] leads to opinion leadership within phases of diffusion, but not across phases" (p. 83). For Brazilian farmers, cosmopolitan contact (frequent visits to nearby cities) strongly influenced early adoption of hybrid corn but was unrelated to opinion leadership. Korean women exhibited a classic two-step flow: the family planning media campaign influenced opinion leadership, which was associated with consistency between system network thresholds. The early family-planning adopters "were considered opinion leaders for the entire village, not just individuals who adopted in their same stage of diffusion" (p. 83).

Network centrality affects decisions to purchase consumer products and services. Faculty at a college of education who received numerous friendship nominations were the earlier adopters of a new computer-based photocopy request service (Durrington et al. 2000). But, at the systemic level, the innovation was considered a failure and the researchers speculated that high homophily within the faculty friendship networks may have acted as a barrier to diffusion. Another project investigated the diffusion of Kijkradio, a free online news program tool, among Dutch children at three public primary schools (Kunst and Kratzer 2007). Children who were more central in their school's friendship network logged

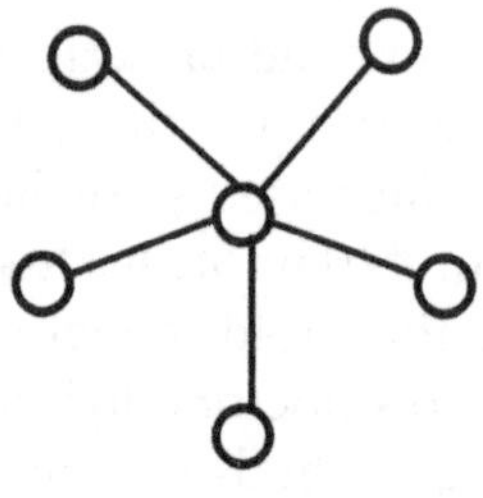

(a) Time 1, exposure 0%

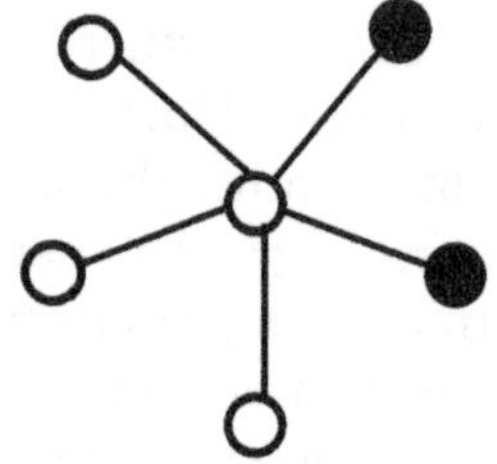

(b) Time 3, exposure 40%

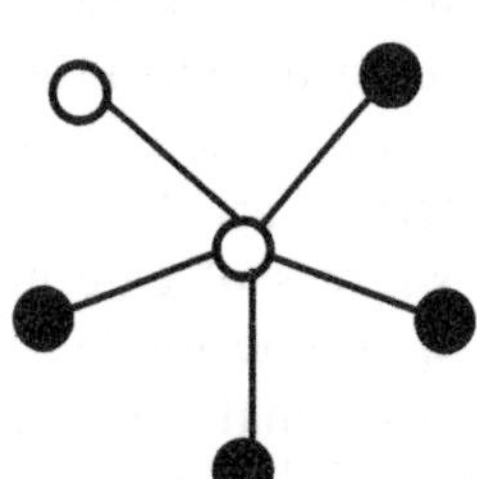

(c) Time 5, exposure 80%

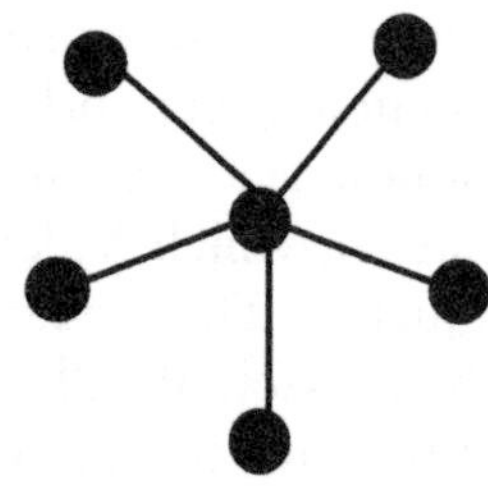

(d) Time 8, exposure 100%

Figure 2.4 Doctor #20's egocentric network exposure to a medical innovation

on more often to the Kijkradio Website. The results supported the hypothesis that "relatively safe and uncontroversial" innovations are more likely to diffuse through strong ties than via weak ties. However, the data offered no support for network threshold hypotheses that children who were either exposed to external influence (mass media campaigns) or involved in new product development activities (as Kijkradio testers, informants, and design partners) were more likely to adopt the innovation. A team of European marketing researchers used an agent-based model to simulate how different network structures affect innovation diffusion at both the market and individual consumer levels (Delre et al. 2010). Their model assumed network structures in which consumers make decisions according to personal preferences and "social influences play a determinative role" (p. 280).

When central actors (VIPs) have many connections to consumers, they increase an innovation's market penetration because they can "immediately spread information about a new product, but VIPs do not have particularly strong power of convincing consumers to adopt a new product." Advertising endorsements by celebrities like Oprah Winfrey, professional athletes, and movie stars raise the public awareness of new products, but high market penetration doesn't guarantee successful levels of adoption. Instead, relatives, friends, and neighbors have considerably stronger social influence on consumer decisions about whether to adopt.

Socially Embedded Consumption

Routine consumer purchases of goods and services – expenditures on food, clothing, furnishings, entertainment – seldom involve major innovative goods or services. Social embeddedness may explain some consumption choices. This subsection examines network approaches to analyzing product brands, conspicuous consumption, and purchases of large-ticket items such as automobiles and houses.

Consumer brands are distinctive names, images, and reputations for products and services intended to attract loyal (repeat-purchase) customers. Perhaps the most successful current brand is Apple, consistently ranked at or near the top of "social brand" surveys, which enjoys fierce customer loyalty to its iPhone, iPad, and iTunes brands (Morrissey 2010). Celebrity persons, such as athletes and entertainers, are also frequently branded. Firms supporting the Tiger Woods brand suffered an estimated $5–12 billion loss in shareholder value after revelations about his off-course sexual shenanigans (Knittel and Stango 2010). Advertising and marketing agents try to generate interpersonal "buzz," an exponentially increasing product awareness that attracts new customers while binding older ones more tightly to their favorite brands. Social relations influence both consumers' knowledge structures – positive and negative memories, feelings, and evaluations they associate with particular brands (Teichert and Schöntag

2010) – and their brand selections. Direct-selling organizations – such as Amway, Avon, Mary Kay, Tupperware, and stock brokerages – expect sales agents to exploit their relatives' and friends' feelings of obligations to buy the firm's products (Biggart 1989), but also to utilize weak-tie connections to expand their distributorships (Lan 2002).

In the Internet age, marketers develop and control their own virtual communities, online sites where consumers can create user-generated content – blogging, texting, chatting, tweeting, and emailing one another about company brands, thereby boosting sales for brand-connected products (Dholakia et al. 2004). The marketing exploitation of existing social networking services, such as Facebook and Twitter, is a twist on traditional word-of-mouth (WOM) campaigns that rely on interpersonal relations to disguise blatant corporate manipulation of consumer tastes and desires. Mobile communication networks, especially popular among adolescents and young adults, are fertile e-WOM terrain for brand promotion. A good illustration is Shintaro Okazaki's (2009) analysis of a mobile-based viral campaign that targeted Japanese male adolescents. To promote a hairstyling wax, the marketers first encouraged Tokyo teens to post images of their own hairstyles on a sweepstakes Website. Any contestant who tried the wax and then persuaded his friend to post a photo using his referral code, received an e-coupon for free music downloads. Post-campaign analyses revealed that, although "face-to-face WOM elicited stronger affective brand commitment and attitude toward the campaign than mobile-based WOM," when measured by the teens' willingness to make referrals, "mobile-based WOM may be persuasive even when adolescents are less interested in the campaign content" (p. 12). Future marketers will doubtless find clever and effective ways to leverage social networking technologies for their clients' advantages.

Prestige-seeking consumer behavior, popularly known as "conspicuous consumption," is economic activity embedded in hierarchical social relations. The ostentatious display of goods intended to impress others has been criticized for centuries on mainly moral grounds as waste and narcissism (Mason 1995). As mentioned in chapter 1, Thorstein Veblen, a founder of the old institutional economics, analyzed the norm of conspicuous consumption in his *Theory of the Leisure Class* (1899). The *nouveaux riche* of the nineteenth-century Gilded Age, who had accumulated enormous wealth from industrialization, were looked down upon by the upper class families whose ancestors traced back to the colonial era. By giving expensive presents and throwing lavish feasts and entertainments, the *arrivistes* sought to flaunt their wealth and to acquire reputations for moral superiority. Subsequently, conspicuous consumption encompassed any consumer product bought to symbolize a purchaser's high status, rather than to be enjoyed for its intrinsic value. This idea is captured by the popular saying, "Keeping up with the Joneses" – who might be next-door neighbors or even a brother-in-law.

Mainstream economics largely ignored Veblen's insights about social influences on consumer demand, with a few notable exceptions. James Duesenberry (1949) assumed that consumer preferences are interdependent, and proposed a "demonstration effect": independently of income or price changes, consumption expenditures would increase through social contacts with other consumers who buy high-quality goods. Hence, relative income drives consumer demand and savings, contrary to Milton Friedman's permanent-income hypothesis (for a history of this debate, see Mason 2000). In addition to Veblen's conspicuous consumption effect, Harvey Leibenstein (1950) discerned two contrasting types of consumer sensitivity to others' choices: (1) the bandwagon effect, where the probability that ego will purchase a product increases as more alters buy it; and (2) the snob effect, where ego's probability of purchase decreases as more alters buy it. Jumping onto passing bandwagons fuels fleeting fashions and fads for the hottest must-have gewgaws, from crazes over pet rocks to aromatherapy and six-sigma management. Bandwagons raise and lower hemlines, underpin speculative bubbles, and generate underground markets for counterfeit Rolexes and Louis Vuitton handbags. Snobby elites, desiring to distinguish themselves from the *hoi polloi*, search ceaselessly for rare items and obscure venues (social clubs, vacation spots) inaccessible to the envious emulative masses. Groucho Marx's quip – "I sent the club a wire stating: 'Please accept my resignation. I don't want to belong to any club that will accept people like me as a member'" – expresses the ultimate snob's aversion to rubbing shoulders with "the little people." The alternative social influences on consumer demand have been formally modeled by economic sociologists (Granovetter and Soong 1986) and economists (Corneo and Jeanne 1997), but none explicitly incorporated social network relations. Future research should investigate how network ties shape preferences and purchases of products that appeal to conspicuous consumers, bandwagon leapers, and snobs.

Paul DiMaggio and Hugh Louch (1998) took a substantial step toward a network theory of socially embedded consumption in their analysis of big-ticket purchases, such as new and used autos, houses, legal services, and maintenance services. Their theoretical framework distinguished two ways that actors might use their social relations to identify and assess potential transaction partners: (1) *search embeddedness*, using social ties to find partners with whom they have no direct or close social ties; or (2) *within-network exchange*, choosing people with whom they had prior noncommercial direct or indirect ties. Arguing that search embeddedness is a well-known strategy for finding potential sellers or assessing goods, DiMaggio and Louch concentrated on mechanisms for within-network exchanges. People might simply prefer to transact with others whom they know because of a generalized reciprocity principle, "characterized by a bias toward in-group exchange," such as buying products only from members of one's ethnic group. Alternatively, within-group exchange could reflect efforts to control others in vulnerable situations. Embedding transactions in pre-existing social relations is more likely if the risk of seller opportunism is higher, such as concealing information about a product's defects:

> Trading with friends or kin reduces risk by embedding transactions in sets of continuous, multipurpose relations. From the buyer's perspective, the seller's willingness to transact with a friend, relative, or compound tie [indirect relation] represents a "credible commit-

> ment" in which the seller's reputation and relations to other network members become hostages to the transaction. (DiMaggio and Louch 1998: 623)

Your close friend is much less likely than a used-car dealer to sell you a "lemon," for not only would it destroy your friendship, but her reputation as dishonest and untrustworthy would quickly spread through your shared social circles.

Drawing from transaction cost theory, DiMaggio and Louch generated four hypotheses where within-network exchanges are more likely for some kinds of consumer transactions than others. Social embeddedness theory predicts that, where uncertainty is high, and "the greater the risk that a transaction poses to consumers, the more likely are consumers to seek out sellers to whom they have preexisting social ties" (pp. 624–5). Risks are substantial for onetime transactions (e.g., selling a home), because sellers are not concerned about repeat business from the buyers, nor their commercial reputations. Therefore, the less that sellers rely on commercial reputation and repeat business, the more likely are within-network exchanges. Within-network transactions are most likely for home purchases, then for buying cars and legal and home-repair services, and least likely for routine furniture purchases.

DiMaggio and Louch tested their "embeddedness-as-control" thesis with data on five types of consumer transactions by 1,444 respondents in the 1996 General Social Survey. Questions asked about use of social connections when purchasing cars in the previous five years, legal or home-repair services in the past 10 years, or ever buying a house. Respondents also reported preferences for within-network exchanges when selling bedroom furniture, a car, or a home, and willingness to reveal whether a car they were selling had "a history of transmission problems" (i.e., concealing a lemon). Almost one-half of the used car purchases from individuals and the home purchases without an agent involved transactions between relatives, friends, or acquaintances. Lower percentages were socially linked to purchases of legal and home-maintenance services. DiMaggio and Louch found general support for hypotheses that the greater the risk in a transaction, the more likely are buyers to deal with people to whom they have social ties outside the transaction. People who sold or bought from relatives and friends reported more satisfaction with the outcomes than people who transacted with strangers. Respondent preferences for in-group exchanges were consistent with expectations that "uncertainty about product and performance quality leads people to prefer sellers with whom they have noncommercial ties" (p. 619). Sellers believed their friends would give better terms of trade than strangers and would be less inclined to conceal unfavorable product information.

Producer Markets

Producer markets, also known as business or industrial markets, consist of buyers and sellers of raw materials, manufacturing equipment, components, and business-to-business services. In contrast to consumer markets involving end-use products by individuals and households, many producer market participants are business firms buying and selling products to be used in further production activities. While consumer products are often mass-marketed to potentially millions of customers, many producer markets involve just handfuls of firms. A familiar example is the petroleum market, where a few giant companies (Valero, ConocoPhillips, BP, Exxon Mobil) control most of the 149 US refineries. Consequently, the thousands of corner retail gas station owners must buy their oil and gas products under terms set by those few producers. Mainstream economics defines a market dominated by a small number of sellers as an oligopoly, and conventionally measures its presence by four- or eight-firm concentration ratios; that is, the proportion of total industry sales accruing to that number of producers. According to a 2009 report of the US Energy Information Administration, the top four petroleum refining firms had 40 percent of the refining capacity and the top eight had 56 percent. The carbonate beverage market was even more concentrated, with the duopoly of Coca Cola and Pepsi controlling 75 percent of the global market. In highly concentrated producer markets, where a few firms transact with many suppliers and customers, the structure of economic exchanges constrains firm behaviors and outcomes. The following subsections examine two network approaches to understanding such producer markets.

Producer Markets as Networks

Network analysts conceptualize a producer market in structural relational terms, as a set of firms purchasing inputs and selling outputs. The firms operating in one market compete to purchase goods or services from businesses operating in other markets and to sell identical or highly similar products to customers in yet other markets. Thus, multiple markets are simultaneously interconnected by exchanges of money for various types of products. Figure 2.5 schematically displays a simplified economy comprising nine firms exchanging in two markets. To offer a substantive example, mining corporations (M) supply iron ore to steel firms (S), which in turn sell their metal products to automobile manufacturers (A). Although companies manufacturing the same product do not transact with one another, the pattern of exchange relations across the iron ore and steel markets reveals differentiated positions or roles. In social network analysis, the concept of *structural equivalence* refers to a subset of actors with identical patterns of ties to all other actors in a network. Importantly, the relations among the actors who jointly occupy a structurally equivalent position are irrelevant. The figure shows that steel companies S_1 and S_2 are structurally equivalent, because both companies buy ore from the same two mining companies and sell steel to the same two automobile firms. Whether the two steel firms interact or ignore one another is irrelevant. Indeed, they're structurally indistinguishable in competing head-to-head to secure both inputs and outputs. In contrast, S_3 is not structurally equivalent to that dyad because it transacts with different firms in the iron ore and steel markets. Two other dyads are structurally equivalent: M_1 and M_2 because they sell to the same customers, and A_1 and A_2 because they buy from the same suppliers. Structural equivalence

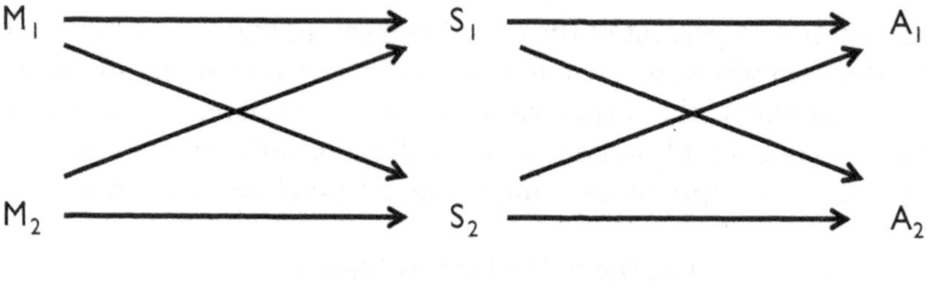

Figure 2.5 Structural equivalence in two producer markets

simplifies a complex network by reducing a large number of individual actors into fewer *jointly occupied positions*. Thus, in figure 2.5, the six firms at the top can be reduced to three structurally equivalent positions, each occupied by two firms. But, the three firms at the bottom cannot be further reduced to fewer positions.

Ronald Burt applied structural equivalence methods to analyze American producer markets, as measured by standard industrial classification codes. His research examined the effects of competition within an industry and among an industry's suppliers and consumers. From economic theories of oligopoly and sociological theories of group affiliation, Burt (1980) developed hypotheses about the "structural autonomy" of network positions in the US economy. Firms jointly occupying a position should enjoy high structural autonomy when: (a) they form an oligopoly, hence have low competition among themselves; (b) they have diverse relations with other positions that are not oligopolies, and thus compete against one another for the oligopoly's business; and (c) an interaction effect occurs; that is, "forming an oligopoly and having conflicting group-affiliations leads to autonomy above and beyond the direct additive effects of either aspect of autonomy" (p. 900). Industries with greater structural autonomy should achieve higher profit margins. Further, firms in a highly autonomous industry will tend to acquire or merge with firms in other industries that are most threatening to the former's continuing structural autonomy. Treating the 335 US manufacturing industries in 1967 as structurally equivalent positions, Burt measured network structural equivalence by sales and purchases with 51 aggregated economic sectors. For example, firms in the food industry bought goods from the livestock, forestry/fishery, and other agriculture sectors. He measured oligopoly by four-firm concentration ratios. Burt found support for most of his hypotheses about firm profits and cooptive merger activity. He concluded that "structural autonomy predicts the relative freedom of corporations in sectors of the economy to set prices independent of other sectors and predicts diversification, joint ventures, interlocking directorates, etc., to develop where constraint on each sector is high" (p. 923).

In subsequent research, Burt extended structural equivalence analysis to other US producer networks. Analyzing purchase and sales transactions for 77 broadly defined commodity markets in four Department of Commerce input–output tables from 1963 to 1977, Burt (1988) found "no obvious groups of commodities that should be combined as structurally equivalent products within a single market" (p. 362). These market boundaries within the US economy were dramatically stable across the two decades. Structural autonomy was highly correlated with three profit measures. The sector with greatest structural autonomy – small numbers of large competitors transacting with many small and disorganized consumers and suppliers – and hence able to negotiate prices "to provide comfortable profit margins," was the communications market exclusive of radio and television broadcasting. Its profit-margin was "a lush 45.3 cents on each dollar of sales" (p. 380). Burt and Carlton (1989) reached different conclusions by applying alternative transaction measures to the 1981–2 input–output tables. Marginal transaction indicators produced a "substantively richer market topology" than proportional measures, "offering clearer distinctions between kinds of market environments in which organizations operate" (pp. 748–9). However, boundaries were highly stable across markets. Burt's theoretical and empirical research program drew attention to the importance of structural relations in producer markets, whose firms operate in complex social structures of competition and interdependent resource transactions. By demonstrating the stability of structurally equivalent market positions, at least during the final decades of the twentieth century, and their impacts on industry profits and merger-acquisition behaviors, it offered crucial insights into the social embeddedness of firms in markets.

Production Markets from Networks

Harrison White synthesized a novel theory of production markets, a "framing for a new economic sociology" that melds "optimization derivations from neoclassical microeconomics with social constructions from network sociology" (2002a: 323). He refined the model through a series of articles (White 1981, 1993, 2002b, 2003) and a book, *Markets from Networks: Socioeconomic Models of Production* (White 2002a). This theory is too richly complex, White's exposition is sometimes so difficult, and the mathematical notation so recondite, that only a nontechnical introduction is provided here. Readers interested in examining White's approach in depth should consult his original publications, particularly the book.

White conceptualized a production market as the social construction of a small number of firms in a highly concentrated industry ("some dozen or so," seldom more than 20; White 2002a: 14). These producers are embedded within "networks of continuing flows" of goods and services, procuring inputs from upstream suppliers and selling their outputs to downstream purchasers (p. 1). Every market involves three distinct economic roles (suppliers, producers, buyers), such as sketched in figure 2.5, with two separate market interfaces (the upstream supplier-producer and downstream producer-buyer boundaries). Thus, White analyzed interconnected sequences of markets, rather than a single producer market in isolation from others. Historically, increasingly interconnected local and regional production markets evolved into the contemporary US national "production economy with networks of intermediate products and services" that "routinely generate net profits for many or all producers" (p. 5). Uncertainty about future flows renders highly problematic each firm's commitments for the coming period – its decisions about investments in production facilities, purchases of equipment, costs, volumes of output. Rather than trying to figure out what their customers will demand in the future, the producers vigilantly search for signals ("cues and clues," p. 5) about what and how much their rival competitors intend to produce. Firm commitment decisions are based on observed activities of this market reference group, particularly peer firms' revenues and volumes shipped. Businesses pick up additional evidence by gossiping "over luncheons with others in the trade, from trade associations, from one's own customers, and so on" (White 1981: 519). The result is a network of firms constantly comparing one another's production activities: "Markets are tangible cliques of producers watching each other" (p. 543). White's examples of industries displaying these features include light aircraft firms, glass manufacturers, marinas, Manhattan grocers, Scottish knitwear companies, professional sports leagues, and Las Vegas casinos. Although several of those producers sell directly to individual consumers, his model also applies to business-to-business producers, such as computer chip and airliner engine manufacturers.

For White, the key production-market mechanism "derives from social construction of a quality order that producers and buyers recognize and regularly reinforce by their commitments" (2002a: 13). A market's quality order is a linear status-ranking, or "pecking order" (p. 14), among the set of producers. This ordering, which emerges "within patterns in structural equivalence among production flow networks" (p. 14), arrays firms and products from the highest to lowest quality. This hierarchy becomes "taken for granted" by each firm when making its own production commitments, and it also signals the products' prestige order to the set of customers who purchase the market outputs. "Existing network ties become folded into and supplanted by relations with a quality ordering, which comes to be perceived in terms of prestige that combines quality for consumption with competitive relations of rivalry" (p. 14). Each firm then chooses a particular volume of production that enables it to maintain its market niche within the quality order. Through its quality-order mechanism, a production market tends toward a self-reproducing role structure of relations among the producers. The status-ranking guides everyone's upstream and downstream production commitments. In their efforts to cope with uncertainties, firms seek secure niches and reliable profits, contributing to a stable market structure over time. At the macro-level, a modern economy is a series of interconnected production markets, each displaying stable quality orderings generated by firms with structurally equivalent inputs and outputs:

> The present economy has grown up around production by firms that make commitments, period after period, within networks of continuing flows of goods and services. Markets evolved as mechanisms that spread the risks and uncertainties in placing these successive commitments with buyers. Firms shelter themselves within the rivalry of a production market. (White 2002a: 13)

As rival producers anticipate procuring necessary inputs (materials, labor) for the next period and planning their optimal production schedules, especially the volumes of output, they signal one another via the quality order. Producers competing for buyers create a "joint interactive profile in revenue for volume" (p. 14). The total revenue, or worth, that a firm receives for its shipment volume (y) is denoted by W(y). Hence, White referred to his theory as the "W(y) model." Figure 2.6 schematically displays the revenue-against-volume positions for all producers strung along a market *profile*, or worth curve, marking the firms' unequal shares of industry gross output and profit. A market profile evolves through the particular histories of firms' trial-and-error searches for advantageous niches within an industry. "Pressures are local, in time as well as network location, and the comparisons are relative, so that not one but many histories can stabilize a market, leading to any one of a predictable array of profiles, a family of similar shapes" (p. 27). Each producer seeks a unique location along the worth curve where it can obtain optimal or maximal profit, given its costs and choice of volume. The locations of rival firms along the W(y) profile send observable signals about their production commitments. Competitors adjust their production in response to information revealed in the profile about one another's performances. Firms acquire some data about peers' volumes and revenues from business press reports, including online sources, but also by networking: "the stuff of managerial conversations, business gossip, and business socializing, through which firms' positions in the market are constituted and recognized" (p. 31). In addition to uncovering the quality pecking order among firms in a market, White argued that his model could explain such observable phenomena as decreasing unit costs with increasing production volumes; why higher quality products have lower cost structures than inferior goods; the rarity of monopoly; and the importance of local variability and historical paths, rather than supply and demand, as determinates of market outcomes (pp. 12–14). White (2002a) demonstrated these principles by applying the W(y) model to explain variations in the market mechanism (a "market plane" consisting of four regions), dynamic evolution among market types, and empirical examples of production markets.

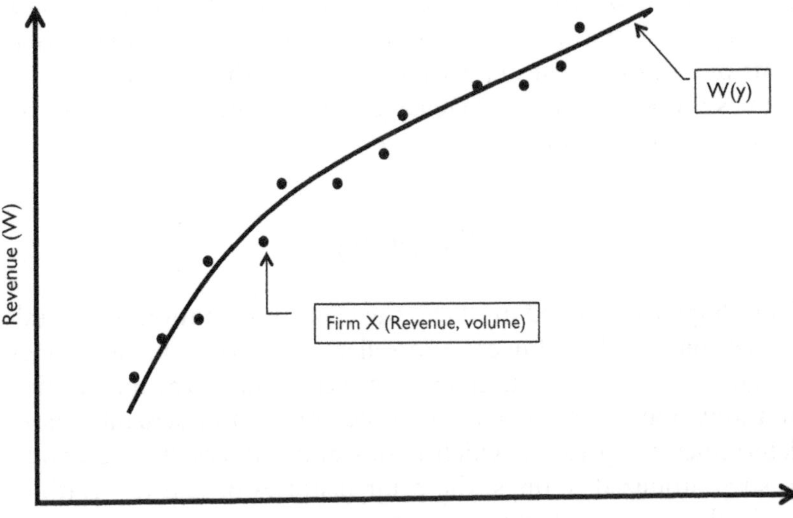

Figure 2.6 A revenue-against-volume market profile

The brilliance of White's market theory drew attention to the multidimensional space within which production firms are distributed and the differential behaviors of firms located in different regions. Its main limitation is the narrow view of how markets are socially constructed, seen through the producers' lens and then only as they spy on one another. What evidence suggests that real producers, even in business-to-business markets, disdain marketing research to gauge buyer interests, shun advertising to stimulate product demand, and ignore their customers when planning their future production schedules? The theoretical scope is reduced to very small markets, perhaps a handful of firms, where stable role structures seem most likely to emerge. And such markets are a decreasing proportion of activity in advanced economies: "Deriving markets from producer firms may not be the best route to choose in an economy where the production sector has been shrinking for decades and accounts for less than 20 percent of the economic activity in Western countries" (Knorr Cetina 2004: 142). Despite the provocative challenge to transcend conventional conceptualizations of markets in mainstream economics, most economic sociologists shirked direct tests of White's theory. His model would benefit from a concerted research program using data from diverse producer markets to test its hypothesis that firms pursue divergent quality niches against the mainstream economics proposition that efficiency constrains them to converge on a common market strategy.

Summary

This chapter examined markets, the central institution of capitalist economies where buyers and sellers meet to exchange money for goods and services. In mainstream economics, the intersection of anonymous participants' aggregate supply and demand curves determines the price at which goods and services change hands. In such atomized settings, the prior histories of market relations are irrelevant to contemporary interactions. In contrast, economic sociologists view market transactions as socially embedded within larger societal contexts where cultural, political, religious, and other network relations affect who exchanges with whom and for how much. Evidence from research on labor markets, consumer markets, and producer markets demonstrates that people and organizations find jobs, purchase homes and autos, and devise production schedules after seeking information, advice, and assistance from others actors to which they are connected. Far from impersonal encounters without past or future, market exchanges are deeply embedded in diverse networks. These connections can be ignored only at the risk of reaching inaccurate and incomplete understanding of market activities.

3

Networks inside Organizations

In the opening scene of Meredith Wilson's *The Music Man*, traveling salesmen on a train discuss how to succeed in business. One advises, "You gotta know the territory." Others demure, pointing out that "Professor" Harold Hill "doesn't know the territory," but he still seduces small towns into buying his musical instruments and uniforms for marching bands. Knowing the territory is the salesmen's metaphor for social networking: knowing who's who and what's what, which can give an edge over the competition. It's building and nurturing relationships with the residents of local communities who can improve the opportunity to make a sale. In fact, Harold Hill is quite adept at getting to know a new territory. His networking aptitude quickly enables him to form close personal ties with River City residents of all ages, gain the trust and admiration of the school board, and extract helpful information from the ladies' gossip network ("pick-a-little, talk-a-little"). Although Hill misapplies his talents as a flim-flam man – but is redeemed at the end by the love of a good librarian – more conscientious people can learn how to develop and deploy social networking skills for positive personal and organizational benefits. This chapter examines theory and research on intraorganizational networks, social relations occurring in a variety of workplaces ranging from offices and factories, to shops and ships, to schools and hospitals. Academics are interested in investigating how networks explain the beliefs and behaviors of people working inside organizations. Their insights have practical implications for employees who want to learn how networking could improve their job performances and career prospects. Managers and supervisors might manipulate networks to exert greater control over their subordinates' work activities to increase firm and agency productivity. Owners and top executives may discover how to make organizations more efficient and, in the private sector, more profitable. As with many results from social research, knowledge about networks inside organizations may be used for diverse, and sometimes conflicting, purposes.

An *intraorganizational network* is a set of actors inside a formal organizational unit boundary and one or more sets of specific relational contents that connect pairs of actors in the unit. The unit boundary may be the whole organization, a subdivision or department, a workplace, or a team. The actors inside a unit could include individual employees (or members in the case of a voluntary association), supervisors, managers, executives, owners, directors, possibly even company stockholders. Relational contents (types of ties) might represent, for example, communication, learning, trust, advice, helping, friendship, competition, antagonism, or hostility among the organizational participants. Understanding an organizational unit may require taking several multiplex relations simultaneously into account. A fundamental premise of intraorganizational network analysis is that actor behaviors and beliefs are influenced by the structural opportunities and constraints arising from embeddedness within both egocentric networks and complete network structures. In turn, participants reshape both micro- and macro-level networks by adding, dropping, or maintaining specific connections to others. Individual choices to change ties may reflect deliberate networking strategies that attempt to improve personal outcomes, captured in shopworn catchphrases "playing office politics" and "sucking up to the boss." More likely, many network transformations are unintended consequences of myriad interactions during routine work activities.

The origin of intraorganizational network analysis can be traced to Max Weber's (1922a) depiction of ideal type bureaucracy as an organization form based on the rational-legal authority type. Among other attributes, bureaucratic "principles of office hierarchy and of levels of graded authority mean a firmly ordered system of super- and subordination in which there is a supervision of the lower offices by the higher ones" (1922a: 197). This vertical authority structure of a bureaucracy – whether governmental, military, ecclesiastical, or private enterprise – is represented in a formal organizational chart that depicts the chain-of-command. Many subsequent investigators of empirical intraorganizational structures disputed Weber's ideal type as an incomplete model of actual bureaucratic organizations. Researchers regularly observed large discrepancies between formal and informal social structures, with the latter exerting great impact on workplace cohesion, employee job performance, and company productivity. A strong implication for managers is that ignoring informal ties among workers can imperil organizational performance. The classic case was research conducted during the Great Depression at the Hawthorne Works, a Western Electric factory outside Chicago (Roethlisberger and Dickson 1939). Observation of 14 men in a bank-wiring room, where they assembled telephone switching equipment, revealed informal "cliques" that developed local norms of behavior control and enforcement mechanisms. Although the workers were paid according to individual productivity, the men decreased their output because they feared the company would cut the base pay rate and fire some employees if they became too productive. The cliques controlled potential rate-busters with sarcasm, ridicule, insult games, and "binging" (punching on the arm) to pressure workers who deviated from the cliques' low-production norms. The employees were far more responsive to informal group norms than they were to the rational controls and monetary incentives provided by management.

As organization scholars began to discover network analysis in the late 1970s and early 1980s, they steadily incorporated this perspective into research on many facets of structure and action inside organizations. In an early exposition of social network analysis ideas and methods to the organization studies community, Tichy et al. (1979: 516) argued that "significant advances can be made in organization theory and research using this approach." Tichy and Fombrun (1979) reanalyzed three firms from the classic Aston Studies of British organizational structures. Their results supported the hypothesis that task-oriented coalitions emerge in loosely structured organic organizations, while in more mechanistic organizations the coalitions are more affective and supportive of individuals. Lincoln and Miller (1979) examined the employee attributes associated with dyad proximities in instrumental (work-with) and primary (friendship) relations in five professional organizations. Race and gender had stronger effects on primary ties, while authority and education co-varied more with instrumental ties in two organizations. An unexpected finding of a center-periphery friendship structure suggested that organizations constrain employees' affective choices to resemble their work relations. In an early effort to specify the connections between informal intraorganizational structures and formal characteristics of organizations and their environments, Jay Barney (1985) proposed an inductively developed contingency model. His blockmodel analyses of student friendship data, from 19 high schools originally studied by James Coleman, revealed an informal structural dimension analogous to the organic-mechanistic dimension of formal structure. These pioneering studies helped to propagate network analyses of organizations over the next quarter century.

Micro-Network Concepts

This section elucidates two important micro-network concepts for investigating the structure of intraorganizational relations: centrality and clique. To illustrate their applications to a real network, I analyze a small communication network displayed in Johnson-Cramer et al. (2007: 95). The authors briefly described it as "the information network across the R&D unit" of a global pharmaceutical firm following a merger between US and European parent companies. As shown in figure 3.1, directed ties connect 22 members of French, German, and American subunits. While Johnson-Cramer et al. did not explain how these dyadic relations were measured, prior articles (Cross et al. 2001; Borgatti and Cross 2003) stated that the R&D professionals were asked how often they had turned to each person "for information or knowledge on work-related topics in the past 3 months," and how often those persons had turned to them, on a five-point scale from "never" to "very frequently." A directed tie averaged the responses to these two information-seeking questions (sum of entries in the GetInfo and transposed GiveInfo matrices), then were presumably dichotomized at the median value to produce the network shown in figure 3.1. Johnson-Cramer et al. (2007: 94) summarized the observed pattern: "Although there were three discernible national subgroups in the network, there appeared to be strong communication ties between the subgroups." To be precise, inspection of figure 3.1 reveals that 102 directed ties occur between dyads within national subunits, but just 16 ties connect pairs of employees in different units. Much can be learned about this network's structure using analytic procedures available in the UCINET computer package (Borgatti et al. 2002). For details about computation of the network measures discussed below, see Knoke and Yang (2008).

Basic descriptions of the R&D communication network include its size (22 employees); dyad-based reciprocity (66 percent of choices are reciprocated); reachability (every employee can communicate with all others, either directly or through one or more intermediaries); and density (0.26, the proportion of the observed ties to all possible dyadic relations). If two actors have a direct tie, the *path length* between them is 1. If communication between a pair must go through one intermediary, their path length has 2 steps; or we can say the distance between that dyad is 2. The shortest directed path between a given pair is called its *geodesic*. In the pharmaceutical company's R&D communication network, the mean geodesic is 2.30; that is, the average length of the shortest paths between two employees is just above two steps. Even some pairs at opposite ends of the diagram, such a G4 and F1, have geodesics with no more than four steps (e.g., from G4 to F1, a shortest path is G4→G1→F8→F6→F1, while a geodesic in the other direction is F1→F2→F9→G1→G4). Thus, interpersonal information

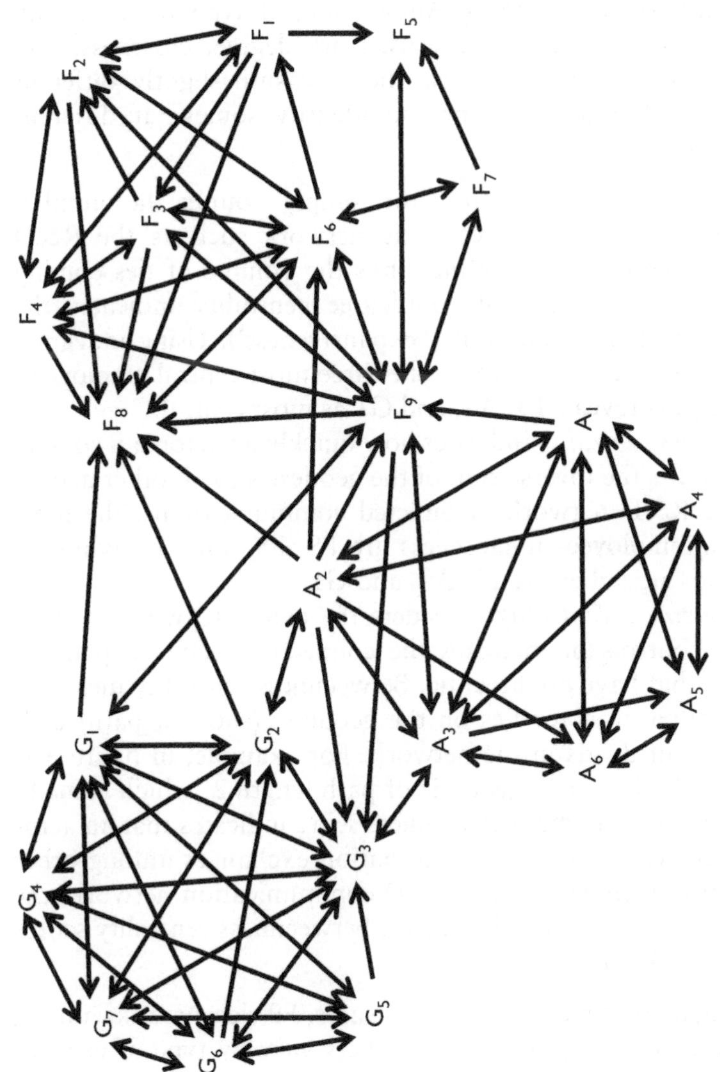

Source: Johnson-Cramer et al. (2007)

Figure 3.1 Post-merger communication in a pharmaceutical R&D unit

could be communicated quite quickly within the R&D unit, probably with few delays or distortions.

An actor's *centrality* within a network indicates how well connected it is to the others. Among several available centrality measures, the most commonly used are degree, closeness, and betweenness centrality. Because they measure slightly different concepts, each indicator tends to identify somewhat different central actors.

- *Degree centrality* of an actor simply counts the number of direct ties. In a directed-tie network such as the R&D unit, indegree centrality measures the volume of ties coming in ("popularity"), while outdegree centrality indicates the quantity of ties going out ("expansiveness'). Using indegrees identifies G3, F8, and F9 as the three most central employees; outdegrees reveals F9, A2, and G1 as most central.
- *Closeness centrality* indicates how quickly an actor can contact others. It's the inverse sum of the geodesics to all other actors. In the R&D network of directed communications, the most central employees in-closeness are F9, F8, and G3, while by out-closeness they are F9, A3, and G1.
- *Betweenness centrality* considers the extent to which a third actor controls or mediates the connection between pairs of actors that have no direct tie. Betweenness centrality measures how often an actor lies on the geodesic (shortest path) connecting all dyads in the network. For example, in figure 3.1, F2 and F7 have one geodesic of path length 2, which is mediated by F6. A higher betweenness score indicates that an actor has greater control over information exchanges among other network members. In the R&D communication network, the three employees with the highest betweenness centrality scores are F9, A3, and G1.

According to all three centrality measures, F9 clearly ranks among the most central employees; but, others vary by type of centrality. The locations plotted in figure 3.1 reflect degree centrality, which is why A2 and F8 appear near the center of the diagram. However, although F8 receives many ties from others, it has just one out-going connection. Thus, F8 cannot control information exchanges, in sharp contrast to F9's high betweenness centrality score due to many in- and out-linkages. In discussing the network, Johnson-Cramer et al. (2007: 96) revealed that F9 is the senior manager of the French subgroup, while F8 is comparable to the other French members in authority. Similarly, A2 is the senior American manager and G1 is one of the three senior German managers. Thus, betweenness centrality scores identified the most powerful network employees based on their strategic positions in the flow of communication.

Each line in figure 3.1 represents a dyadic relation, but a variety of larger network subsets may also be investigated. Many social network theories and methods emphasize *triads*, a subset of three actors and their possible ties. For example, triad {G1, G4, and G7} all mutually communicate with one another, but only two of the six possible ties occur in triad {F1, F5, F6}. In his classic essay on triads, Georg Simmel (1950) drew attention to the *tertius gaudens* (translated from Latin as "the third who enjoys" or "the third who benefits"). A *tertius* can derive advantages from a conflict between two others: "he may also, inversely, make the interaction that takes place between the parties and between himself and them, a means for his own purposes." The *tertius gaudens* takes two basic forms: "either two parties are hostile toward one another and therefore compete for the favor of the third element; or they compete for the favor of the third element and therefore are hostile toward one another" (p. 155). As an economic example, Simmel observed that a buyer in a modern market economy, confronted with goods offered by competing producers, "can base his purchases almost wholly on his appraisal of quality and price of merchandise" (p. 156) by playing merchants off one another to get the best deal. The egocentric strategy deployed by the *tertius* relies on actively working to keep two alters unconnected, controlling the flow of information between them, thus manipulating and exploiting transactions to the *tertius*' benefit. But, Simmel (pp. 146–7) also described another "non-partisan" third actor who mediates the conflict between two adversaries, such as a conciliator in labor-management bargaining:

> The non-partisan either produces the concord of two colliding parties, whereby he withdraws after making the effort of creating direct contact between the unconnected or quarreling elements; or he functions as an arbiter who balances, as it were, their contradictory claims against one another and eliminates what is incompatible in them.

Subsequent theorists argued that benevolent third parties may also derive benefits from introducing and facilitating collaborations among others who are not hostile but simply unacquainted with one another (Nooteboom 2006). An actor who deploys this *tertius iungens* ("the third who unites") strategy brings unconnected parties together to develop mutually beneficial opportunities (Obstfeld 2005). An entrepreneur who identifies and arranges new network connections is called a *broker*. Familiar examples are entertainment and sports agents – the fictional Ari Gold in *Entourage* and Jerry Maguire in the eponymous movie – who bring together clients and producers to negotiate movie contracts and product endorsements. In the figure 3.1 triad {G2, G3, A3}, employee G3 could broker an introduction of his German colleague G2 to the American A3, fostering more communication and possibly greater cooperation between the two R&D subunits. Alternatively, A3 could forge another completely connected triad by introducing A6 and G3 to one another.

Other important network subsets can be identified by clique analysis. A *clique* is a set of three or more actors who all have direct ties to one another (i.e., density = 1.00). The R&D communication network contains 11 cliques: three German cliques with five members each (e.g., G1, G4, G5, G6, and G7); three American cliques with four members each; and four French cliques with just three members apiece. Importantly, no clique contains members from two subunits. However, by relaxing the requirement of direct contact, lower-density subgroups called *n-cliques* can be identified, where *n* is the maximum length of geodesics connecting pairs of actors. The R&D network has seven 2-cliques, and each has at least one member from the three national subunits. The largest 2-clique encompasses 13 of the 22 employees (F2, F3, F4, F5, F6, F7, F8, F9, A1, A2, A3, G1, G3). This subgroup contains all of the most central employees according to the centrality analyses above. Furthermore, the three senior managers of each subunit (F8, A2, and G1) are members of this 2-clique and they also belong to four of the other six 2-cliques (A2 belongs to all seven 2-cliques). Despite the concentration of communication ties within the three national subunits, these key employees maintain sufficient cross-boundary ties to knit the R&D unit into a relatively integrated network. The basic social network concepts and measures described and illustrated in this section recur below, along with some more advanced analytic measures of employee networks.

Social Capital

Financial capital is familiar in mainstream economics as the funds provided by lenders and investors to entrepreneurs and businesses for purchasing land, labor, equipment, and material inputs to produce goods and services. Human capital is also familiar in labor economics as the knowledge and skills gained when persons, employers, and governments invest in education, job training, and work experience to increase worker productivity. Social capital is a relatively less familiar form of capital investment. Primarily developed by sociologists and political scientists, social capital involves forming social relationships for the purpose of improving social, political, or economic benefits. In network conceptualizations of social capital, the key idea is that an ego-actor's social capital consists of the resources controlled by the alters to whom ego is directly or indirectly connected. Social capital resides neither in an individual's attitudes and beliefs, nor in group norms, but involves the actual or potential transfer of control over resources through the relations among actors. Network ties facilitate exchanges of diverse types of resources, including transfers of financial and physical goods, information and knowledge, expert advice and political influence, and emotional support.

In addition to popularizing the closely related concept of cultural capital, Pierre Bourdieu defined social capital as "the aggregate of the actual or potential resources which are linked to possession of a durable network of more or less institutionalized relationships of mutual acquaintance and recognition – or in other words, to membership in a group – which provides each of its members with the backing of the collectivity-owned capital" (1986: 249). The quantity of an ego-actor's social capital varies with the number of connections to alters, and with the amount of capital – economic, cultural, or symbolic – possessed by the persons to whom ego is connected. Bourdieu is widely considered the inspiration for subsequent network treatments of social capital. James Coleman's (1986, 1988a, 1988b, 1990) approach to social capital emphasized both individual and collective actions within a social structure. Like Bourdieu, Coleman conceptualized social capital as relational: it "inheres in the structure of relations between persons and among persons" (Coleman 1990: 302). He stressed the obligations and expectations, norms and sanctions, trust and authority relations generated through social network connections. Connectedness purportedly increases with denser, stronger ties and "network closure." In a closed network, most actors are linked directly or indirectly to many other group members by ties exhibiting high levels of communication and emotional bonds. Coleman emphasized the social cohesion benefits of closure, which enable effective enforcement of sanctions against violators of group norms and encouragement of laggards who shirk their obligations. For example, in a "religious community surrounding a religiously-based school," the social capital for children's development "resides in the functional community, the actual social relationships that exist among parents, in the closure exhibited by the structure of relations, and in the parents' relations with the institutions of the community" (Coleman 1988b: 387). In communities replete with network closure, strong ties tend to foster obligations of mutual assistance, promote prosocial behaviors, and socially control deviant behaviors. A negative example is the greater high-school dropout rates in inner-city neighborhoods where impoverished residents lack sufficient social capital to support children's struggles to graduate.

Social capital analysts adopting the Bourdieu and Coleman perspectives investigated how people obtain resources through their network connections. Nan Lin (2001: 12) defined social capital as "resources embedded in a social structure which are accessed and/or mobilized in purposive action," where resources can be material or symbolic goods. Lin classified resources along three dimensions: resources embedded in a social structure (embeddedness); accessibility (opportunity); and use. His theoretical propositions applied to social mobility within a hierarchically stratified social system, for example, finding a better job through social connections. (See chapter 2 for discussion of Lin's empirical research on labor market networks.) Henk Flap and Ed Boxman (2001: 168) measured social capital in a job-search network as "the product of: (1) the strength of the tie and (2) the resources of alter, summed over all network members." Tie strength is alters' willingness to help ego, an unweighted sum of four elements: number of years ego and alter have been acquainted; frequency of contact; intensity of contact; and frequency with which ego provides services to alter. Resources are the alters' occupational prestige score, with higher scores implying access to better job information and assistance. Hence, social capital is greatest for persons with strong ties to many others who possess high-quality resources. Elaborating on this weighted-tie method, Johnson and Knoke (2004: 247) observed that Granovetter's strength-of-weak-ties hypothesis implies that "weak ties reflect casual relationships, nonredundant connections, and better access to more numerous and varied resources." Consequently, social capital should capture the uncertainty of social relationships, by taking into account the "probabilistic nature of ego accessing the resources of a given alter." Alters differ in how much assistance, advice, support, and money they're willing and able to offer if ego requests help. (How much money could you borrow from your neighbors compared to your relatives?) Further, ego's access to others' resources changes over time due to competing claims and the rise and fall of fortune. Figure 3.2 illustrates this probabilistic conceptualization of social capital for an egocentric network with five alters. Alter resources are indicated by the relative size of their labels, while line thickness indicates ego's subjective perception of how likely the alters are to provide their resources. Although ego has two very resource-rich

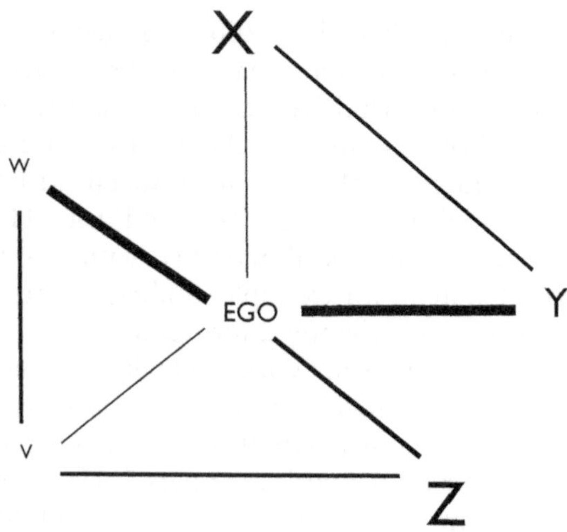

Figure 3.2 Ego's social capital as probability of accessing alter resources

alters, X and Z, the probabilities of access are low and moderate, respectively. Ego has greater chances of obtaining resources from Y and W, but those alters can provide only medium and low amounts. Johnson and Knoke's point was that it's not just whom you know, nor how rich they are, but whether they're willing to give you a loan when you need one.

Taking a similar network perspective on social capital, Ronald Burt (1992: 12) defined it as "at once the resources contacts hold and the structure of contacts in a network." Shifting away from Coleman's collectivist orientation toward an individualistic reference point, Burt depicted social capital as the informational and control advantages accruing to an ego actor who can spot opportunities and seize advantages in a network. His approach integrated ego's access to alters' information and resources with control over particular network structural features. Burt extended ideas about brokerage into a novel social capital concept, the structural hole. A *structural hole* occurs where the members of two or more network subgroups lack direct ties to one another. Either they can communicate only indirectly through multi-step paths, or, in the absence of any indirect paths, the subgroups are entirely disconnected. A hole presents an opportunity for someone who can fill that hole to gain a competitive advantage. By forging new ties that uniquely bridge the gap between subgroups, a broker gains access to nonredundant information circulating within each subgroup. A broker also gains some control over any joint activities and projects which bring together people from opposite sides of the hole. Social capital in a network accrues to persons occupying structural positions that enable them to broker connections among otherwise unconnected alters. Social entrepreneurs who can identify and fill structural holes, thus serving as a bridge between subgroups, can charge a commission for rendering valuable services to the groups. "Compensation, positive performance evaluations, promotions, and good ideas are disproportionately in the hands of people whose networks span structural holes" (Burt 2004: 349). In Burt's structural hole perspective, brokers are Simmelian *tertius gaudens* who seek personal advantages by manipulating the relations among others.

Some basic features of the social capital of structural holes are illustrated in figure 3.3, an artificial communication network among employees of three subunits, A, B, and C (which might represent the advertising, marketing, and public relations departments of a mid-size company). It's a stylized version of Burt's (2005: 14) more elaborate diagram, "an information Polynesia in which the clusters are islands of opinion and behavior." In a communication network, the resource that actors exchange is information useful for performing their jobs. A large volume of information obtained from redundant sources is less valuable than high-quality new information acquired through connections to diverse sources. In figure 3.3, the two named actors, Carol and Mike, have identical communication degree-centralities (four direct ties apiece), indicating no formal distinction in the quantity of information they receive through their direct contacts (employees A_1, B_2, and C_1 also have four degrees). But, their egocentric networks are quite differently structured by quality of relations. All of Mike's connections are to workers in subunit B, who themselves only have direct ties with other members of B, including Carol. Carol has ties within subunit B through two people,

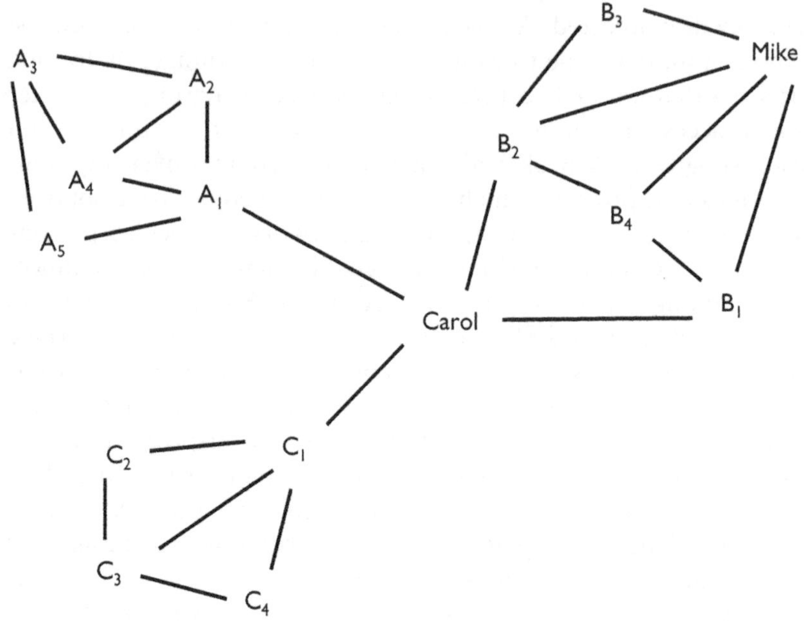

Figure 3.3 The social capital of structural holes

but her other two contacts provide direct access to information resources that Mike lacks. Through alter A_1, Carol can connect to most members of subunit A with path distances of length two. Through alter C_1, her path distances to subunit C members are also two steps. Carol's ties to alters A_1 and C_1 are both *bridges*: if those ties were cut, none of the subunits could communicate with one another. (Carol is also a *cutpoint*; if she leaves the firm, the communication network would fall apart into three disconnected subcomponents.) As discussed in the preceding section, Carol is the most central person in the network whether measured by closeness centrality (mean geodesics, or shortest paths, for Carol to reach all other employees) or by betweenness centrality (how many geodesics involve her).

Compared to Mike, Carol's network position confers three structural advantages: "access to wider diversity of information, early access to that information, and control over information diffusion" (Burt 2005: 16). Her direct contacts to the three subunits bring her less redundant information than any other employee can obtain. As the main person through whom information flows between the three groups, Carol can more quickly learn about new activities occurring in each location and could act as an opinion leader (see chapter 2). She's also "more likely to know when it would be rewarding to bring together separate groups, which gives [her] disproportionate say in whose interests are served when the contacts come together" (p. 17). The structural holes between Carol's four contacts mean that she can broker communication while displaying different identities and opinions to each subgroup. She occupies a classic *tertius gaudens* position. Carol's personal benefits might be a material commission (like a sports or entertainment agent's fee), higher status and prestige within the firm, or power and influence over the network and its outcomes. "The social capital of structural holes comes from the opportunities that holes provide to broker the flow of information between people, and shape the projects that bring together people from opposite sides of the hole" (p. 18). Of course, the social networks of real organizations are likely to be more complex than the simple example in figure 3.3. The following sections discuss classic and recent research on intraorganizational networks that applied the analytic principles and methods described above.

Forming Employee Networks

Networks of social relations connect employees inside work organizations, ranging from small Mom-and-Pop corner stores to huge multinational conglomerates with thousands of branches across a hundred countries. Multiplex intraorganizational ties encompass cognitions about workplace relations, such as knowledge about who has authority and expertise; subjective perceptions about affective bonds, such as friendship and trust; and specific behavioral interactions, such as communicating information and assisting others in performing their tasks. Networks underpin the socialization of newcomers into organizational practices and routines; facilitate the transfer of complex tacit knowledge; permit the formation and diffusion of group norms; create and maintain organizational cultures and subcultures. The more that participants become aware and understand the multiplex networks within which they are embedded, the more effectively they can learn how to use existing connections and forge new ties that improve their work performance. This section examines the formation of employee networks, beginning with the hiring of new employees. Formal organizational relations exert important constraints on informal relations among workers. Learning and trust relations are two important informal networks that affect workplace behaviors.

The Hiring Process

Many employers use personal networks as one of several mechanisms to recruit, screen, and select new employees. Organization staffing practices mirror the individual job searches examined in chapter 2. On the labor supply side, job-seekers use their network connections to learn about job openings and to obtain referrals and recommendations to employers. On the demand side, firms and agencies collect and process information about the qualities of applicants. Widely used recruitment techniques include formal channels – advertising, sign postings, employment agencies, executive recruiters (headhunters) – and informal channels, such as referrals by coworkers and business or professional contacts. In a 1991 national sample of US establishments, Peter Marsden (1996) asked how often employers had used six methods in the past two years to hire a "core worker," defined as the job title of employees most directly involved in the main product or service at the worksite. He found that 37 percent of employers frequently used employee referrals, followed by newspaper ads (36 percent; this study occurred before Internet classified ads became prevalent), unsolicited inquiries by phone, mail, or in person (24 percent), professional referrals (23 percent), posting signs on buildings (15 percent), and employment agencies (13 percent) (p. 138). In recruiting managers, the most frequently used employer methods were newspaper ads (32 percent), professional referrals (30 percent) and employee referrals (26 percent).

Some studies of recruitment at particular organizations underscored the huge importance of social ties in screening and hiring job applicants. Research using the hiring records for four entry-level office jobs at a retail bank examined 18 recruitment sources, such as newspaper ads, walk-ins, campus recruiting, and employee referrals (Fernandez and Weinberg 1997). Being recommended by a current bank employee conferred "advantages at both the interview and job-offer stages compared to external nonreferral applicants" (p. 883), even after controlling for more appropriate résumés and applications during more favorable labor market conditions. The researchers speculated that social ties provide employers with valuable information about job candidates' qualities and their likely post-hire job performance which is unavailable from other sources. Research on entry-level hires at a bank's credit-card phone center found that employee referrals produced better hiring outcomes; that is, "savings in screening costs due to referrals being more appropriate for the job at application" (Fernandez et al. 2000: 1351). Data on all 38,512 job applicants to a US high-tech company revealed that more than half involved referrals by a friend (Petersen et al. 2000). "Personal networks, through a friend, and professional networks, from having been a previous contractor, cover 67.7% and 13.2% of those receiving an offer, a total of 80.9% of offers" (p. 777).

Structural holes may affect the hiring process at organizations using professional headhunters to find higher-level employees. Headhunters are brokers who find candidates for clients (employers), and they are paid only if their candidate accepts a client's job offer. An example is a recruiter who places paralegals and legal secretaries in law firms. Working in a highly competitive environment with low entry requirements, headhunters are particularly vulnerable to opportunism by employers who may offer the job instead to a more attractive candidate turned up by a rival agent. In a survey of 98 headhunting firms and interviews with 34 job brokers in a Southeastern US city, Finlay and Coverdill (2000) found that successful headhunters follow two contrarian strategies. First, they try to reduce risks by identifying structural holes between firms and candidates – "they seek out opportunities to broker a match between employer and job candidate" – particularly developing close ties to regular clients that generate job orders (p. 381). They also decide whether to undertake a given candidate search, and how much effort to put into it, by assessing the likelihood of placing someone with the client and thus earning the brokerage fee. Second, because strong ties to an employer increase their vulnerability to client opportunism, headhunters try to mitigate those risks by pursuing a strategy of "reciprocal opportunism in which they specify the circumstances under which opportunism toward clients can be condoned" (p. 381). They may decide to take a candidate away from the original client and instead to market that person to another employer, thereby creating brokerage opportunities for themselves with new clients. These alternative strategies reflect the headhunters' powerlessness vis-à-vis clients, widespread beliefs that clients are disloyal, and "a lack of embedded ties between clients and headhunters that could create a basis for enforceable trust" sanctioned by larger business networks (p. 377).

Formal and Informal Relations

Formal work relations among employees are explicitly prescribed by their job descriptions, their positions in an organization chart, their locations in the physical layouts of offices or plants, and their assignments to particular routine tasks and special projects. The formal structure of a workplace – its system of interdependent work roles – is an organizational design planned and implemented independently of the persons who occupy designated positions. As an institution, the formal structure constrains employees in those roles to behave according to rules and regulations. Violators of organizational norms are subject to sanctions ranging from reprimand to firing. The intraorganizational networks generated by the formal work designs are primarily intended to achieve, sustain, or improve organizational performance outcomes. A variety of formal work networks can be observed across diverse organizations. A hierarchically structured bureaucracy may have lengthy vertical authority channels through which commands flow downward, from managers to supervisors to subordinate staff, while reports on work results flow in the opposite direction. In contrast, a decentralized "flat" organization has fewer vertical ties but numerous horizontal communication exchanges. In a multidivisional corporation, the lower-level employees of different divisions dwell in distant sites and rarely or never contact one another. But, the senior managers of its divisions intensively communicate and coordinate actions with one another and with headquarters officials. Firms that regularly reassign workers to different teams for new projects induce intraorganizational networks quite different from firms that keep the same team members together from one project to the next.

Formal organizational roles markedly shape the opportunities for informal employee relations to emerge. "If formal relationships provide a skeletal structure for an organization, informal relationships are the glue that holds an organization together and makes it work" (Hardcastle et al. 2004: 259). Employees usually cannot choose their job placements but must work where, and with whom, the organizational authorities assign them. Newly hired, just-promoted, and recently transferred employees acquire formal ties to other workers with whom they previously had little or no contact. How informal networks subsequently develop, and which forms and contents those relations take, are constrained by employees' embeddedness in the organization's formal structural relations. Company policies about job assignments may amplify or limit opportunities for informal relations to emerge. A business that routinely rotates its staff among positions in several departments and divisions at diverse geographic locations will generate informal networks rather distinctive from a firm whose employee career paths occur entirely within one silo (Gulati 2007). Merged and acquired units also instigate the formation of new formal ties among strangers. A humorous illustration occurred in an episode of *The Office* when Dunder Mifflin's Scranton branch absorbed employees from the closed Stamford branch. Jim Halpert returned as the office's number two, provoking Dwight Schrute and Andy

Bernard to bicker about who would be number three. In subsequent episodes, alliances, pranks, romances, and breakups ensued as the merged employees jockeyed for petty advantages.

Although variations in formal work relations are important for understanding workplace behaviors, researchers have known for decades that informal relations among employees exert important impacts (Roethlisberger and Dickson 1939; Blau and Scott 1962). Numerous informal ties originate directly in employees' efforts to perform their work duties. They communicate across formal role boundaries, seek and share information, transfer knowledge, offer advice, and give help. Other informal employee ties arise less from work activities than through primordial bonding motives, which may be positive or negative. The ubiquitous human preference for homophilous affiliations – captured in such pearls of folk wisdom as "birds of a feather . . ." and "like attracts like" – is a driving force for friendships and socializing among employees of similar race, ethnicity, gender, social class, or shared interests in sports and hobbies (Kilduff et al. 2008). Intensely intimate relations such as confiding, emotional support, and romantic attachment are typically more deeply rooted in the dynamics of interpersonal attraction than in formal work obligations.

Learning and Trust Networks

Organization scholars have long argued that continuous learning is indispensable for organizations to stay competitive in rapidly evolving environments. Only recently have they investigated organizational learning as network processes through which individuals learn how to perform their jobs better and organizations learn how to adapt to changing circumstances. At the heart of organizational learning are employee networks for exchanging information and transferring knowledge, as exemplified in three studies. First, in a contract R&D firm in a medium-size Midwest city, Ray Reagans and Bill McEvily (2003) showed that both network cohesion and network range facilitated easier knowledge transfer among the employees, beyond tie strength as measured by emotional closeness and communication frequency. Scientists and engineers with more cohesive (denser) networks and whose network range was more evenly spread among diverse knowledge pools (e.g., mechanical engineering, chemistry) achieved better knowledge transfer from a source to a recipient. Second, Steve Borgatti and Rob Cross (2003) proposed "a formal model of information seeking in which the probability of seeking information from another person is a function of (1) knowing what that person knows; (2) valuing what that person knows; (3) being able to gain timely access to that person's thinking; and (4) perceiving that seeking information from that person would not be too costly." For information scientists and genomic researchers in two global pharmaceutical corporations, both knowledge of another person's expertise (transactive memory) and perceived access to that knowledge mediated the relation between employees' physical proximities and information requests. "In terms of transactive memory, a key question is: What relationships need to exist for a group to leverage its collective expertise?" (Borgatti and Cross 2003: 442). Without collective agreement among employees about "who knows what," an organization cannot recognize new information and efficiently mobilize it for new purposes. Third, Wenpin Tsai (2001) investigated intraorganizational networks providing "new knowledge or expertise" among 24 business units of a petrochemical company and 36 units of a food-manufacturing firm. The more centrally positioned units of each company produced more innovations (number of new products introduced relative to annual targets) and achieved higher performance (profitability relative to targeted returns on investment). This centrality effect was larger for units with high "absorptive capacity," the ability to assimilate and replicate new knowledge from external sources. Centrality "provides opportunities for shared learning, knowledge transfer, and information exchanges" (p. 1002), and central business units with high absorptive capacity better acquired and applied the knowledge developed by other firm units.

Theory and research on the importance of trust burgeoned in recent years. To interact effectively with one's coworkers requires substantial confidence in their integrity. Suppose manager Martha asks subordinate George to complete an important report for her presentation at tomorrow's client meeting. She trusts he will do quality work, even if he has to stay late to finish. In turn, George trusts that Martha has his back, that she'll reward his hard work on a performance evaluation, rather than claiming full credit for herself for a successful presentation. If either person were to fail the other's expectations, their trust in one another could be damaged, if not destroyed. Although scholars in psychology, economics, and sociology do not agree on a universal definition of trust, two useful ones emphasize vulnerability to others and expectations about others' actions. Mayer et al. (1995: 712) defined trust as the "willingness of a party to be vulnerable to the actions of another party based on the expectation that the other will perform a particular action important to the trustor, irrespective of the ability to monitor or control that other party." More succinctly, Rousseau et al. (1998: 395) defined trust as "a psychological state comprising the intention to accept vulnerability based upon positive expectations of the intentions or behavior of another." Neither a behavior nor a choice, trust is "a psychological condition that can cause or result from such actions." Any trust relation involves risk-taking because a trustor is deliberately vulnerable to potential betrayal by a trustee. The trustee might behave deceitfully, engage in opportunism or "self-seeking with guile" (Williamson 1975), and produce a loss or harm to the trustor. Trust and risk are intimately intertwined because "risk creates an opportunity for trust, which leads to risk taking" (Rousseau et al. 1998: 395). Psychological theories of trust emphasize the attributes of trustors and trustees. Personality traits or general dispositions toward risk-taking and trusting others begin in childhood experiences with benevolent caregivers. "Blind trust" – proclivity to trust others unconditionally, bordering on naïveté – renders gullible trustors more susceptible to manipulation and exploitation by unscrupulous operators. (Professor Harold Hill relied on this type of trust in the small towns he bilked; so did Bernie Madoff for his ginormous Ponzi scheme.) A related psychological dimension is the trustworthiness of the trustee. People are more willing to trust others they see as benevolent, competent, honest, and predictable (Mayer et al. 1995). The homophily principle asserts that trust is more likely to occur within identity groups, among people sharing similar ascribed attributes, achieved statuses, and beliefs and attitudes. Trust in a specific individual increases through an accumulation of positive experiences, but can evaporate after even a single instance of betrayal.

Socially, trust is a set of directed relations among actors, which may be reciprocal or asymmetric, that can be analyzed using network methods. The grammatically incorrect question "Who do you trust?" asks employees to name the others on whom they depend to accomplish their work. Network theorists emphasized how organizational structures influence the formation of employee trust ties. Rafael Wittek argued that an actor's "position in the role structure of the informal network has an impact on the formation of interpersonal trust relations in organizations" (2001: 110). He assumed that people working in competitive environments try to reduce uncertainty about the trustworthiness of possible trustees by imitating the social choices of people in their networks. Wittek proposed three testable hypotheses: (1) positional trust, that employees trust others who occupy similar network positions as themselves; (2) mimetic trust, that employees trust others who are trusted by persons in their own network positions; and (3) advisory trust, that employees trust people occupying a position of advisor rather than persons in other positions. Wittek reanalyzed data collected in 1954–7 by Cecil French (1963) from a 25-salesmen network in the furniture department of a retail sales store, "one of first longitudinal network studies in a real-life organizational setting" (p. 117). The model estimates, fitted to the sociometric choices of salesmen in four role positions spanning three periods, supported both the mimetic and advisory trust hypotheses but not the positional trust hypothesis. Wittek concluded that "imitating the behavior of those who occupy a similar position in the role structure of the informal network as oneself seems to have played a crucial role for the creation and maintenance of social relationships in a highly competitive environment" (p. 136).

Theorists concur that high levels of trust within organizations mostly produce beneficial consequences, including "more positive attitudes, higher levels of cooperation and other forms of workplace behavior, and superior levels of performance" (Dirks and Ferrin 2001: 451). High trust presumably facilitates collaboration among employees, such as sharing information and rendering assistance with job tasks; reduces conflicts and decreases such transaction costs as monitoring performances and enforcing conformity; encourages organizational citizenship, commitment, and job satisfaction; and improves organizational innovation, adaptation, and effective response to crises. The dominant theoretical explanation is that trust directly affects organizational outcomes, while an alternative account depicts trust as mediating the effects of other factors on outcomes (Dirks and Ferrin 2001). Research by Daniel Levin and Rob Cross (2004) on employees of three companies showed that competence- and benevolence-based trust mediated the connection between strong advice ties and the receipt of "useful" knowledge or information (perceived as having a positive impact by knowledge seekers). Indeed, when both types of trust were controlled, the net effect of tie strength became negative, meaning that *weak* ties led to more useful knowledge, consistent with Granovetter's strength-of-weak-ties hypothesis. Competence-based trust was especially important for acquiring tacit (uncodifiable) knowledge. That is, "the more that a knowledge transfer involve tacit knowledge, the more crucial it was . . . that the knowledge receiver trust the competence of the source" (p. 1485). A third theoretical model specified two broad causal pathways by which trust influences important organizational properties: (1) by *structuring* a system of positions and ties among employees in social space, where "trust influences the density, multiplexity, stability, and nonredundancy of social structure"; and (2) by *mobilizing* actors "to contribute their resources, to combine, coordinate, and use them in joint activities, and to direct them toward the achievement of organizational goals" (McEvily et al. 2003: 94 and 97).

Network Outcomes

Employees are embedded in multiplex networks with diverse implications for work attitudes and behaviors. Networks enable some employees to perform their jobs better than others, and thus to receive better rewards, such as pay and promotions. Employees occupying advantageous network positions enjoy more positive outcomes such as higher job satisfaction, and experience fewer negative outcomes such as work stress, burnout, and turnover. On the dark side, some relations hinder individual performance, which can negatively impact organizations. Women and minorities frequently face distinctive obstacles to networking relative to white males, but those impediments may be decreasing. This section examines exemplary research on network outcomes at work.

Job Performance

Job performance encompasses diverse behaviors, ranging from productive tasks, such as making goods and selling services, through contributions to achieving group and organizational goals (Campbell 1990). Employees who are more central in learning, trust, and other workplace networks obtain more accurate task-specific knowledge and gain quicker access to confidential information about work-related matters. Through connections to diverse coworkers, employees can obtain more resources with less dependency on others. The more support, advice, help, and encouragement that employees receive from coworkers, the stronger is their motivation to accomplish work tasks and receive higher performance evaluations. An employee who fills a structural hole between subgroups, thereby achieving control over information flows and resource exchanges, enjoys greater power to influence others' behaviors, for example, by coordinating projects and solving problems. In contrast, employees who occupy more peripheral and marginalized network positions receive fewer resources and less social support from coworkers, hindering their job performance.

Several analysts documented the importance of workplace networks for employee job performance and rewards. Research on 236 salaried employees in a large high-tech engineering and manufacturing corporation demonstrated how informal social ties affected their career advancement prospects (Podolny and Baron 1997). Upward advancement was enhanced for employees with "buy-in" relations (ties to people who had "fate control" over their job-related initiatives). But, career mobility was diminished for employees whose mentors were located outside the buy-in network. Evidence at a major commercial bank supported two paradoxical tie-strength hypotheses: under conditions of high economic uncertainty, bankers relied on dense, strong-tie trust relations with their colleagues for advice and support of their deals (Mizruchi and Stearns 2001). But, "embeddedness in strongly connected networks is precisely the condition that makes it more difficult to close deals" (p. 667). So bankers who used sparse, nonhierarchical approval networks were more likely to close their deals successfully. The analysts attributed the finding to unanticipated consequences of intended rational actions: despite engaging in purposely rational behavior, the bankers who used strong ties to manage job uncertainties actually produced counterproductive outcomes. Research on 101 engineers in a petrochemical company and 125 consultants in a strategy-consulting firm found that greater betweenness centrality in an information network and an awareness network (knowledge of others' expertise) were both related to higher performance ratings (Cross and Cummings 2004). "Centrality in an information network reflects one's ability to tap expertise for current concerns, while centrality in an awareness network reflects one's ability to take action on new opportunities by leveraging others' expertise" (p. 934). Another project studied networking by employees in the top fifth of performance reviews in diverse organizations (Cross and Thomas 2008). Top performers occupied key network positions where they could "leverage the network around them better when implementing plans" (p. 166). They also tended "to invest in relationships that extend their expertise and help them avoid learning biases and career traps." They focused on forming high-quality ties, not just large networks.

Individuals who fill structural holes carry out their tasks more effectively, receive personal recognition, and are rewarded for superior job performance. Burt (2004) examined idea brokerage among 673 managers in charge of the supply chain for a large American electronics company. Managers were first asked, "From your perspective, what is the one thing that you would change to improve [the company's] supply-chain management?" (pp. 376–7). If a manager had discussed the idea with anyone, she or he was then asked, "More generally, who are the people with whom you most often discuss supply-chain issues" (p. 360). Burt measured idea brokerage as a network constraint. A highly constrained manager either talked directly with many others or shared information indirectly through a central contact. Because more constrained networks spanned fewer structural holes, both job performance and the quality of ideas were negatively correlated with network constraint. "Managers who often discussed supply-chain issues with managers in other groups were better paid, received more positive job evaluations, and were more likely to be promoted" (p. 369). Burt asked two senior managers to judge how much value would be generated for the firm if each managerial idea were "well executed." For example, the judges rated highly a suggestion to involve supply-chain managers in the proposal process, which would improve the firm's win rate. They rated poorly a wordy, incomprehensible idea to modify the computerized ordering system. Consistent with the brokerage hypothesis, good ideas tended to come from managers having the fewest network constraints, particularly managers in the more senior ranks. But, managers constrained in closed discussion networks of redundant social contacts were less likely to generate good ideas. The evidence indicated that "managers whose networks spanned structural holes were more likely to express an idea and discuss it with colleagues, . . . have the idea engaged by senior management, . . . and have it judged valuable" (p. 386). Good ideas are not intrinsically valuable, but acquire their importance through the audiences they reach via social connections:

> The brokerage value of an idea resides in a situation, in the transaction through which an idea is delivered to an audience; not in the source of the idea, nor in the idea itself. . . . People with connections across structural holes have early access to diverse, often contradictory,

> information and interpretations, which gives them a competitive advantage in seeing and developing good ideas. People connected to groups beyond their own can expect to find themselves delivering valuable ideas, seeming to be gifted with creativity. This is not creativity born of genius; it is creativity as an import-export business. An idea mundane in one group can be a valuable insight in another. (Burt 2004: 388)

Ironically, although the corporation was riddled with structural holes providing numerous opportunities for brokerage, most managerial ideas had very little impact on changing the firm's supply-chain activities. Managers talked about ideas with colleagues located predominantly in dense informal discussion networks segregated from the formal authority hierarchy. "[I]deas were not discussed to change business practice so much as they were discussed to display competence and to entertain familiar colleagues" (p. 391). Few managers attempted to mobilize support for implementing their ideas. Burt concluded that "the potential value for integrating operations across the company was dissipated in the distribution of ideas" (p. 394). Although less constrained networks provided personal benefits to managerial brokers, they prevented amassing of support to implement good ideas that might benefit the organization.

As discussed above, Burt's approach to social capital depicts structural holes as leveraging resources via brokerage opportunities created by sparse, diversified ties. In Coleman's contrasting approach, social capital ensues from network closure, the strong cohesive ties that promote group trust and cooperation. To adjudicate the Coleman–Burt debate, Martin Gargiulo and Mario Benassi (2000) tested the opposing hypotheses with data from a newly created unit of an Italian multinational computer subsidiary. Its mission was to promote alternative forms of horizontal cooperation in the subsidiary, which was undergoing global reorganization. This difficult job required the new unit's 19 managers to coordinate their work through informal communication ties and to adapt their networks to a continually changing task environment. Gargiulo and Benassi found that managers with cohesive communication networks (strong ties to a cohesive group of peers) experienced more frequent coordination failures, as measured by the frequency of dyadic task interdependence coupled with weak communication. In contrast, managers with communication networks rich in structural holes adapted better to organizational transformations in the new unit. The authors concluded that a cohesive network is detrimental to cooperation because it restricts a manager's autonomy to initiate and sustain cooperation beyond existing network boundaries. "Paradoxically, this 'dark side' of cohesive networks is the unintended consequence of the very mechanism that makes such networks a warranty against defection from cooperation" (p. 193). Research on a large sample of investment bankers, working in the equity division of a large international financial services firm, found contrasting effects of network closure on job performance, as indexed by year-end bonuses (Gargiulo et al. 2009). When a banker acquired information, closure within a strategic information network improved his or her job performance. But, when the banker provided information, network closure decreased it. This paradox reflected asymmetric normative control arising from network closure: "Control may benefit people when they need to induce others to behave according to their preferences, but it may hurt them when it forces them to behave according to the preferences of others" (p. 326). Both studies showed that benefits accrue to employees who fill structural holes which free them from constraints while performing their jobs. However, the differential impact of network closure in the investment banker project suggests that debate over social cohesion versus structural holes remains inconclusive.

Other researchers who studied network brokerage inside organizations drew different conclusions about the impact of structural holes on job performance. Shi et al. (2009) elaborated a theoretical brokerage typology, originated by Gould and Fernandez (1989), to identify eight brokerage roles of middle managers and their contributions to achieving strategic goals. Whereas Gould and Fernandez considered only brokers in a *tertius gaudens* situation (playing two separated alters against another), Shi et al. recognized that *tertius iungens* situations (predisposition to bring alters together) are also prevalent inside many organizations. They proposed 16 theoretical hypotheses about the brokerage roles in which managers would be more disposed to choose the *gaudens* or the *iungens* strategy. David Obstfeld (2005) investigated the networks of 182 engineers, designers, and managers who worked on new vehicle designs for a Detroit automotive manufacturing firm. Dense social networks, diverse social knowledge, and an *iungens* orientation – but notably not the *gaudens* orientation implicit in Burt's constraint measure of structural holes – predicted greater involvement in each of 73 product and process innovations. The results also have important implications for markets and collective action. "A grasp of markets as constituted by both *gaudens* and *iungens* activity captures a substantial amount of market activity that an exclusively competitive framework overlooks" (p. 125). Simon Rodan (2010) analyzed ego-network density and alters' knowledge heterogeneity for 106 middle managers of a Scandinavian telecommunications service provider. He found that structural holes were not used to exploit individual autonomy, nor to create competition among alters, nor to gain advantages by seizing opportunities earlier. Instead, managers who were exposed to alters' more heterogeneous knowledge exhibited greater creativity and innovativeness, and received higher job performance ratings from senior managers. In a caution about scope limitations of the structural-hole hypothesis, researchers who investigated social capital in four Chinese firms concluded that China's collectivist culture is incompatible with network brokerage (Xiao and Tsui 2007). The control benefits of structural holes clash with the Chinese familial-collectivist value system:

> Although structural holes may bring positive returns to individual actors in a market-like, low-commitment organizational culture, it is network closure that will bring advantages to the actors, by facilitating trust, reciprocity, and reputation, in a clan-like, high-commitment organization with a strong cohesive culture. Further, to the extent that brokering runs counter to the way of doing things in high-commitment, collectivistic organizations, brokering is a risky venture in those firms. (p. 23)

These studies underscore the need for carefully designed network research to uncover the multifaceted and culturally contingent effects of structural holes on individual job performance.

Satisfaction and Stress

Employee workplace networks and social capital induce beneficial effects beyond improving job performance, such as greater job satisfaction and reduced psychological stress. On the dark side, *hindrance networks* may negatively impact workers, leading to harmful effects including illness, absenteeism, burnout, and job turnover.

Social ties influence employee job satisfaction and organizational commitment primarily through alters who provide strong social support. Dense egocentric networks composed of coworkers, as well as off-the-job friends and kin, offer the greatest protection against inevitable adversities and disappointments at work. A supportive network buffers workers against heavy job demands, pressures by supervisors, unpleasant working conditions, and other unrewarding aspects of work. Coworker support is a resource component of social capital, providing sustenance that ego may access when most needed. Respondents in the 1985 General Social Survey expressed higher job satisfaction if their egocentric networks included coworkers, implying that colleagues offer socio-emotional support that helps people cope with job problems (Hurlbert 1991). Network analysts of work behaviors increasingly conceptualized social support as multidimensional, exerting differential impacts on job satisfaction. One theoretical classification scheme identified six types of support (e.g., sharing, listening, counseling, encouragement) that vary along five dimensions, such as intimacy, emotional energy, and expressive-instrumental function (McGuire 2007). An instrumental-affective dichotomy emerged in some empirical investigations of network impacts on job satisfaction. A test of the buffering hypothesis, using full-time employees in the 1997 National Employee Survey, showed that both instrumental and affective support independently increased job satisfaction (Ducharme and Martin 2000).

That is, workers whose colleagues provided help, advice, and assistance with job problems (instrumental support) or who care about, take a personal interest in, and appreciate them (affective support) tended to express greater satisfaction with their jobs. Data from 506 staff members of a German municipal administration were consistent with a buffering hypothesis that organizational commitment moderates the links between work stress and psychological burnout (Schmidt 2007). "The effects of high stress on the burnout dimensions of exhaustion and depersonalization were reduced with increasing commitment to the organization" (p. 26).

Research on two Dutch governmental agencies found differential effects of network social capital on job satisfaction (Flap and Völker 2001). Open networks of instrumental ties that were rich in structural holes increased employee satisfaction with instrumental aspects of the job, such as income and career opportunities. Dense networks providing solidarity, trust, and identification with others produced greater satisfaction with the social side of the job, such as cooperation with coworkers and social climate. But, "a network with a bow-tie structure (i.e., where a focal actor is the link between two or more mutually exclusive cliques) generally has strong negative effects on satisfaction with the social side of the job; although a bow-tie type network of trusting ties does increase satisfaction with the social side" (p. 297). Across a variety of public and private sector organizations, researchers discovered that dense personal networks, high social capital, and strong coworker support reduces absenteeism, burnout, emotional exhaustion, and quitting (Wegge et al. 2007; Boyas and Wind 2010). High levels of job satisfaction among trusted coworkers are contagious (Agneessens and Wittek 2008). And a tight coupling between friendship networks and formal authority networks leads to both organizational identification and internalization (Kuipers 2009). Overall, evidence is quite compelling that emotionally strong, supportive networks inoculate employees against many plagues and pitfalls of the workplace.

Four investigations of public employees demonstrated that workplace networks also contributed to reduction in psychological stress and psychosomatic symptoms and to improved employee health. Research on 209 employees of a New England public child welfare organization revealed that high social capital predicted less job stress and emotional exhaustion (Boyas and Wind 2010). Greater support from supervisors also reduced job stress, but coworker support had no effect. A survey of social capital and health among 6,028 public sector employees in eight Finnish towns found that both high coworker support and moderate employment security contributed to better self-rated health, especially for women (Liukkonen et al. 2004). A multi-level longitudinal survey of 9,524 initially healthy Finnish employees in 1,522 governmental units calculated that the odds for subsequent health impairment were higher for employees working in units with low social capital, and that "an increase in individual-level social capital from low to high was associated with sustained good health" (Oksanen et al. 2008: 644). A longitudinal epidemiological study of 7,770 employees in Malmo, Sweden, showed that absence of social support in high-stress workplaces increased the likelihood of heart attack and stroke among women, but found no relationship between psychosocial work conditions and cardiovascular disease among men (Andre-Petersson et al. 2007).

Hindrance networks, the exact inverse of support networks, involve active efforts by some employees to block and subvert others. Actions range from disliking to antagonism to hostility toward coworkers. In their most severe form, hindrance networks may tear apart an organization, thwart job performance, and destroy collective productivity. Social liabilities may be more potent than positive relations for explaining many employee outcomes. For example, hindrance relations reduce organizational commitment, increase psychosomatic symptoms, worsen job performance, and induce withdrawal behaviors such as absenteeism and turnover (Labianca and Brass 2006). Social undermining actions intentionally directed by supervisors or coworkers at other employees – gossip, ridicule, rejection, unconstructive criticism, physical assault – have obvious negative consequences for targeted individuals, but also for organizations that tolerate such workplace abuses (Duffy et al. 2006). Undermining and other deviant behaviors may be rare relative to more prevalent prosocial supportive relations, but the harm they cause can far outweigh the beneficial effects of most workplace social networks.

Gender, Race, and Ethnicity

An old-boy network – a.k.a. "good ole boys" and "the establishment" – traditionally refers to strong informal ties among white male members of an upper social class, the legal and medical professions, elite business firms, or prestigious college alumni. Old boys mutually assist one another and perform favors for their fellows in business and political transactions. Such networks may reward and promote less competent people to positions of higher status and power ahead of more meritorious outsiders. A renowned comedic skewering of an old-boy network among Britain's higher civil servants is the BBC series *Yes Minister*, first broadcast in the 1980s. Other familiar examples are white-shoe law firms that recruit WASPs from Ivy League law schools; academic departments that hire and tenure the graduates of particular universities; and coaching staffs in professional sports that give preference to former teammates. In the corporate world, old-boy networks provide opportunities to meet, converse, and cut business deals at private golf courses, fraternal and social clubs, stadium executive sky-boxes, and similar exclusionary venues where women, blacks, Hispanics, gays, and other minorities have little or no access. In her classic study, *Men and Women of the Corporation* (1977), Rosabeth Kanter described the virtual exclusion of women from top management positions during that era as a structural outcome of *homosocial reproduction*. Because people are generally more comfortable with others similar to themselves, especially in situations of high uncertainty, the white men occupying upper corporate echelons sponsored and advanced the careers of other white males, effectively closing managerial positions to people who were different. In the decades since, much US legislation was enacted to eradicate discrimination in employment by gender, race, age, and disability status. However, enforcement has often been sporadic and ineffectual. The question persists whether female and minority employees still confront substantial network barriers to career advancement in the workplace.

Theory and empirical research on the effects of gender, race, and ethnicity on social networks underscore persistent differences in homophily – the tendency of egos to choose alters like themselves – that generally disadvantage women and minorities. In an early investigation of gender networks in a newspaper, Daniel Brass (1985) found that female employees were more adept than men at building informal networks (workflow, communication, and friendship) and were more central than men in overall interaction networks. But, these networks were heavily segregated by gender, meaning that women were less central within the men's networks and particularly lacked ties to the nearly all-male dominant coalition. As a result, women were rated by their supervisors as less influential than men and received fewer promotions. However, a handful of women belonging to integrated work groups were perceived to be equally influential as men. In the 1990s, Herminia Ibarra analyzed gender differences in intraorganizational networks. She hypothesized that women's inequality in organizational power was reinforced through two network mechanisms: (1) gender differentials in homophily; and (2) men's greater ability to convert their personal attributes and network positional resources into such advantages as pay and promotions (Ibarra 1992). Evidence from a New England advertising and public relations agency revealed that the male employees formed stronger homophilous ties across multiple networks. But, the female network ties were differentiated: women obtained friendship and social support from other women, and acquired information, advice, and influence through their connections to men. Because men occupied higher positions in the firm hierarchy, "homophily contributed or had no effect on men's centrality, while it decreased women's centrality" (p. 440). Ibarra (1993) argued that the organizational contexts within which employees' personal network are embedded produce structural constraints on women and minorities. For example, where women and minorities are underrepresented in positions of corporate power and authority, aspiring female and black employees have fewer opportunities than white males to develop beneficial professional relations based on identity-group homophily preferences. Thus, organizational demography constrains personal networks, both directly and indirectly by shaping available alternatives. Based on interviews with 63 middle managers at four large corporations, Ibarra (1995) contrasted minority and female employee networks with those of whites and males, respectively. She found that the minority managers (mostly African Americans, but also some Hispanics and Asian Americans) had fewer homophilous contacts and fewer intimate relations. However, managers who had been put onto a "fast-track" (high-potential program) for corporate advancement, had higher proportions of same-race ties than their nonfast-track peers. They had more out-group contacts, fewer high-status ties, and less overlap of their social and instrumental relations, suggesting a strategy of developing work ties to white sponsors while relying on other minorities for psychosocial support. Similarly, Ibarra (1997) found that women's networks were less homophilous than men's networks. Fast-track female managers differed from male peers in having "closer and broader ranging information network ties, [which] suggested that women may need greater quantities of the resources provided by close and external ties, or may need them in a broader array of network types" (1997: 98). Such patterns suggest that women and minority employees may need greater sponsorship or mentoring than white males, an issue briefly discussed below.

Other researchers generally depicted the network disparities of women and racial/ethnic minorities as arising from structurally disadvantageous positions inside organizations, within authority hierarchies and in physical locations, rather than from homosocial preferences for same-sex or same-race affiliations. For example, Gail McGuire (2000) analyzed employee assistance networks – "who made an effort to give you job, career, or personal help?" – for a sample of 1,150 full-time employees of a large financial services firm, of whom a majority were women and 39 percent were people of color. Women and minorities had alters with less control over company resources and decision making than the alters of male and white employees, primarily because "[w]omen and people of color were less likely than men and Whites to have the resources and positions that would put them into contact with high-status employees" (p. 517). They tended to work on floors with mostly female employees, hence to have workplace networks composed of relatively powerless women. Further analysis (McGuire 2002) revealed that even when white women and blacks controlled organizational resources and had high-status white male alters, they received less work-related help than their white male competitors. She concluded that network and sociological assumptions about gender-neutral workplaces overlook "the ways in which organizational norms, values, and positions have been constructed to privilege men and disadvantage women" (p. 317), as well as racial minorities. Julie Kmec (2007) studied the impact of social capital, measured as an applicant referred by a current employee, on the job turnover of 300 entry-level workers at a private research firm. White and minority networks had similar effects on their referrals' turnover, but same-race contacts and applicants had marginally more involuntary departures than employees recruited via racially mis-matched referrers and non-contacts. One interpretation is that "employers may hold referrals provided by minorities to a tougher standard than referrals provided by whites" (p. 499). Alternatively, if minority contacts fear losing their jobs or their employer's trust by making a bad referral, they may refer only exceptional applicants who are less likely than whites to quit. A study of black and Latino contacts and applicants in a multi-city survey showed that using an outside minority contact was associated with higher pay (but an insider contact was not), while the minority contact's influence was most beneficial if his or her race and ethnicity were unknown to the firm's hiring agent (Kmec and Trimble 2009). Undoubtedly, the impacts of employee race, ethnicity, and gender on social capital, workplace networks, and job outcomes are quite complex and likely also contingent on firm and industry contexts. Opportunities abound for improved theorizing and empirical investigations of diverse organizational settings.

Remedies for the network disadvantages of women and minorities frequently include company assigned-mentor and fast-track programs to groom promising young employees for rapid intraorganizational promotion. Despite intensified mentoring of women managers at many multinational corporations, high-potential candidates continue to lag behind their male counterparts in promotion to executive leadership positions (Carter and Silva 2010). Incessant transformation of the global economy and accompanying organizational restructuring suggest a developmental network approach could be more beneficial for people whose careers increasingly span multiple employers (Higgins and Kram 2001; Dobrow and Higgins 2005). In a developmental network strategy, diverse "developers" with varied weak and strong ties to a protégé, both inside and outside organizations, can contribute actively to moving a young person along an upward career trajectory. Protégés themselves must energetically forge new contacts and regularly modify their social capital connections to create structures more conducive to attaining goals at different career stages. For a mid-career high-potential candidate to break through the final glass ceiling into senior management, a crucial developmental relation is "sponsorship – in which a mentor goes beyond giving feedback and advice and uses his or her influence with senior executives to advocate for the mentee" (Ibarra et al. 2010: 82). More than brokers who merely make introductions to top-echelon people who might help their protégés' careers, sponsors must actively advocate and fight to get them plum assignments, challenging opportunities, and meaningful promotions. A sponsor's dilemma is how best to change white-male perceptions of women and minorities as "not ready" and "risky" appointments, while helping a protégé to avoid appearing either "too aggressive" or "not aggressive enough." An ideal sponsor may well be an older white man, competent in playing the politics of structural holes, yet willing to fill the gaps to benefit younger people of a different gender, race, or ethnicity. How many such altruists exist?

Burt (2010) cautioned against the naïve belief that programs which encourage junior employees to network with well-connected senior colleagues would necessarily bring substantial career benefits. His research on the purported advantages of *neighbor networks* (the networks of ego's alters, i.e., two-step linkages or friends-of-friends) in five managerial populations revealed that the strong correlation between a manager's performance and her ties to well-connected alters disappeared after holding constant the manager's own network. That is, if a manager's ego-network lacked connections to many diverse alters, then only having ties to well-connected alters gave her no spillover advantages through indirect access to her alters' structural holes. Burt concluded that "the advantage of network brokerage is not about quick, early access to distant, novel information so much as it is about what happens to a person who has to manage communication across a network full of structural holes" (p. 9). This perspective restores the primacy of social psychology in networking. A junior employee who undertakes serious efforts to learn how to manage diversified, even contradictory, relations in networks with numerous structural holes between subgroups, can develop her cognitive and emotional skills; identify opportunities for integrating ideas and practices across groups; and derive career advantages by bringing those opportunities to realization. Because neighbor networks generally fail to produce spillover benefits to novice networkers, most corporate mentoring and sponsorship programs "operate somewhere between irritating and irrelevant. For any such program that has proven valuable, the factor responsible for its value would have to be something other than neighbor networks" (p. 7). That factor appears to be ambitious junior managers who widely affiliate with other employees engaged in diverse ideas and practices.

Team Networking

Corporations, government agencies, and nonprofits increasingly deploy teams as fundamental workplace units. A *team* is a subgroup within an organization whose members are connected through interdependent work tasks. Team members typically possess complementary skills, engage in coordinated actions, share consistent perceptions and beliefs, and focus on collective achievements and rewards. A sports team is the paradigmatic type, whose members strive to defeat opposing teams in athletic contests regulated by rules of the game. In economic organizations, a team may be a formally designated corporate entity (e.g., "Target India" at Target Corp.), may have shorter or longer duration according to project requirements, or may be an informal network of employees who interact and assist one another at work. Formal membership requirements can establish a clear boundary between a team and its larger organizational environment. Alternatively, a team's boundaries may be fuzzy and porous, with a floating membership based on such ambiguous criteria as frequently working together and exchanging information. Team-based organizations make high-stakes wagers that improve structural configurations, particularly social networking among team members, boost productivity and performance outcomes. Well-functioning teams are particularly crucial when high task interdependence requires strong interpersonal ties – frequent, intense, emotional bonding – to generate "unit cohesion," high morale, and group solidarity. Well-known examples are army platoons, naval patrols, flight squadrons, SWAT teams, smoke-jumper crews, and surgical units. Even organizations engaged in more mundane production and services, such as manufacturing, sales, and accounting, can benefit from teamwork. This section asks two questions about team network relations and social capital: What are the origins and evolution of team networks? How do the demographic composition and network structural properties of teams affect group performances?

Analysts know relatively little about the formation and evolution of team networks, in particular how prior social structures influence subsequent structures and outcomes. However, two longitudinal studies of temporary production teams in cultural industries disclosed some important dynamics. First, Brian Uzzi and Jarrett Spiro (2005) investigated the formation of 474 Broadway musical teams from 1945 to 1989, when 2,092 artistic and financial participants incessantly collaborated on projects, then dispersed and formed new freelance production teams to create new musicals. They found that a team's success (turning a profit, getting favorable critical reviews) was curvilinearly related to connections among cohesive clusters based on the members' prior collaborations:

> When there is a low level of *Q* [a small-world property; see chapter 4], there are few links between clusters, and the links are more hit-and-miss, on average, in the sense that they are not disproportionately formed through credible third-party or repeat ties, isolating creative material in separate clusters. As the level of *Q* increases, separate clusters become more interlinked and linked by persons who know each other. These processes distribute creative material among teams and help to build a cohesive social organization within teams that support risky collaboration around good ideas. However, past a certain threshold, these same processes can create liabilities for collaboration. Increased structural connectivity reduces some of the creative distinctiveness of clusters, which can homogenize the pool of creative material. At the same time, problems of excessive cohesion can creep in. The ideas most likely to flow can be conventional rather than fresh ideas because of the common information effect and because newcomers find it harder to land "slots" on productions. (Uzzi and Spiro 2005: 464)

Second, Akbar Zaheer and Giuseppe Soda (2009) traced co-membership patterns of 501 production teams in the Italian television industry across 12 years. Television teams were short-lived, continually dissolving and reforming to produce new TV serials and movies. The network structural holes spanned by a new team originated in the high-performance status, centrality, and structural holes of the prior teams to which its members belonged. If the members' prior teams were strongly cohesive and produced similar artistic content, a new team spanned fewer structural holes. But, spanning more structural holes was associated with superior team performance, as measured by the commercial success of its productions (e.g., TV audience share). "Overall, our results provide considerable evidence for the notion that structural entrepreneurs are able to actively exploit opportunities, although inertia and homophily also play a role, in the genesis of network structure" (p. 27). A fascinating question for future research is whether these network evolutionary dynamics of creative teams also occur among teams in noncultural industries?

Theorists diverge on the question of whether demographic diversity – measured by race, gender, age, class, or other social attributes – among team members hinders or helps group performance. Diversity can be problematic when member preferences for homophily renders coordination more difficult among people with incompatible assumptions, beliefs, and experiences. In contrast, diversified teams may perform better because heterogeneous members bring complementary knowledge, skills, and perspectives that enhance learning and collective problem solving. Among 76 work teams in 48 organizations, gender diversity was associated with low advice-network density and greater team fragmentation, and was negatively related to team performance as measured by leader and member reports (Henttonen et al. 2010). Research on 57 Dutch high school teams, composed of teachers from different functional areas, found no impact of demographic diversity. But, in teams with high social capital, homogeneity of attitudes toward teaching was associated with improved team effectiveness, role performance, and satisfaction (van Emmerik and Brenninkmeijer 2009). Ray Reagans and Ezra Zuckerman (2001) took a sociometric approach to the diversity-performance debate in analyzing productivity and network relations of 224 research and development teams in 29 corporations. Team productivity was assessed by the volume of papers, proposals, patents, and reports produced. Productivity increased with greater R&D team social capital, as indicated by: (1) network density, high communication between team members; (2) network heterogeneity, frequent contact among scientists joining the organization many years apart (tenure diversity); and (3) interaction of network density and heterogeneity, that is, "communication across demographic boundaries appears to be more valuable when such relations are relatively strong than when they are weak" (p. 512). Reagans and Zuckerman concluded that the evidence was most consistent with a structural hole approach to R&D team social capital. It "emphasizes the importance of interchange among individuals with a wide range of skills, information, and experiences, for maximizing a group's capacity for creativity and effective action." A related project examined the impacts of internal density and external range on the performance of 1,518 project teams in a contract R&D firm (Reagans et al. 2004). Event history analysis of project durations revealed that demographic diversity, measured by average difference in tenure among project members, had no effect on performance. But, both network variables were associated with better team performance, as indicated by quicker project completion. A practical implication for organizational managers is to avoid futile efforts to manipulate demographic balance in assigning employees to teams. A better strategy for building effective teams is to apply network-based criteria that are "more precise and proximate indicators of the causal mechanisms than are demographic variables" (p. 128) and which better predict team performance.

Other research on team performance identified facets of team networks that promote successful collaboration or lead to counter-productive conflicts. A meta-analysis summarizing 37 team studies discovered that dense ties, leaders who are central within their groups, and teams that are central in intergroup networks were more viable (committed to staying together) and achieved their goals (Balkundi and Harrison 2006). Another meta-analysis of 72 team studies demonstrated that greater information-sharing contributed to higher team performance, cohesion, decision satisfaction, and knowledge integration (Mesmer-Magnus and DeChurch 2009). Apparently, network diversity rather than demographic diversity is a key to better team performance. Researchers investigating 19 teams at a wood-product firm found neither ethnic nor gender diversity related to structural holes in friendship networks (Balkundi et al. 2007). However, "structural holeyness" was curvilinearly related to team performance: both low and high proportions of structural holes were associated with lower team performance than were moderate levels of structural holes. Further analysis of those teams showed that the type of leader centrality affected conflict among members (Balkundi et al. 2009). Teams with more prestigious leaders, measured by how many members sought their advice, experienced less conflict and were more viable. However, teams whose leaders brokered advice relations among unconnected team members had greater conflict and lower viability, regardless of the leader's network prestige.

In sum, researchers have consistently identified strong, dense ties among members as conducive to team cohesion and high performance outcomes.

Summary

Multiple types of social networks connect workers inside organizations, allowing them to perform their jobs more effectively and their companies to achieve goals more efficiently. Formal organizational structures, embodied in job descriptions and organizational charts, constrain the informal ties that employees develop. In turn, social connections in the workplace influence job performance and individual outcomes. Social capital, comprising the resources controlled by alters to whom ego is connected, generally creates benefits such as career advancement, job satisfaction, and lowered stress and burnout. On the dark side, some negative social relations can hinder employee morale, generate conflict, and damage organizational well-being. Women and racial and ethnic minorities still face impediments to networking as effectively as their white male coworkers, although the obstacles may be eroding. As teamwork grows increasingly crucial in organizational design, better understanding of the interplay between demographic attributes and team members' network relations becomes imperative.

4

Networks among Organizations

In 1947, two Swedish multinational companies launched a highly effective strategic alliance that endured more than four decades before ending in bitter divorce. Combining Sandvik Rock Tool's advanced tool-making technologies and hard-metal competence with Atlas Copco's global marketing capabilities gave their alliance unique competitive advantages for selling rock-drilling equipment in global mining and road-building markets. "This initial collaboration offered both of the firms a first chance to get to know one another and build trust, based on the fact that both firms were founded in the same culture during the same period of industrialization. Their geographical proximity also facilitated communication" (Hyder and Ericksson 2005: 788). By the 1960s, the "Swedish Method" of producing and selling rock-drilling products had captured more than half the world markets. But, as those markets gradually changed, fewer drilling projects required Sandvik's hard-metal technologies, and competitors had time to catch up. After the alliance reached its original goal of international growth and expansion, it no longer satisfied the two firms' motives and desires. "When trust began to decline in the latter part of this stage, however, collaboration became difficult and things that had functioned well earlier did not work anymore" (p. 794). In June 1988, the alliance ended abruptly when Sandvik surprisingly broke the contract and sought complementary resource exchanges with other partners. To acquire marketing competence quickly, Sandvik poached sales staff from Atlas Copco, which retaliated by marketing its own rock-drilling brand to the confusion of former customers. In the ensuing price war, both firms suffered lost profits, shrunken market shares, and damaged reputations. "During the 1990s, relations between the previous partners were frosty, but not hostile. No further collaboration took place in the fields of marketing or product development" (p. 791). Eventually, Sandvik and Atlas Copco regained competitive vigor and both found success as individual firms.

This Swedish saga exemplifies one of several types of interorganizational relations that are neither hierarchies nor markets, but cooperative activities among two or more competitors with complementary capabilities and expectations of mutual gains at lower costs than the parties could attain through their separate efforts. Such beneficial expectations may be realized, as in the early years of the Sandvik–Atlas Copco alliance, but many collaborations sour and fall apart before fully accomplishing their aims. Theoretical bases for interorganizational network research include transaction cost economics, resource-based views of organizations, trust, status, power and control, signaling, and social capital theories. With such diversity in theory, methods, measures, and samples, research findings remain poorly integrated. As one overview pithily summarized, "much of the work has borrowed from traditional theoretical frameworks (such as resource dependency) in order to explain the theoretical mechanisms that link network phenomena to organizational outcomes (often performance). Unfortunately, as a cumulative body of work, this approach has resulted in a lack of coherence and parsimony" (Zaheer, Gözübüyük and Milanov 2010: 63). This chapter examines four prevalent types of interorganizational relations – business startup networks, business groups, interlocking boards of directors, and strategic alliances – from network perspectives on their origins, structures, and consequences.

Business Startup Networks

Most businesses begin life very small – often with just a sole entrepreneur/owner and no paid workers. Many never survive beyond infancy, and among businesses lasting beyond five years, most will stay small throughout their life spans – typically an owner and fewer than a dozen employees. Theory and research on new firms tend to emphasize heroic efforts by creative entrepreneurs facing long odds, but dogged perseverance by conventional business men and women is more common. Personal relations and inter-organizational networks can give both types of leaders advantages that may affect a startup company's chances of survival, growth, and prosperity or its ultimate extinction. "The web of external relationships that surrounds any small business . . . is capable of providing a wide variety of tangible and intangible benefits" (Street and Cameron 2007: 240). These outcomes include access to crucial financial and social resources, business development opportunities, competitive edges, organizational performance, and success in achieving business goals.

An *entrepreneur* is a person who undertakes economic risks in an uncertain environment by investing time and money to create and cultivate a business producing a new product or service. She or he identifies a market opportunity, assembles the resources necessary to launch an enterprise, expands and nurtures its activities, and either reaps the profits or suffers the losses. Under the broadest definition of an entrepreneur – anyone who starts a new company – the United States is an entrepreneurial nation. A 2002 survey of more than 2.3 million firms revealed that most were "self-made" businesses (US Census Bureau 2006). However, more nuanced definitions differentiate the large majority of conventional small businesses from a much smaller number of genuinely entrepreneurial ventures. For example, an entrepreneur has "a preference for creating activity, manifested by some innovative combination of resources for profit," in contrast to a small business owner "who establishes and manages a business for the principle purpose of furthering personal goals" (Carland et al. 1984: 357–8). Other distinctions consider whether an entrepreneurial firm is an industry outsider (an independent startup) or insider (a spin-off sponsored by an established firm, or an incubator-driven venture), and whether the type of innovation involves merely incremental changes or radical economic or technological disruptions (Elfring and Hulsink 2007). This section concentrates on the relatively uncommon entrepreneur who introduces innovative ideas that fundamentally challenge conventional economic wisdom.

Several mainstream and heterodox economists proposed explanations of entrepreneurship centered on a singular individual's bold actions. Frank Knight (1921) argued that an entrepreneur is a rational risk-bearer who acts only after calculating the probability of future profit. Josef Schumpeter depicted entrepreneurs as the drivers of modern capitalism's "creative destruction," by promoting innovations that revolutionize economic production. Entrepreneurial skills are rare: "To act with confidence beyond the range of familiar beacons and to overcome that resistance requires aptitudes that are present in only a small fraction of the population and define the entrepreneurial type as well as the entrepreneurial function" (Schumpeter 1942: 132). He extolled heroic visionaries who possess "willpower adequate to breaking down the resistance that the social environment offers to change" (p. 417). Likewise, Israel Kirzner's visionary "pure entrepreneur" subconsciously discovers a market opportunity for making a gain by buying and selling, finances a venture by borrowing money from a capitalist lender, then pays back the capitalist with interest, and pockets the "pure entrepreneurial profit" (Kirzner 1973: 49–50). Economic theorists steered research attention to the psychodynamics of entrepreneurial personalities, for example, their drive for achievement, confidence and optimism, propensity to take risks, and problem-solving styles. Similarly, early sociological accounts stressed the individual traits of entrepreneurs, such as their social class, gender, nationality, and ethnic origins (Thornton 1998). In recent years, the center of entrepreneurial research shifted from micro-toward macro-level influences on demand for entrepreneurs, such as market development, technological changes, national public policies, and rates of organizational founding.

Social network approaches to entrepreneurship integrate individual and group explanations of new enterprise creation. Launching a startup requires a nascent entrepreneur to forge connections with numerous economic actors: banks, technical advisors and consultants, headhunters and employment bureaus, advertisers and marketers, trade associations, regulators. For a fortunate few, venture capital (VC) firms provide seed funding to especially promising high-risk companies deemed likely to produce above-average returns on investment. Some recent examples are startups in technology-intensive industries like biotech, communications, and electronics. VCs create partnerships and syndication networks to broker connections between an entrepreneur and institutional investors, such as pension funds and university endowments, in effect granting the entrepreneur access to the VC's funder network (Sorenson and Stuart 2001). Unfortunately for most prospective entrepreneurs, VC startup resources are simply beyond reach. Instead, they mostly turn to their egocentric networks – embedded in families, friends, religious communities, or ethnic enclaves – in the quest for crucial seed money, unpaid labor, and moral support (Dubini and Aldrich 1991). Aldrich and Zimmer (1986) claimed that the majority of new small businesses are funded informally by the owner's personal savings, family, and network of friends. The Census Bureau's 2002 survey concurred: more than 60 percent of business owners reported using their own savings or family assets to start their companies. Almost 30 percent of all "entrepreneurs started or acquired their business with no capital at all" and one in ten used credit cards to finance a startup or acquisition (US Census Bureau 2006). Many worked out of spare rooms or proverbial garages in their homes until sufficient earnings allowed them to move the business to a separate site.

Research on entrepreneurial networks grew substantially over the past two decades. Analysts expended more effort investigating the impacts and consequences of networks on startup performance and outcomes than on examining entrepreneurial organizing processes at either the dyadic or complete network levels of analysis (Hoang and Antoncic 2003). To explain network change, typical approaches "depicted or described using a developmental event sequence" (Slotte-Kock and Coviell 2010: 33). Process or phase models portray an entrepreneurial venture evolving through an orderly series of stages, such as planning, startup, growth, maturity, succession (Jiang and Zhao 2009). Entrepreneurial network structures, contents, and dynamics vary according to the enterprise's developmental stage. A family-and-friends nexus helps to nurture and sustain a nascent company through precarious planning and startup phases (Peng 2004). "As firms emerge, their networks consist primarily of socially embedded ties drawn from dense, cohesive sets of connections. We label these networks identity-based" (Hite and Hesterly 2001: 275). A homophily hypothesis asserts that dense, strong-tie relations among homogeneous alters are notoriously inbred and feckless at tapping new information and ideas. An impacted egocentric network may severely constrain an entrepreneur's awareness of, and access to, timely information and other vital resources available outside her cozy circle of intimates. Sustaining an innovative organization necessitates reaching across subgroup boundaries to connect with diverse economic actors who have less interest and commitment to the startup. A too-heavy reliance on the solidary bonds within one's egocentric network could strangle an infant company before the entrepreneur can forge valuable weak-tie links to the business community that might help to secure important externally provided resources, such as legitimacy, advice, assistance, and business leads. Thus, a prominent hypothesis in network explanations of successful entrepreneurship is the evolution from homogeneous strong-tie networks in the initial startup stage toward intentionally constructed and calculative networks of heterogeneous weak ties during later growth stages (Hite and Hesterly 2001).

Empirical support for a process model of entrepreneurial networks is equivocal. Although some researchers found strong ties at the beginning stages (e.g., Batjargal 2003; Jack 2005), others observed evolution from weak to strong ties (Lechner et al. 2006). In an attempt to reconcile conflicting findings, Elfring and Hulsink (2007) examined changes in the personal networks of 32 founders of info-tech startups in The Netherlands. They identified three distinct patterns of entrepreneurial network evolution in which initial founding conditions and subsequent processes influence changes in tie-formation:

(1) *Network evolution*: Spin-offs and incubatees that pursue an incremental strategy of competing in new markets start life

with strong ties to their parent firm or incubator, then add increasing numbers of weak ties.

(2) *Network renewal*: Spin-offs and incubatees pursuing radical innovations begin with a mix of strong and weak ties and maintain this balance by dropping and adding weak ties, and turning some weak ties into stronger ones.

(3) *Network revolution*: independent startups pursuing radical innovations start with large numbers of weak ties, "the result of a frantic search for private information on business opportunities and access to ties in the inner circles of the IT industry" (p. 1864). Search becomes more focused and efficient if a prominent IT player connects to the startup, forming multiplex ties that benefit the new player.

Elfring and Hulsink's research was a major stride in understanding that entrepreneurial network processes follow no universal pattern, but vary according to a firm's founding conditions and innovation strategies.

Few researchers examined gender difference in the networks of entrepreneurs and small-business owners. Research in two North Carolina counties using data from the early 1990s found that, compared to men, women had a higher proportion of kin and homogeneity in their core business discussion networks. That mix isn't helpful for gaining access to diverse people with whom "to discuss your ideas for a new business or your ideas about representing or running your current business" (Renzulli et al. 2000: 533). Women's more restricted social capital, not their gender nor the higher proportion of females in their networks, may explain why they were only half as likely as men to start their own businesses. Further analyses of the North Carolina data assessed when business owners would activate their core network to obtain legal, loan, financial, and expert advice (Renzulli and Aldrich 2005). Business resource providers were more likely to come from inside core networks that had higher density, occupational heterogeneity, and a greater proportion of men. However, women business owners were as likely as men to activate their core networks, suggesting that "women business owners have adapted to the same competitive conditions as men and continuing competitive pressures require similar behaviors, regardless of gender" (p. 336). Researchers comparing the business discussion networks of female and male small business owners in upstate New York in the late 1990s found fewer female disadvantages (Loscocco et al. 2009). Although women's networks still had more kinfolk, they were somewhat larger (2.37 alters versus 1.95 alters for men), and the proportions of female alters were the same (40 percent) for both genders. Although the evidence for change is slim, businesswomen may be closing the business network gap with their male peers, and possibly developing innovative ways to turn networks to their advantage.

Business Groups

Ownership of large- and medium-sized corporations is heavily concentrated, for both privately and publicly held firms, across diverse societies at varying levels of economic development around the world. Sometimes a national state is the controlling owner, but more typically a founding entrepreneur or family descendants occupy the key management positions and control multiple subsidiary firms via pyramidal stock-holding structures (Almeida and Wolfenzon 2006). Family-controlled businesses are very common in Asia, Latin America, Africa, the Middle East, and some parts of Europe, such as Germany, Belgium, and Italy. Notable exceptions are the United States and United Kingdom, which have better legal protections for minority shareholders, resulting in more dispersed ownership of public firms run by professional managers (La Porta et al. 1999). In many countries, corporate concentration takes the form of a *business group*. Mark Granovetter defined business groups as "sets of legally separated firms bound together in persistent formal and/or informal ways" (2005b: 429). Other definitions explicitly emphasize collaboration among the member firms of a business group: they conduct "business in different markets under common administrative or financial control" (Leff 1978: 663); their "reciprocal commitments stem from long association and strong collective identity" (Lincoln et al. 1996: 83); and they are "accustomed to taking coordinated action" (Khanna and Rivkin 2001: 48). One effort to synthesize the huge business-group literature argued that they comprise multiplex networks of interrelated firms, with an institutionalized logic of reciprocity and "intersubjective interpretation or recognition of individuals inside and outside the groups" (Smångs 2006: 896). Particularly in emerging economies, where underdeveloped market institutions function poorly, business groups allegedly provide important benefits to their members by internalizing exchanges of financial capital and human talent, thus reducing the higher transaction costs of market exchanges. Their origins and specific forms are as diverse as the historical, political, and socioeconomic conditions of each nation. The primary concerns in this section are the network structural features and the performance outcomes of business-group member firms.

Japanese *Keiretsu*

Under the Empire of Japan, the paradigmatic family-centered business conglomerate was the *zaibatsu* (financial clique), a holding company using financial and director interlocks to connect manufacturing, mining, trading, and banking firms (Lonien 2007). The companies belonging to a *zaibatsu* cooperated with one another and competed against the rival oligopolies' firms. The Allied Occupation after World War II, intent on breaking *zaibatsu* domination of Japan's economy, made holding companies illegal. But, intercorporate alliances called *keiretsu* quickly emerged – particularly the "Big Six" horizontal keiretsu: Mitsubishi, Mitsui, Sumitomo, Fuji, Dai-Ichi Kangyo, and Sanwa. Keiretsu are comprised of major financial institutions, trading companies, and multi-industry producers linked to sets of smaller affiliated suppliers and distribution firms (McGuire and Dow 2009). Although member firms operate without central keiretsu control, one formal institution is the presidents' council (*shacho-kai*) which meets regularly. Although some analysts regarded presidents' councils as merely social gatherings, others argued that councils facilitate

Japanese business group coordination (e.g., Lincoln and Gerlach 2004: 180–1). A secondary form is the vertical keiretsu organized around one major manufacturing firm with its suppliers, subcontractors, and distributors; for example, Toyota and Hitachi. The Big Six horizontal keiretsu dominated for decades, enabling Japan to become the second largest economy on the planet. But, starting in 1988, Japan experienced a financial bubble as frenetic speculation by major banks and industrial firms ran up stock prices and real estate values to unsustainable levels. After the bubble burst in 1991, followed by a "lost decade" of stagnation and recession from which Japan never fully recovered, economic realities and institutional reforms altered the connections among the keiretsu member firms. The Big Six shrank to four when Sumitomo and Mitsui merged in 2000 and Sanwa joined the Mitsubishi group a year later. The alleged competitive advantages for firms in horizontal keiretsu include access to stable financing, insulation from market pressures, risk reduction, information monitoring, and mutual assistance (McGuire and Dow 2009: 335). But, critics charged that, by propping up weaker "zombie firms," keiretsu distort efficient resource reallocation in the Japanese economy (Hoshi 2006). The weakening and transformation of traditional keiretsu ties during the recession cast doubt on the presumed firm-performance benefits.

Relational approaches to business groups analyze patterns of ties among firms to identify jointly occupied social structural positions. Among relevant relational contents are equity shareholding, banking borrowing, and board of director interlocks. Michael Gerlach (1992) used blockmodel methods to study those networks among the 40 largest Japanese industrial firms and 20 largest financial firms in 1980. Blockmodel analysis applies structural equivalence methods to simplify ties among many actors by aggregating a subset into a jointly occupied position if their ties to other positions are the same or very similar. (See figure 2.5 in chapter 2 for an example of structural equivalence in producer markets.) Gerlach found eight blocks occupied by the 60 firms, with Blocks A, B, and C consisting of the financial institutions and Blocks D to H industrial corporations. Between-block densities varied by type of tie. For example, 37 percent of the banks in Block B sent equity ties to the industrial firms in Block G, 61 percent sent lent money, but only 8 percent sent board directors. Gerlach's blockmodels revealed that a financial hierarchy was pervasive in all three networks and that the composition of an industrial block was largely determined by the firms' keiretsu memberships. Figure 4.1 displays the sociogram of the equity network, for tie densities of 10 percent or higher. The three financial blocks, located at the center, had three directed ties to one another. But, none of the five industrial blocks, located at the periphery, directly connected to another industrial block and only five of the 15 possible industry-bank ties occurred. A closer look at the industrial composition of the blocks confirms that these interblock ties reflected the organizations' predominant keiretsu identities. For example, Block H was constituted mostly of Sumitomo-affiliated companies and sent equity ties to the Sumitomo and Fuji banks residing in Block B. Similarly, Block G contained firms of the Fuji and Sanwa keiretsu and also sent equity to Block B banks. The industrial firms in Block D belonged to the Mitsubishi group, while Block F's firms were affiliated with the Mitsui and Dai-Ichi Kangyo (DKB) keiretsu. Both industrial blocks sent equity to the Block A, which included those groups' banks. No industry invested in Block C which consisted mainly of nonlife insurance companies. Gerlach concluded:

> Together, these results indicate that the Japanese corporate network represents a relatively well-ordered structure of relationships among highly differentiated firms and that understanding the precise contours of this structure requires consideration of a set of complex and overlapping structures. . . . Unlike the relatively fragmented, loosely organized ties typically discerned in the American corporate network, the reality in Japan appears far closer to one of coherent and enduring cliques among affiliated financial institutions and industrial firms. (Gerlach 1992: 135)

In a subsequent book, *Japan's Network Economy* (2004), James Lincoln and Michael Gerlach investigated the changing relations among the 200 largest industrials, 50 financials firms, and 9 major trading companies at seven intervals from 1978 to

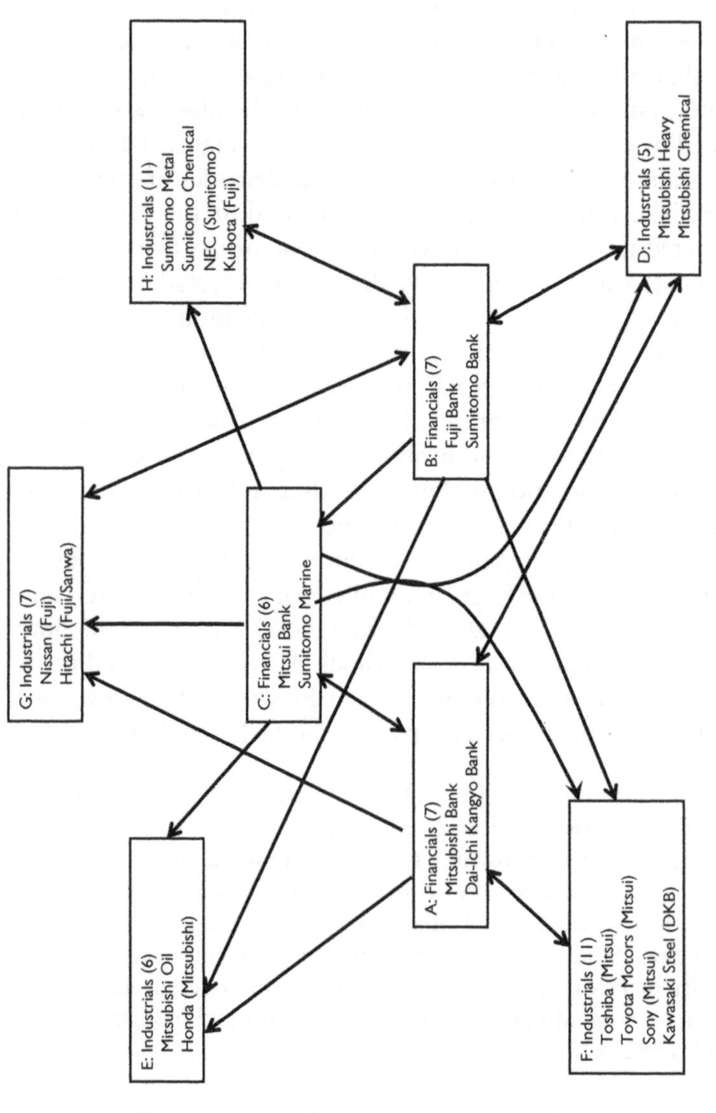

Source: Gerlach (1992)

Figure 4.1 Network of equity ties among eight Japanese blocks

1993. They operationalized group cohesion by network density (the ratio of direct ties to possible ties in equity, director, lending, and trading networks) and by connectivity (the ratio of direct and indirect ties to possible ties). Although density rose dramatically across the two decades, connectivity peaked in the mid-1980s then declined as fewer Japanese firms were indirectly linked through long-chain connections. Cross-shareholding became instruments of individual firms' strategies instead of "threads from which a macro-network web is spun" (p. 46). Director interlocks had "less to do with the macro-network fabric of keiretsu than with the means whereby one firm establishes control over another" (p. 100). Lincoln and Gerlach attributed this change to the declining importance of the keiretsu system after Japan's economic bubble burst. Their blockmodel analyses revealed that positions in the Japanese economy became less related to keiretsu membership and more industry-based. Declining block cohesion was consistent with an economic modernization model of disintegration in which "networks fray and fragment as economies mature" (p. 102). Although interfirm ties remain important in the Japanese economy, corporations take their keiretsu commitments less for granted and more closely scrutinize new alliances for cost-effectiveness and strategic utility.

Business Group Performance

Key questions for business group research are: Do member firms benefit from a group's ability to spread risk and raise economic returns? Do groups create collective value by sharing resources such as capital pools, brands, technologies, and managerial skills? Or do business groups foster inefficiencies and poor performances by sheltering weaker companies from the harsh discipline of direct market forces? Do poor performers sap the vitality of their stronger brethren? Comparative research by Tarun Khanna and colleagues yielded mixed results. Khanna and Rivkin (2001) examined business groups in 14 emerging markets in the 1990s. Group affiliates clearly enjoyed higher profitability, measured by return on assets, than comparable unaffiliated firms in India,

Indonesia, Israel, Peru, South Africa, and Taiwan. But independent firms performed better in Argentina, Chile, and the Philippines, while no differences occurred in Brazil, Korea, Mexico, Thailand, and Turkey. Further analyses showed that business groups facilitated mutual insurance among affiliated firms (measured by lower variation and lower levels of profitability) in Korea, Thailand, and Japan, but not in nine other countries (Khanna and Yafeh 2005). Finally, Khanna and Yafeh (2007) noted that business groups emerge and evolve under diverse historical conditions, including differing types of government support. Groups sometimes compensate for underdeveloped economic institutions, but at other times may harm social welfare by rent-seeking or monopoly power. The researchers reached "no clear verdict on the extent to which groups should be viewed as 'paragons' or 'parasites,' and the answer is likely to vary across countries, groups, and possibly time periods" (p. 334).

Research on firm performance in Japanese, Korean, Chinese, and Indian business groups arrived at similar mixed conclusions. Studies of Japan found either no difference between keiretsu firms and independent firms or a negative impact of keiretsu membership on firm performance. The lower cost of capital among keiretsu firms, due to efficient insider monitoring and financing by the main bank, may be offset by higher debt costs and "pressures toward overinvestment in order to draw on financing from the main bank . . . leading to lower financial performance" (McGuire and Dow 2009: 336–7). Lincoln and Gerlach (2004) documented the tendency of firms in the Big Six horizontal keiretsu to underperform independent firms in return on assets and sales growth. In effect, the economically healthy firms pay an insurance premium to maintain a safety net that supports and bails out financially distressed members, thus dragging down overall group performance.

> The benefits to weak affiliates go without saying. Why the best performers of a group maintain their membership is one of the mysteries of the keiretsu. . . . The networks within which Japanese economic action is embedded give corporations limited freedom to chart their own course, to pick and choose alliances (or whether to align at all)

> on the basis of unilateral calculations of advantage. There is a collective – embedded network – logic to the keiretsu phenomenon that is not reducible to rational optimizing on the part of individual firms. (p. 287).

Thirty large South Korean *chaebol*, family-controlled conglomerates such as Samsung and Hyundai, comprise about 40 percent of the economy (Chang and Hong 2000: 429). Debt guarantees, equity investments, and internal trade extensively supported poorly performing affiliates at the expense of profitable companies. Group effects on firm profitability were small and decreased from the 1980s to the 1990s (Chang and Hong 2002). A corporate "diversification premium" enjoyed by chaebol-affiliated firms, which enabled them to out-perform unaffiliated competitors, eventually diminished to a "diversification discount" (Lee et al. 2008). During the 1997–8 Asian financial crisis, collapsing Korean export prices triggered 25 chaebol bankruptcies, with many second-tier groups either downsized or absorbed into larger groups, such as Kia into Hyundai (Feenstra et al. 2002; Feenstra and Hamilton 2006). The International Monetary Fund intervened, forcing many market-oriented institutional reforms (Chang 2006). During the reformation, Korean manufacturing firms affiliated with business groups were less successful than independent firms at international diversification to improve performance, as measured by market-to-book values (Kim et al. 2010). However, after "business-group-affiliated firms embrace the market-oriented institutional logic, they show stronger abilities than independent firms to facilitate improved performance in relation to international diversification" (p. 1156). The surviving chaebol members were subsequently better situated than unaffiliated companies to overcome the international diversification discount and emerged as efficient, high-performing multinational corporations.

China arrived late among emerging markets, but quickly made up for the delay. Prior to the 1978 market reforms, all enterprises were state-owned and politically controlled by the Communist Party. In the mid-1980s, the Chinese government began encouraging firms to form business groups (*qiye jituan*), which developed intricate trading, lending, ownership, and social relations (Keister 1998a). However, after three decades, Chinese business networks continued to be smaller and less densely connected than their Western counterparts, more regionally fragmented, and without a dominant national center (Ren et al. 2009). Using panel data on 535 member firms in China's 40 largest business groups during the early market transition (1988–90), Lisa Keister (1998b) found that firms in business groups with a finance company and interlocking directorates produced higher profits and greater output per worker than the firms in groups without such relations. Analyzing 800 private firms and state-owned enterprises during a later period (1994–9), Keister observed a shift in the formation of interorganizational networks:

> In the early stages of development, processes originating outside the groups had the strongest influence on the formation of ties. As time passed, the role of external social relations and other external indicators of the trustworthiness and reliability of potential partners decreased. Yet processes originating within the business groups became more important. Firms increasingly sought to ally with group members with whom they had other ties and who were central players in the network of interfirm ties within business groups. (Keister 2009: 1728)

As the market reforms stabilized, Chinese business groups grew less beneficial for firm performance, implying that "China's economy may be becoming competitive enough that firms that compete openly are stronger than those that remain protected by business groups" (2009: 1724). Analyzing 76 Chinese business groups in 2006, Xinxiang Chen (2010) showed that firm performance depended on the mode of Chinese government intervention in their economic affairs. Direct state intervention – such as ownership, officials, and Chinese Communist Party members at the business group level – failed to produce beneficial economic impacts. Chen's research demonstrated the state's positive economic role in promoting the emerging market, for example, through loans from state-controlled banks as financial support for business groups. His results partially supported both political economy perspectives and developmental state theories, as well as the usefulness of a contingency framework for understanding the Chinese state's impact on the transitional economy. Other studies reached similar conclusions about the negative effects of Chinese government ownership on business group performance. As China's economic evolution continues, its business group networks will undoubtedly change as well.

After the Soviet Union collapsed in 1991, state socialism in Eastern Europe rapidly shifted toward mixed and market economies. Between 1987 and 2001, Hungary's large firm sector went from 98 percent state ownership to 25 percent and foreign ownership rose from 1 percent to 53 percent (Stark and Vedres 2006: 1368). Social sequence analysis of the ownership histories of 1,696 large enterprises revealed that the most cohesive business groups and networks included the participation of foreign firms. Hungary's post-socialist transformation "did not occur despite its interorganizational property networks but, in part, because of and through these networks" (p. 1399). Further analyses of interpersonal ties, among the Hungarian firms' 72,766 senior managers and directors and with 16,919 political officeholders, identified *intercohesion* occurring at *structural folds*, locations in entrepreneurial activity where recombination and innovation occur:

> Actors at the structural fold are multiple insiders, participating in dense cohesive ties that provide close familiarity with the operations of the members in their group. Because they are members of more than one cohesive group, they have familiar access to diverse resources. (Vedres and Stark 2010: 1156)

Although intercohesion did not buffer against declining firm revenue, it strongly predicted high growth. But, groups with more structural folds were more likely to break into smaller fragments, suggesting that "structural folding stresses the fabric of cohesion. Actors who are ambiguously committed produce destabilizing tensions inside these groups" (p. 1174). Business groups, whether formally named institutions or informal clusters as in the Hungarian case, are often simultaneously creative and disruptive.

Finally, research on Indian business groups also yielded mixed conclusions about their impact on firm performance. Like China and Hungary, the Indian economy experienced an era of heavy state regulation followed by market reforms as economic globalization accelerated. During the 1990–7 Indian market deregulation, research on the 18 largest business groups found increases in both the strength of economic and social ties connecting member firms and the groups' intermediation efforts. Firm performance was "consistent with the proposition that the strengthening of the role of these groups is associated with an improvement in profitability" (Khanna and Palepu 1999: 303). However, in the post-reform era, business group-affiliated firms performed either similarly or worse than unaffiliated firms (Singh and Gaur 2009). The Chinese, Hungarian, and Indian experiences in transforming from state-dominated toward market-oriented economies underscore the importance of context and history for understanding business groups. The performance benefits of group affiliation seem strongest when market institutions are weak or undergoing radical change. But, as markets grow more efficient and institutional reforms level the playing field, group affiliation may turn into a liability. Contingent relationships between markets, states, and interorganizational networks caution against reaching too facile explanations of business group dynamics.

Interlocking Directorates

A board of directors interlock between two corporations is created when one person sits on the boards of both firms. Interlocks occur through both inside directors (the chief executive officer (CEO) or top executive of a focal firm also sits on another firm's board) and outside directors (a focal firm director is affiliated with another firm). Reciprocal CEO interlocking, where CEOs of two firms sit on one another's boards, occurred among one-seventh of large US corporations in the 1990s (Fich and White 2005). Director data are readily available about publicly trade corporations, enabling researchers to construct two-mode network matrices showing which corporations have ties to which individual directors. Although two-mode data can be used to investigate individual-to-individual connections via shared board memberships, almost all research on interlocking boards focused instead on firm-to-firm connections via common individual directors. Some theorists argued that interlocks reflect corporate efforts to coopt sources of resource dependence. A firm would allegedly offer a board seat to the representative of a bank to which it was heavily indebted. However, a majority of ties broken by retirement or death of a board member were not replaced, indicating that resource dependence involved only a minority of observed interlocks (Westphal et al. 2006). Yet, among the 625 largest publicly traded corporations, the "average path length between nodes in the largest connected component is remarkably stable over time," despite almost complete turnover in directors and major changes in both firm population and corporate governance practices (Davis et al. 2003: 317). The average shortest path (i.e., geodesic) for firms was 3.38, 3.46, and 3.46 in 1982, 1990, and 1999, respectively. Other findings were mixed on whether firms that coopt sources of their resource uncertainties performed better or worse than firms that did not coopt (Mizruchi 1996: 275). An alternative hypothesis about interlock choices is that banks use board placements to gather business information and to control firms in financial difficulty. For example, research on the largest US firms of the 1960s revealed that "the interlock network is dominated by a handful of major New York banks and insurance companies. Since densely interlocked companies carry the potential to coordinate intercorporate action, these institutions are prime candidates for that role" (Mintz and Schwartz 1981: 865–6). Other analysts concluded that "nearly any collection of firms that share directors with a few random ties will end up appearing like a well-connected elite, without intentional design" (Davis et al. 2003: 322). Summarizing the twentieth-century research literature, Mark Mizruchi concluded that "interlocks remain a powerful indicator of network ties between firms" (1996: 272) and the evidence is "overwhelming" that interlocks explain some corporate behaviors, such as mergers and corporate financing (p. 292).

Interlock research generally uncovered negative outcomes, such as weaker corporate governance, collusion, and poor firm performance. Interlocking directors may contribute to board ineffectiveness by poorly monitoring chief executive officers, acquiescing in substantially higher levels of CEO compensation (Fich and White 2003), and allowing CEO private interests to supersede company shareholders' interests (Bebchuk et al. 2002; Fich and White 2005). Analysis of 2,942 US firms for 2001–3 showed that corporations with lower performances – measured by industry-adjusted return on assets and Tobin's Q (ratio of a company's market value to the replacement value of its assets) – more often had interlocked directors (Devos et al. 2009). Furthermore, "a negative stock price reaction to the announcement of director appointments that create interlocked directors [suggests] that shareholders view the presence of interlocked directors as an indication of weak monitoring and entrenched management" (p. 884). Research on 1,669 Italian firms for 1998–2007 found director interlocks negatively related to company performance as measured by market-to-book ratio (Drago et al. 2011). Director networks are important conduits that facilitate the diffusion of experience, knowledge, and innovative corporate practices among firms (Shropshire 2010). For example, if a US public firm had a currently interlocked director who experienced prior private-equity takeover at another firm, it was 42 percent more likely itself to be targeted for a takeover (Stuart and Yim 2010). "These results support the interpretation that past experiences are transmitted across the links in the board network" (p. 176). Similarly, if a firm had a director who was interlocked to another company that had engaged in the highly controversial – and potentially fraudulent – practice of backdating executive stock options, then the firm had a 33 percent greater likelihood of also backdating its own executive's options (Bizjak et al. 2009). "Diffusion of crime across industries and firms is of critical importance and more work needs to be done to understand what mechanisms and characteristics facilitate or retard its spread" (Snyder et al. 2009). Chapter 5 considers the structure of interlocks among transnational corporate boards and its implications for the globalizing world economy.

Strategic Alliances

Over the past three decades, organization researchers invested much energy in explaining the formation, structure, and consequences of strategic alliances among various types of organizations such as business firms, nonprofits, and governmental agencies. Industries where alliances are especially prevalent include biotechnology, pharmaceuticals, telecommunications, airlines, and social services. (For overviews, see Gulati et al. 2000; Elmuti and Kathawala 2001; Baker and Faulkner 2002; Todeva and Knoke 2005.) Analysts quickly recognized that alliances comprise a distinct type of interorganizational relation – nondirected ties among collaborating organizations – which allows the application of social network concepts and data analytic methods. Most researchers concentrated on micro-level processes, using either individual organizations or dyads as the unit of analysis. This section considers those processes from several perspectives, while the following section examines macro-level structures and the evolution of large alliance systems.

Defining Strategic Alliances

The adjective "strategic" refers to organizational struggles to survive and thrive in highly competitive economic environments: alliances "are often 'strategic' in the sense that they have been formed as a direct response to major strategic challenges or opportunities which the partner firms face" (Child and Faulkner 1998: 5). A *strategic alliance* involves two or more partnering organizations that: (1) are legally independent after their alliance is formed; (2) share in the benefits and maintain managerial control over the performance of assigned tasks; and (3) make continuing contributions in one or more strategic areas, such as technology or products (Yoshino and Rangan 1995: 5). Organizations collaborate to achieve diverse goals such as organizational learning, legitimacy, coping with uncertainty, R&D innovation, penetrating international markets, formulating industry standards, even undertaking collective political actions. Risk-sharing enables partners to learn from one another, to acquire new knowledge and skills, and to transfer technologies and organizational competences. In addition to sharing any revenues generated by a successful joint project, agreements often specify opportunities for employees to observe and participate in each partner's R&D facilities, manufacturing plants, or distribution centers. Such interactions allow firms to gain mutual access to some of the other organization's resources, including expertise and proprietary knowledge, even its political clout with legislative and regulatory bodies. "Partners' resources may include financial assets and extensions of credit; timely information, scientific knowledge, or expert advice; proprietary technologies or patents; marketing expertise or penetration into new countries and cultures; organizational prestige, status, or corporate or brand reputations; trustworthiness and low risk (moral hazards)" (Knoke 2009: 1696). Hence, an ego-organization's *corporate social capital* is its set of connections to alter-organizations and the resources controlled by those partners to which it may gain access.

Many organizations maintain large and continually changing *alliance portfolios* of suppliers and customers, joint ventures, equity co-investments, and less formalized transactions that confer cumulative advantages beyond any benefits derived from a particular alliance dyad (Wassmer 2008). Executives are more likely to create high-performing alliance portfolios "when they visualize their portfolios in the context of the entire industry as opposed to a series of single ties and when they simultaneously form ties with multiple partners" (Ozcan and Eisenhardt 2009: 246). Generous organizations facilitate their partners' move into new business lines by brokering business contacts and customer relations and speeding new products and services to market. Through repeated alliances, an initial partnership may evolve into a sustained integration of technological capabilities, shared customer bases, product cross-branding, marketing know-how, cross-cultural entrée, and access to credit sources. The alliance between Sandvik Rock Tool and Atlas Copco, discussed at the beginning of this chapter, initially yielded many such mutually beneficial outcomes. Because organizations can boost their competitive advantages through judicious selection of interorganizational relations, rational choice theory hypothesizes that firms prefer to form new partnerships, increase their network centrality, and build alliance portfolios that enhance their corporate social capital (Preston 2004). In other words, organizations tend to behave strategically in choosing their strategic allies.

Explanations of alliance formation and outcome vary with the type of collaboration under investigation. A few analysts created typologies for classifying interorganizational relations based on forms of governance for coordinating and regulating joint project activities and distributing the payoffs. An early classification system defines three forms of governance structures – joint ventures, minority investments, and contractual alliances – that differ in the magnitudes and types of hierarchical controls (Gulati and Singh 1998). Empirical evidence on 1,570 announced alliances among firms in the automobile, biopharmaceutical, and new materials sectors between 1970 and 1989 showed that coordination costs and concerns about partner appropriation of payoffs predicted which governance structures were adopted. Another typology placed strategic alliances midway between unstructured industrial districts and highly structured intracorporate networks (Inkpen and Tsang 2005). Similarly, Emanuela Todeva and Knoke (2002; 2005; Knoke 2001) situated diverse interorganizational relations between arm's-length transactions among firms based solely on market prices and the vertical integration inside bureaucratic hierarchies. They identified an array of 11 governance mechanisms, ranging from lobbying coalitions, research consortia, industry standards groups, licensing and franchising, to equity investments (one firm purchases a majority or minority stake in another's shares) and joint ventures (two or more parent firms create, jointly own, and control a new legal organizational entity). Alternative alliance classification schemes examine partner motivations or the primary goal of collaborative activity, regardless of the particular governance form chosen. An early assessment distinguished among motives related to basic and applied research or technological development, motives related to concrete innovation processes, and motives related to market access and search for market opportunities (Hagedoorn 1993). Other analysts restricted their investigations only to alliances formed for conducting R&D, marketing, coproduction, supply procurement, or cross-border alliances. Such heterogeneity among alliance typologies may hinder the generalizability of research results.

Who Allies with Whom?

Research on strategic alliance formation often focused on individual organizations or dyads. Related issues are the choice of network governance forms, alliance management, financial arrangements, and creating trust among partners. Investigators analyzed the effects of organizational attributes such as firm status and market position, motives for collaboration such as reducing transaction costs, egocentric network measures such as density, and dyadic similarities such as firm size. Theory and research typically hypothesized that prior network structures and processes generate subsequent network structures. For example, by repeatedly collaborating with the same partners, firms typically reinforce mutual obligations and dependencies, thereby reducing reliance on equity investments and contractual forms of governance in favor of informal mechanisms of social control. Firms that are poorly embedded in a network structure are less likely to form alliances than firms enjoying extensive alliances, given their difficulties in acquiring information and reputational benefits (Ahuja et al. 2009). Alliance data on 97 leading global chemical firms from 1979 to 1991 demonstrated that poorly embedded firms could overcome these constraints by forging asymmetric ties to more embedded and central partners than by allying with other peripheral firms. However, the more central member of a dyad "is more likely to secure more favorable terms of trade, in the form of a majority ownership position in joint ventures, when allying with a less embedded partner" (p. 955). Unfortunately, a strategy of accepting minority positions in an alliance tends to hinder the poorly embedded partner's social mobility by constraining its participation in subsequent partnerships. "Creeping toward the center" of the network is likely to be gradual rather than dramatic. Research that uses network structural properties to explain organizations' network actions risks generating biased results; that is, reaching erroneous conclusions by omitting important explanatory factors. To avoid this problem, network analysts of strategic alliance formation must also take into account other influences on interorganizational behavior identified by relevant theories and prior research.

Dyadic indicators of organizational (dis)similarities enable tests of two competing hypotheses about interorganizational relations. The *homophily principle* in social network analysis is that actors prefer to affiliate with others who are most similar to themselves on salient dimensions, such as race, gender, recreational activities, and attitudes. Applied to interorganizational relations, the homophily hypothesis is that firms are more likely to form an alliance when they have similar sizes, share national origins and cultural identities, or possess equivalent organizational prestige and status. The strong tendency for Japanese companies belonging to the same keiretsu to ally with one another illustrates homophilous preference. In contrast, the *functional interdependence* hypothesis argues that interorganizational relations are motivated primarily by complementarities arising from firms' differential locations within interdependent R&D, production, and distribution chains. A specialized organization often requires additional competences – skills, tacit knowledge, technology, equipment, and other resources – which can better be provided by another firm possessing quite different capabilities. The resulting alliance synergies may add value to both partnering organizations. For example, in 2009 Perot Systems Corp. of Plano, Texas, announced an agreement with China Telecommunications Corp. to deliver information technology services to the Chinese healthcare industry. Said Perot's president, "By combing our leading-edge technology, data-center management, and deep industry knowledge with China Telecom's network and data-center operations, the companies can create and deliver transformational IT solutions to healthcare providers" (PRNewswire 2009). An implication is that, without the sponsorship of a strong Chinese partner, a lone American firm could not gain access to that vast emerging consumer market.

Organizations are more likely to form new alliances when they have complementary organizational capabilities or resource requirements (Chung et al. 2000); are strategically interdependent (Gulati 1995b); and have equivalent organizational status rankings (Podolny 2005). Semiconductor firms enjoying higher prestige (strong track records of seminal inventions) and participating in crowded technological segments formed alliances at higher rates (Stuart 1998). "Particularly when one of the firms in an alliance is a young or small organization or, more generally, an organization of equivocal quality, alliances can act as endorsements: they build public confidence in the value of an organization's products and services and thereby facilitate the firm's efforts to attract customers and other corporate partners" (Stuart 2000: 791). Firms in the global chemical industry possessing accumulated technical, commercial, and social capital were advantaged in forming interfirm linkages, but firms lacking those resources could still make connections if they generated radical technological breakthroughs (Ahuja 2000). Researchers studying international alliances of 853 German biotech startups between 1995 and 2006 hypothesized that a firm's prior alliance experience represents a stock of externally acquired knowledge making it attractive to new partners (Al-Laham and Amburgey 2010). Event history evidence showed that "by accumulating that stock of external knowledge a biotech firm accumulates valuable capabilities that foster its innovativeness, and thereby increase its attractiveness as a network partner for firms sourcing for knowledge" (p. 317). The speed of new alliance formation among 847 US biotech firms was a nonlinear function of prior collaborative experience, suggesting that they "learn how to learn more effectively from multiple research alliances" (Al-Laham et al. 2008).

Alliances occur more frequently among organizations that can access larger social capital through their CEOs' personal networks, interlocking boards of directors, or joint participation in cooperative technical organizations. Software firms tend to follow strategies of balancing exploration and exploitation in alliance formation decisions, shifting over time among exploring new knowledge with new partners and collaboratively exploiting existing knowledge with old partners (Lavie and Rosenkopf 2006). A review of more than 40 alliance formation studies identified four major influences on partner attractiveness and selection: trust, commitment, complementarity, and value or financial payoff (Shah and Swaminathan 2008). Evidence was mixed about which organizational characteristics – size, age, financial resources, product diversity, R&D intensity, market position – affect firms' alliance participation. Effects may be contingent on industrial, national, or environmental conditions. Incompatible organizational and national cultures, legal systems, and political institutional environments can impede the formation and success of international joint ventures (IJV), in which at least one equity owner is headquartered outside the country of operation (Salk and Brannen 2000; Sirmon and Lane 2004). However, more extensive experiences with diverse international operations encourage cross-national collaborations among multinational corporations (Castellani and Zanfei 2004).

Different alliance governance forms (e.g., nonequity and equity investments, joint ventures, licensing) represent alternative methods that partners may adopt to manage and safeguard their mutual dependencies and vulnerabilities. Organizations are less likely to insist on detailed contracts, to install monitoring committees, or to create hierarchical joint ventures when they have high levels of interfirm dependency, reciprocity, and mutual trust, that is, confidence that the partners will not opportunistically exploit vulnerabilities. Renegotiations of alliance governance forms are more likely for projects having broader scope, lower division of labor, and greater relevance to the partners (Reuer et al. 2002). Because trust minimizes uncertainties and reduces the chances of partner opportunism (self-interest with guile), organizations tend to repeat alliances with the same partners. Ranjay Gulati's (1995a) research on alliances among US, European, and Japanese firms in the automobile, biopharmaceutical, and new materials sectors affirmatively answered the question, "Does familiarity breed trust?" Challenging the hypothesis from transaction cost economics that firms form alliances when costs are not high enough to justify an organizational merger, Gulati found that firms decided the form of their alliance not only based on the type of activity (R&D) but on the trust emerging through repeated ties. Over time, as partners gained confidence in one another, their subsequent alliances were less likely to be equity-based: "Firms placed in a social network of trusting relationships can significantly reduce their search for new partners when they decide to ally with an entity they already trust" (Gulati 1995a: 107). Research on supplier–buyer relations at Ford and Chrysler uncovered a nonlinear dynamic: if the interaction between the automakers' lead buyers and the suppliers' agents survived an ambivalent two-year threshold, interorganizational trust markedly improved (Gulati and Sytch 2008). During the early stages, partners apparently probed one another's trustworthiness and quickly broke off unsatisfactory relations.

Alliance Outcomes

Do organizations derive benefits from participating in strategic alliances? Researchers almost unanimously believe that collaborating with a high-quality partner confers competitive advantages and other benefits unavailable to a firm operating alone. Studies of diverse industries and nations supported a general proposition that alliance relations improve organizational performances. Researchers investigated how strategic alliances affect such firm performance indicators as organizational survival, productivity improvements, stock market values, profitability, and the creation of innovative products and services. Fewer analysts assessed subjective performance measures, such as managerial satisfaction with project outcomes.

Survival chances increase for firms belonging to alliances by facilitating scale economies, permitting greater access to more diverse information and network resources, assisting knowledge transfer and learning opportunities, and reducing the risks of intra-alliance rivalries. Organizational survival chances in the New York better dress industry were optimal at intermediate levels of personal and interorganizational network embeddedness (Uzzi 1996). Data on 559 alliances formed by 137 shipping line operators from 37 nations between 1988 and 2005 showed that firms better matched on resource compatibility (similar ship ages of alliance partners) had higher survival rates than mismatched partners (Mitsuhashi and Greve 2009). Analysis of 5,192 IJVs operating in China from 1999 to 2003 discovered that foreign equity share had an inverted U-shaped effect on IJV productivity, measured by value added per employee normalized to average industry productivity (Li et al. 2009). The authors concluded that, "while foreign ownership in general benefits IJV productivity by enhancing commitment of foreign partners and motivating foreign partners to transfer advanced knowledge (that is, control benefits), overly dominant foreign ownership may reduce commitment and knowledge contributions of local partners, thus reducing collaboration benefits" (p. 880). An optimal ownership structure would achieve a balance between the two types of benefits.

Share prices of partnering firms often increase following an alliance announcement, because stock markets anticipate the collaborators will create higher quality products and services, attract more customers, lower production costs, and increase cash flows. Researchers found asymmetric financial impacts on shareholder value for 222 new product development alliances between pairs of larger and smaller firms in the computer, software, and communications equipment industries between 1993 and 2004 (Kalaignanam et al. 2007). Although market values rose following alliance announcements, the benefits were much greater for the smaller partner. Broad-scope alliances created higher financial gains for larger firms than did narrow-scope alliances. Smaller firms tended to gain more from scale alliances, where partners' resources are pooled for performing activities at the same stage in the value chain, than from link alliances, where their resources are exchanged. Research on 367 software firms found that market performance improved with competitive intensity among partners (Lavie 2008). Firm- and relation-specific factors may also affect the impacts of accumulated alliance experience on stock prices. Stock market returns from new joint venture announcements by 184 Fortune 300 firms between 1987 and 1996 were higher for firms having prior experience with the same partners than for all prior alliances with any partner (Gulati et al. 2009).

Announcements of 230 marketing alliances by 103 computer software companies from 1988 to 2005 were followed by "abnormal stock returns," measured as higher prices during a 20-day event-window surrounding the announcement day compared to the preceding six months (Swaminathan and Moorman 2009). Two network characteristics, density and efficiency, and marketing alliance capability had positive impacts on value creation. Consistent research findings of increased short-term stock values pose questions concerning whether some firms opportunistically announce collaborative agreements just to manipulate share values.

Profits are another important financial indicator of firm performance influenced by strategic alliances. Researchers investigating alliances among 54 facilities-based service providers in the US telecommunications industry between 1991 and 1998 measured organizational profitability by return on invested capital (ROI) and return on assets (ROA), two widely used indicators (Bae and Gargiulo 2004). Consistent with structural hole theory, firms with sparse alliance networks performed better than firms whose partners had mutual alliances. However, "organizations embedded in dense alliance networks were more likely than those with sparse networks to benefit from having nonsubstitutable partners," that is, partners so resource-rich that they cannot be excluded without endangering its access to those resources (pp. 853–4). For a telecom facing a nonsubstitutable partner, the effective strategy is to embed the alliance in third-party ties, thus allowing indirect leverage on those partners. Analysis of 198 joint ventures between Chinese and foreign firms in Jiangsu province revealed that economic integration of the parent firms' resources – "effectively combined in an alliance's value chain system such that if one party withdraws, the alliance will not be able to survive and the other parties will suffer great loss" – increased alliance profitability, measured by return on investment (ROI) over three years, and stability of four types of growth rates (Luo 2008: 618). Mutual dependency created by tighter integration reduced the partners' temptations to opportunism by increasing trust and procedural justice. Researchers investigated the impact of alliance portfolio internationalization (API) – the extent of foreign partners in a firm's set of alliance relations – on firm profitability, as measured by annual ROA for 330 US software vendors from 1990 to 2000 (Lavie and Miller 2008). They found a curvilinear pattern, with moderate API levels contributing to higher profitability, but at high API levels "internationalization precludes successful adaptation to nationally distant partners, because the firm's collaborative routines are ineffective in bridging geographical, cultural, institutional, and economic differences" (p. 638).

A study of alliance activity by 195 US firms in the computer, steel, pharmaceutical, and petroleum industries examined ROA across 13 years (Lin et al. 2009). Partners with high resource complementarity boosted firm performance when those partners also had high network status: "intangible institutional benefits may affect firm performance by improving the resource flow in both quality and quantity" (p. 935). Multinational automobile firms whose alliance portfolios had greater organizational and functional diversity and lower governance diversity enjoyed higher net profit margins (Jiang et al. 2010). But, Anthony Goerzen dissented from the prevailing wisdom that alliances improve firm profitability. Data from a 1999 survey of 13,529 subsidiaries of 580 very large Japanese multinational corporations showed that firms with more diverse partners had lower returns on assets, sales, and capital (Goerzen and Beamish 2005). Further analysis demonstrated the more often that equity-based alliances were repeated with the same prior Japanese or host-country partners, the more inferior was the corporate economic performance on those three indicators (Goerzen 2007). He attributed the negative impact of repeated alliances to suboptimal information acquired through redundant interorganizational networks, particularly in environments with high technical uncertainty: "The problem for the firm is that these over-lapping relationships often do not truly improve the quality of the network so much as simply enlarge it, lessening its efficiency and weakening its effectiveness over time, since fewer new ideas flow into the group through these already familiar contacts" (p. 492). A challenge for alliance managers is how best continually to renew portfolios with fresh, diverse partners that sustain their organization's competitive advantages.

Innovation is an explicit goal for many strategic alliances, whether collaborating on basic R&D, producing new products and services, or developing new markets. Researchers frequently used patent citation counts to identify important innovations in high-tech industries. For example, Stuart (2000) found evidence that semiconductor producers allying with large and innovative firms experienced higher patent rates and sales growth than comparable firms lacking such partners. This effect interacted with partner characteristics, with smaller and younger firms gaining more than their older and larger partners, consistent with status-transfer theory. A study of 1,106 firms in 11 high-tech industries from 1990 to 2000 found higher rates of patenting by firms embedded in alliance networks displaying both high clustering and high reach, that is, shorter average path lengths to diverse firms (Schilling and Phelps 2007). The patenting rate of 839 US biotech firms from 1973 to 2003 was higher for joint research alliances transferring highly firm-specific knowledge than for licensing agreements only giving access to external knowledge (Al-Laham et al. 2010). A study of 762 alliances among 85 chemicals, automotive, and pharmaceutical firms from 1986 to 1997 identified three network factors influencing "explorative patents" – the number of patents a firm received within patent categories where it had been inactive during the previous five years (Gilsing et al. 2008). Technological distance between partners, network betweenness centrality, and total network density of each industry had curvilinear effects on company patent rates. The authors concluded that "the three elements of network embeddedness need to be considered jointly in order to understand their complementary effects on both novelty creation and absorptive capacity" (p. 1729). Another analysis of the dataset found that two types of alliance redundancy differentially affected technological innovations, as measured by patent citations (Vanhaverbeke et al. 2009): a firm's egonet redundancy linearly increased the creation of core technology and had an inverted U-shaped relation to non-core technology, but its component density had only a curvilinear relation to core technology.

Surveys of more than 1,800 Dutch companies conducted in

1998 and 2000 discovered that innovator firms maintained broader alliance portfolios than imitator firms, providing greater access to novel information and deriving benefits from both intensive (exploitative) and broader (explorative) use of external information sources (Duysters and Lokshin 2011). Alliance complexity had an inverse-U relation to innovative performance, measured as the share of new products introduced by a firm into the market in the previous two years, implying that "firms will at a certain stage reach a specific inflection point after which marginal costs of managing complexity are higher than the expected benefits from this increased complexity" (p. 570). In a survey 127 German firms collaborating between 2000 and 2005, alliance scope and type of governance (equity joint venture or contracts) indirectly increased self-reported innovative performance, by improving management of knowledge creation and sharing processes (Jiang and Li 2009). This analysis was an important attempt to uncover the mechanisms connecting alliance structures to innovative outcomes.

Terminating Alliances

Less theory and research explains how and why strategic alliances come to an end, and under what conditions. Some studies estimate that between 30 and 70 percent of alliances fail, either not attaining goals set by the parent companies or falling short of delivering expected benefits (Reuer and Zollo 2005; Lunnan and Haugland 2008). Network and other social factors seem to drive alliance breakups. Exits from cliques in Canadian investment banks resulted more from inequality and complementarity than from similarity and cohesion (Rowley et al. 2005). Withdrawals from global liner shipping alliances were triggered by market competition and time-dependent effects of direct and indirect ties with other alliance members (Greve et al. 2010). Network structures in which global chemicals firms were embedded affected the unplanned dissolutions of joint ventures (Polidor et al. 2011). Positional embeddedness from combined partner centrality did not stabilize alliances, and possibly contributed to instability. But structural embeddedness from having common partners seemed to preserve ventures, especially among positionally unequal and highly competitive firms. Some analysts argued that more successful outcomes depend on how well the partners jointly coordinate activities and build trust during the implementation stage. Given the frequency of repeated alliances, both with prior and new partners, a firm that institutionalizes a dedicated alliance function – specialized staff engaged in learning, codifying knowledge, and monitoring on-going interorganizational relations – could improve the quality of its partner choices, strengthen its alliance portfolio, and achieve higher success rates.

Corporate social capital generates obligations and commitments among alliance partners based on norms underpinning legitimate social conduct, such as reciprocity, balance, proportionality, solidarity, and trust. But, if collaboration produces undesirable, even illegitimate, expectations for one organization to satisfy the unreasonable demands of a partner, then the concept of *corporate social liability* is more apt. A common occurrence is the inability to fulfill the terms of an agreement, for example, failure to deliver products on time because of a warehouse fire or workers going on strike. A more sinister termination involves opportunism by a firm intending either to acquire a partner's proprietary knowledge for its own uncompensated use, or to appropriate the lion's share of the benefits resulting from a joint project. Some alliances deteriorate into technological "learning races" when competitive aspects overwhelm cooperative features. Partner betrayal is "a consequence of each firm's attempt to also use its partners' know-how for private gains, and of the possibility that significantly greater benefits might accrue to the firm that 'finishes' learning from its partner(s) before the latter can do the same (as it is then free to leave the alliance and deny its partner(s) access to its know-how)" (Khanna et al. 1998: 194). Transaction cost theorists hypothesized that a firm making fewer investments in alliance-specific assets has great bargaining power and ability to negotiate a larger share of alliance quasi-rents, or "value above and beyond what could have been generated through general purpose investments" (Dyer et al. 2008: 141). Despite the inherent structural potential for opportunism and exploitation, only a few researchers have investigated liabilities in strategic alliances and firm reactions to self-serving partners. Alliance managers at 212 companies revealed that, when relational capital between alliance partners is based on mutual trust, the better is their ability to protect core proprietary assets while still achieving knowledge transfer from partners (Kale et al. 2000). A study of accommodation in 174 international marketing alliances demonstrated that consistent constructive responses to a partner's competitive acts "may reverse the self-serving partner's opportunism and lead to a performance upturn" (Bello et al. 2010: 87). Evidence on 344 US joint ventures from 1985 to 2003 supported the transaction cost hypothesis that "the partner with less valuable resources is likely to extract higher private benefits and gain more when it has greater bargaining power and absorptive capacity. Conversely, the partner with more valuable resources is likely to protect itself better from appropriation when it has JV capabilities" (Kumar 2010: 232). An obvious implication is that firms must proceed cautiously in selecting partners, creating trust, and safeguarding against exploitation.

The circumstances of alliance termination can affect future alliance activities. If a project outcome was mutually beneficial, or if its failure was not blamed on one's partner, a dyad seems more likely to form a new alliance. But, under the principle of "once bitten, twice shy," a negative outcome seen as the fault of a partner would probably discourage repetition. Theoretical discussions about repairing relationships between organizations promise eventually to turn empirical attention toward mechanisms for re-establishing trust and collaboration after alliance failures (Gillespie and Dietz 2009; Ren and Gray 2009). Network positions can be expected to influence tie-restoration behavior. For example, a pair of structurally embedded firms with many ties to common third organizations is more constrained to continue collaborating. However, the inherently unequal relation between a central firm and a peripheral one only invites further opportunistic exploitation that the less powerful organization is well advised to avoid.

Evolution of Interorganizational Networks

Compared to organizational- and dyadic-level research on strategic alliances, relatively fewer analysts examined interorganizational relations at the complete network level by applying evolutionary and ecological perspectives to explain how macro-level structures emerge and change over time (Provan et al. 2007; Ulset 2008). Organizational evolution theory, which draws its inspiration from biological models of speciation, emphasizes how random and systematic factors generate variations in organizational forms, structures, and practices. External environments – consisting of legal, political, cultural, and technical conditions – then select the most successful forms for retention within an organizational population (Romanelli 1991; Aldrich and Ruef 2006). Unfortunately, few organizational evolutionists explicitly incorporated network concepts and principles to explain organizational evolution. Howard Aldrich (1999) was a notable exception in stressing the social network contexts through which entrepreneurs obtain scarce resources to launch new businesses (pp. 81–7), and the growth of extensive social networks as a complement to an increased density hypothesis about the legitimization of new organizational forms (pp. 274–7). This relative neglect of social networks in organizational evolution opens opportunities for theoretical and empirical syntheses to explain the evolution of strategic alliance networks.

Organizations participating in numerous alliances with diverse collaborators generate complex webs of indirectly tied "partners of partners." An emergent social structure at the level of organizational populations is the *strategic alliance network*, a "set of organizations connected through their overlapping partnerships in different strategic alliances" (Knoke 2001: 128; Todeva and Knoke 2002). A strategic alliance network is a type of *field network* (field-net), "the configuration of interorganizational relations among all the organizations that are members of an organizational field" (Kenis and Knoke 2002: 275). To illustrate, figures 4.2 to 4.4 depict structural change in a strategic alliance network among 13 computer and software firms in the Global Information Sector

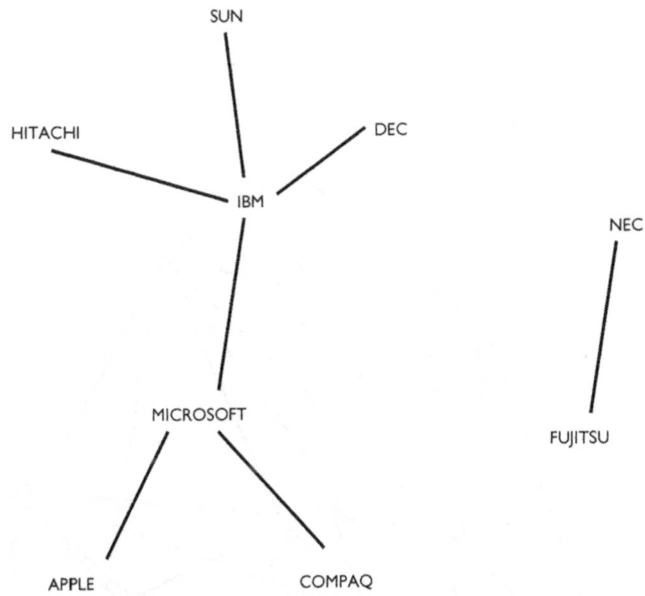

Figure 4.2 Alliance network among 13 Global Information Sector computer and software companies 1990

(GIS) across the last decade of the twentieth century (more below about the GIS). In 1990, as the field-net was just developing, very few firms announced any alliances. Only IBM and Microsoft had more than one ally, a single Japanese dyad was unconnected to the large component, and four organizations were isolates. Network density was just 0.09 (figure 4.2). By 1995, just one corporation (Dell Computer) was isolated while all other firms engaged in multiple partnerships in the large component, which had a density of 0.60 (figure 4.3). In 2000, every firm was connected through multiple alliances in the component and its density had increased to 0.79 (figure 4.4).

Some analysts investigated the emergence and evolution of alliance networks from a complete network perspective. A fundamental hypothesis is that structural characteristics of networks, such as centralization and density, influence transactions among organizations, which further changes the complete network

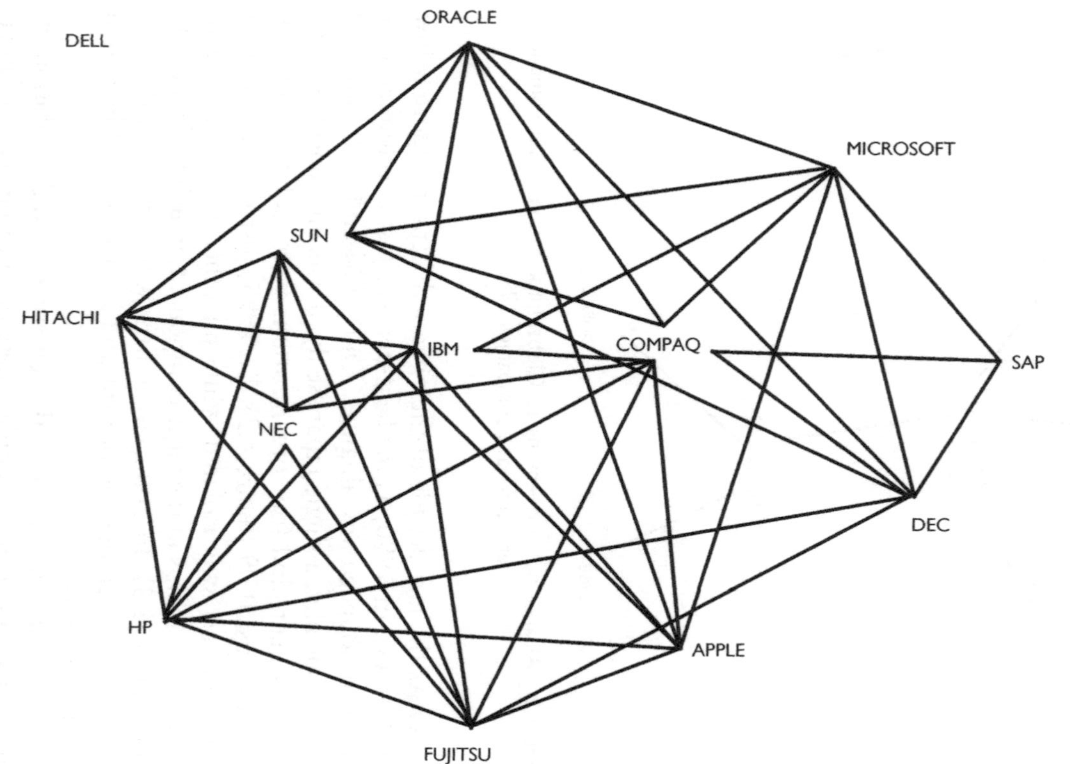

Figure 4.3 Alliance network among 13 Global Information Sector computer and software companies 1995

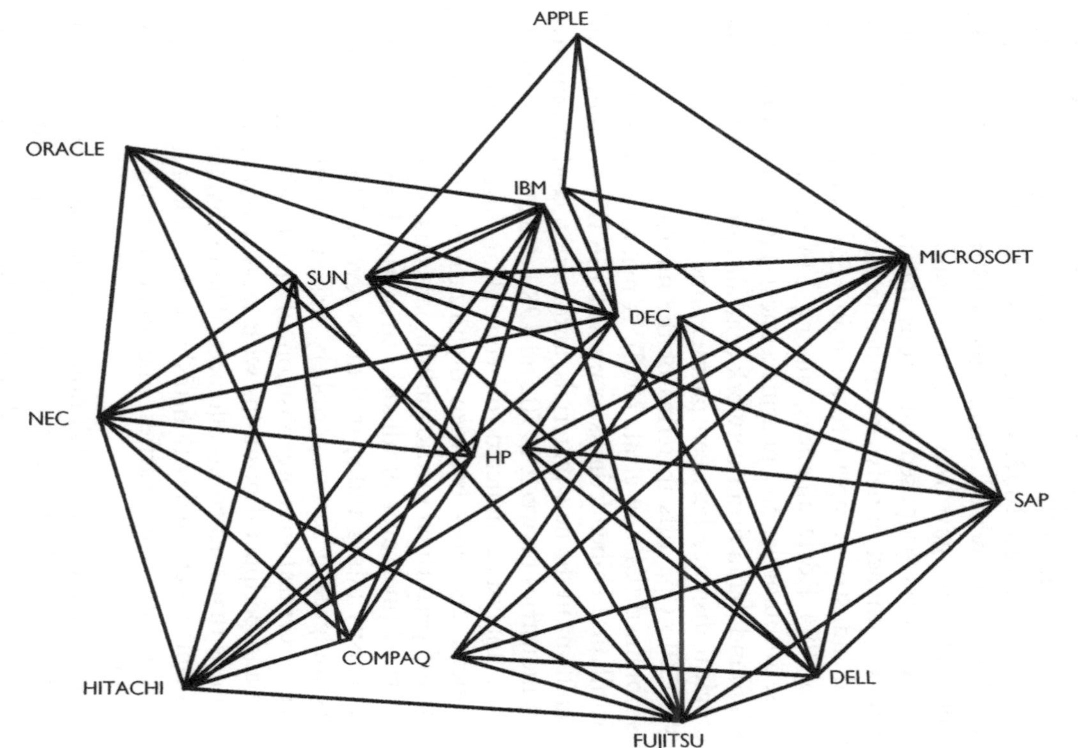

Figure 4.4 Alliance network among 13 Global Information Sector computer and software companies 2000

structure. The most comprehensive macro-level analyses used the MERIT-CATI dataset, a compilation of four decades of R&D partnerships among global firms in the computer, telecom, pharmaceutical, and other high-tech industries (for descriptive trends, see Hagedoorn 2002; Cloodt et al. 2006). Strategic technology alliances increased during the 1980s and early 1990s, while joint ventures gave way to diverse contractual agreements. Project researchers proposed numerous theoretical propositions to explain the impact of network embeddedness on rates of innovation and industry competitive intensity. For example, a panel analysis of 994 R&D alliances, among 116 companies in the chemicals, automotive, and pharmaceutical industries from 1986 to 1997, found that a firm's network centrality interacted with the technological distance between partners and with total network density to affect payoffs in terms of the number of explorative patents obtained (Gilsing et al. 2008). A macro-level analysis of strategic alliance embeddedness examined 166 US, Japanese, and European firms in the new materials, automation, and automotive products industries between 1970 and 1989 (Gulati and Gargiulo 1999). The analysts conducted role-equivalent cluster analyses of the Euclidean distances between organizations' triadic alliance patterns, and performed metric multidimensional scaling of proximity matrices (measures of alliance strength). Inspection of the resulting density tables and spatial maps revealed four distinctive positions comprising a core-periphery structure within all three industries: a central or core position of strong alliances, semi-periphery and peripheral positions with weaker ties, and isolated organizations that formed no alliances. The probability of a new alliance forming increased with firms' interdependence, their prior alliances, common third parties, and joint centrality within the alliance network.

Initial research on the evolution of a network among 400 firms in the human biotechnology industry emphasized learning processes (Powell et al. 1996). Pharmaceutical firms and startup research companies formally collaborated to gain access to and competitive advantages from, respectively, new scientific knowledge and investment funds for research leading to marketable medical innovations. Subsequent work on biotechnology alliances from 1988 to 1999 investigated the changing logics of attachment among 482 biotech firms (White et al. 2004; Powell et al. 2005). Organizations well connected to a diverse set of partners deployed four successive attachment mechanisms – accumulative advantage, homophily, follow-the-trend, and multiconnectivity – at different periods to occupy the most structurally cohesive positions in the network. As the number and diversity of biotech collaborative activities increased over time, cohesive subgroup components emerged that conditioned and reinforced subsequent firm preferences for affiliations with diverse, well-connected partners. The biotech field's primary activities evolved from commercialization to finance and R&D partnerships. Frequently recombining ties between biotechnology firms and different network participants (e.g., universities and pharmaceutical companies) resulted in firms simultaneously collaborating and competing on different projects. A small core of central players dominated the biotech network: "This suggests an open elite, accessible to novelty as the field expands" (Powell et al. 2005: 1189).

The structure and evolution of interorganizational networks can be tracked by examining their small-world properties. As defined by Duncan Watts and Steven Strogatz (1998; Watts 1999), a small-world network has large size, low density, high local clustering, and short average path length. Local clustering means that a large proportion of triplets are transitive; i.e., three nodes directly connected to one another. Even a few random ties connecting local clusters would decrease the network's mean path distance (geodesic) between dyads, thus generating a small-world structure. Figure 4.5 schematically exemplifies a small world with high local clustering and low average path distance. The relatively few short paths linking the dense local clusters enable information, knowledge, and resources to flow more efficiently through a small-world network. Researchers discovered that small-world properties characterized diverse interorganizational networks, including: ownership ties of the largest German corporations, banks, and insurance companies (Kogut and Walker 2001); interlocking boards of directors among the largest US

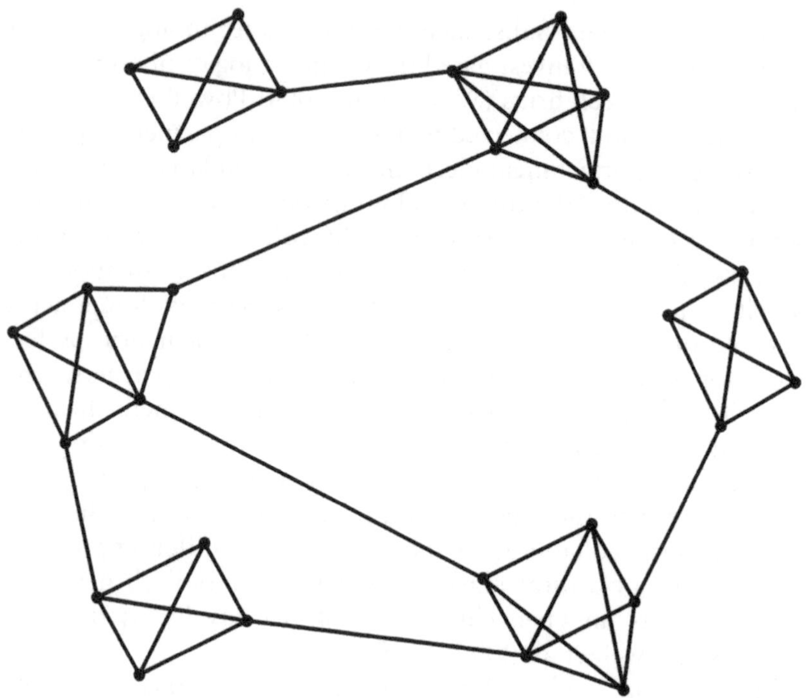

Figure 4.5 A small world with high local clustering and low average path distance

firms (Davis et al. 2003); owners of Italian enterprises (Corrado and Zollo 2006); and owners of Swedish companies (Stafsudd 2009). Several projects also found the networks were scale-free; that is, having skewed distributions of ties among organizations consistent with a power law (Barabási and Albert 1999). Such distributions typically arise by a preferential attachment process, in which organizations acquire new ties in proportion to the number of existing ties – a "rich-get-richer" dynamic prevalent in many competitive situations. Central "hubs" attract high volumes of connections, particularly from new organizations entering a field. Preferential attachment offers a calculative rather than a random mechanism to explain how an emergent network evolves toward a small-world structure.

Concerning strategic alliance networks, a handful of investigators uncovered small-world structures. Technical alliances in the chemicals, food, and electrical fields exhibited small-world features favorable to knowledge transfer (Verspagen and Duysters 2004). Research on 1,106 firms involved in 3,663 alliances in 11 US high-tech industries at three intervals from 1990 and 2000 (in all, 66 network "snapshots") revealed substantial variation across industry and over time (Schilling and Phelps 2007). Firms that participated in alliance networks combining high clustering with greater reach (number of firms connected via a firm's geodesics) created more knowledge, measured by numbers of patents, than firms lacking those attributes. "Both *local* density and *global* efficiency can exist simultaneously, and it is this combination that enhances innovation" (p. 1124). Another small-world study, of 960 technology innovation agreements among 603 smart card industry firms across three sub-periods from 1992 to 2006, found that small-world criteria emerged only in the second and third intervals (M'Chirgui 2010). Preferential attachment to central firms holding patents for key technologies described the structure of 739 antibody-related deals among 557 biotech firms between 1987 and 2004 (Gay and Dousset 2005). The scaling values of the antibody alliance network, which also displayed small-world properties, evolved consistent with a "fitter-get-richer" dynamic in which firms with cutting-edge technologies attracted the most partners. "The data show that preferential attachment to central hubs is limited by the shift of relations towards new technologies. Successive waves of new technologies shape the overall evolution of the network" (p. 1465). Lori Rosenkopf and Giovanna Padula (2008) investigated how network shortcuts are created and how new entrants connected to a main network component. Analyzing the strategic alliance network of the US cellular communication industry from 1993 to 2002, they found that ties between local clusters formed more often among firms of similar centrality. Within dense local clusters, alliance formation involved repeated partnerships. New participants in the main component mostly connected to the local clusters.

Dalhia Mani and Knoke (2011) investigated the alliance

network among US corporations between 1988 and 2008. They used graphic methods developed by Moody and White (2003) to analyze structural cohesion and visualize the skeletal structure of the largest component, which contained the majority of US firms at three intervals. The method successively splits the largest component into one or more bicomponents (where at least two paths connect every dyad), then into tricomponents (three paths), 4-components, and so on. Like peeling an onion, the resulting skeletal diagram depicts nested levels of smaller and increasingly dense *neighborhoods* (subgroups) and reveals whether the largest component's network resembles a small-world structure (many k-components of fairly equal sizes) or a core-periphery structure (one large k-component and many small ones). For 1988–90 when the US economy was in recession, figure 4.6 shows the skeletal structure of the largest alliance component, consisting of 454 firms. A clear pattern is evident: four bicomponents with a 1:3.8 *neighborhood ratio*, indicating that almost four times as many firms resided in the largest bicomponent as in the three smaller ones combined. This skewed neighborhood ratio implies that the largest component more closely resembles a core-periphery than a small-world structure. However, considerable atomization occurred, with 37 percent of US firms residing outside that component. Figure 4.6 shows that the alliance network was nested 15 levels deep, indicating moderate vertical complexity. In 1998–2000 at the height of the dot.com bubble, the largest component swelled to 2,491 firms in 42 bicomponents, with a more unequal neighborhood ratio of 1:4.9, and 43 nested levels (and atomization increased to 46 percent). By 2007–9, with the Global Financial Crisis tipping the economy into the Great Recession, the alliance network reverted toward its prior structure: the largest component had 4,835 firms in 18 bicomponents, a neighborhood ratio of 1:4, and nestedness of 19 levels, while atomization leaped to 72 percent of firms outside the component. The changing pattern suggests that alliance structures track economic boom-and-bust cycles.

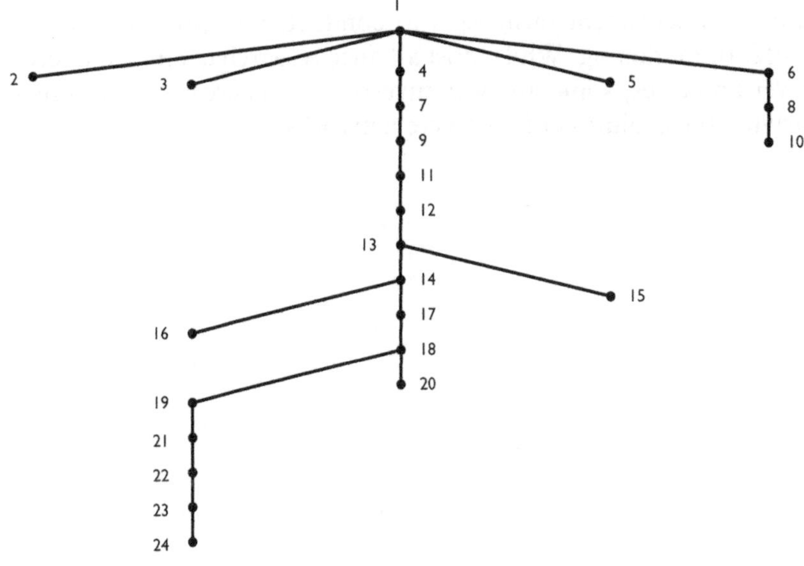

Source: Mani and Knoke (2011)

Figure 4.6 Skeletal structure of the largest component in the US alliance network 1988–90

Summary

A variety of relations create interorganizational networks among businesses that can affect their performances in competitive national economies. Business startups depend heavily on entrepreneurs' personal connections for access to vital resources that influence whether new enterprises will survive, grow, or die. Business groups are multiplex networks of integrated firms, particularly in emerging economies with weak market and legal institutions, that provide support unavailable in markets. But, as in the case of the Japanese keiretsu, business groups may prevent market forces from weeding out poorly performing firms. Interlocking directorates among large corporations imply network connections and may account for such behaviors as mergers and financing. Strategic alliances are collaborations among independent businesses to conduct joint projects such as R&D or marketing. While most alliance research examined micro-level processes, some analysts investigated macro-level dynamics driving the evolution of complete networks.

Skip 160-163

5

Global Networks

After Cambridge economist John Maynard Keynes became bursar of King's College in 1924, he made a small fortune for the university by selling properties and investing in stocks right through the Great Depression and World War II. Ironically, as an academic analyst, he was contemptuous of the economic function of financial speculation, which he defined as an effort to forecast market psychology:

> Speculators may do no harm as bubbles on a steady stream of enterprise. But the position is serious when enterprise becomes the bubble on a whirlpool of speculation. When the capital development of a country becomes a by-product of the activities of a casino, the job is likely to be ill-done. The measure of success attained by Wall Street, regarded as an institution of which the proper social purpose is to direct new investment into the most profitable channels in terms of future yield, cannot be claimed as one of the outstanding triumphs of *laissez-faire* capitalism - which is not surprising, if I am right in thinking that the best brains of Wall Street have been in fact directed towards a different object. (Keynes 1936: 159)

As policymakers in capitalist societies adopted Keynesian economics, financial markets were more tightly regulated, public financial institutions dealt with market failures, and severe financial crises nearly disappeared. Yet, seven decades after Keynes' prophetic warning, the best brains of newly deregulated Wall Street firms placed huge speculative bets that sliced-and-diced credit default swaps – bonds referencing derivatives-based subprime mortgages made to numerous homebuyers without sufficient incomes to make balloon payments – would continue to rise ceaselessly in value. When the housing bubble began bursting in 2007, it nearly brought down the entire global economy.

Global interorganizational networks, examined toward the end of this chapter, contributed to the financial crisis and ensuing Great Recession. To set the stage, I review theories and research on international networks, supply and commodity chains, the world cities network, and an emerging transnational capitalist class. As ever, the "vast and continually expanding literature on economic globalization continues to generate a miasma of conflicting viewpoints and alternative discourses" (Dicken et al. 2001: 89). Network analysis provides valuable theoretical and methodological tools for dissecting and illuminating the multi- and cross-level ties comprising the increasingly complex web of the global economy.

International Networks

Economic globalization involves increasing integration of local, regional, and national economies into international economic networks, through such dynamic relations as exports and imports, foreign direct investment, financial capital flows, labor migration, technology transfers, and diffusion of knowledge and innovations. Some analysts stressed noneconomic relations – political, military, cultural, scientific – as additional ties sustaining and strengthening global economic interdependence. Recent studies of transnational diffusion of public policies and institutions emphasized how economic networks facilitate the spread of information and ideas, and the adoption of policies and practices, from nation to nation. For example, Mauro Guillén and colleagues identified effects of network cohesion and structural equivalence on the worldwide diffusion of ISO 9000 quality certification standards (Guler et al. 2002); on the spread of central bank independence (Pollilo and Guillén 2005); and four market-oriented infrastructure reforms

(Henisz et al. 2005). Nations with close proximity in networks of transnational portfolio investments and exports were more likely to adopt similar top corporate tax rates, primarily through policy learning and emulation processes (Cao 2010). "We find evidence of the network socialization mechanism in the networks of IGOs [intergovernmental organizations] and the evidence is much stronger in the IGO networks that facilitate policy learning than in the IGO networks that facilitate policy emulation" (p. 850). These and other studies underscore the importance of economic ties among nations in the modern era of globalization.

Globalization is not a contemporary phenomenon. The extensive Silk Road network of trade routes connecting Chinese and Indian markets to the Mediterranean flourished from the first century BCE. Western European voyages of discovery and subsequent colonization of overseas territories began in the fifteenth century. Much globalization theorizing and empirical research concentrates on the past 500 years and the twentieth century in particular. Modernization and development theorists in the 1950s argued that traditional societies would follow a single evolutionary path from poverty to prosperity by integrating into the world economic and sociopolitical systems. Advanced industrial democracies could assist "underdeveloped" countries to modernize their economies and societies through such policies as free trade, direct capital investment, government foreign aid, and people-to-people assistance programs like the Peace Corps. The belief that globalization generally promotes economic development and prosperity everywhere still echoes in popular treatments such as Thomas Friedman's *The World Is Flat* (2005).

Beginning in the 1960s and 1970s, two Marxist-influenced theories that rejected the proposition of progressive economic modernization came to dominate debates in the sociology of development. Dependency theorists hypothesized that a core of rich capitalist nations, through their control of the global economy and ability to compel unequal terms of exchange with a periphery of poor countries, whose economies are based on agriculture and raw materials extraction, actually create and sustain continual underdevelopment (Frank 1966). World systems theorists refined this core-periphery dichotomy into a stratified model of three ideal types: core, semiperiphery, and periphery. Immanuel Wallerstein (1974) hypothesized that an international division of labor began in the fifteenth century as European feudalism transformed into industrial capitalism. Core nations possess sufficient financial capital and skilled, high-wage labor forces to industrialize and they use their market power to exploit peripheral economies of low-paid, labor-intensive production. Semiperipheral countries also exploit the periphery, but may benefit from favorable transactions with the core, for example, from relocation to their shores of auto factories and call centers. The world system is dynamic, as some nations gain or lose status over time. Hegemonic power shifted across three centuries from the Netherlands, to England, to the United States. Although the world systems model emphasized unequal economic relations among nations, research by Wallerstein and others relied primarily on historical methods to document long-range, holistic narratives of structural changes in the global economy. In parallel, some network-oriented sociologists applied formal network methods to search for dichotomous and tripartite structures of relations among nations.

World-system and dependency models informed David Snyder and Edward Kick's (1979) analysis of economic networks among nations. But, they also emphasized the importance of noneconomic international linkages, especially political-military relations, in globalization processes. Consequently, they simultaneously blockmodeled matrices of four networks – trade flows, military interventions, diplomatic relations, treaty memberships – among 118 nations in the mid-1960s. They successively split the four matrices into structurally equivalent positions, finally stopping at a ten-block partition, and used the within- and between-block densities to further simplify the model into four 10 × 10 binary image matrices. Based on visual inspection, "[i]n general, though with some deviations, we interpret the pattern of bonds depicted in the image matrices as a core-semiperiphery-periphery structure" (p. 1110), with one core block, six peripheral blocks, and three semipheripheral positions. The core contained the capitalist nations of Western Europe, North America, Japan, Australia, and

South Africa. One semiperipheral block consisted of the Soviet Union, Eastern Europe, Cuba, and nine mostly Middle Eastern nations. The peripheral positions were populated by all African and many South American and Asian developing countries. To test the hypothesis that structural position affected national economic welfare, Snyder and Kick estimated multivariate regression models with change in gross national product (GNP) per capita for 90 nations from 1955 to 1970 as the dependent variable. Net of other factors such as school enrollment rates, nations in the periphery or semiperiphery lagged the core nations by $500 per capita. They concluded that "the effects of structural position on the economic growth of nations from 1955 to 1970 are highly consistent with world-system/dependency formulations, although they do not differentiate between the economic costs of peripheral versus semi-peripheral location" (p. 1123). In subsequent research, Kick and Davis (2001) expanded the dataset to more nations and into the 1970s, finding generally similar results that implied great stability of the international structure of economic and noneconomic relations.

In the most recent iteration, Kick et al. (2011) blockmodeled four networks (trade, arms transfers, intergovernmental organizations, and embassies) for 1995–9. Their ten-block solution identified a center core block of six nations (US, UK, France, Germany, Italy, Netherlands) and two other central blocks whose ties to other positions closely resemble the center core. The Western European block contained 13 members from that region plus Brazil, Israel, and Turkey, while the Asian block had nine nations from that continent, including China, India, and Japan, but also former British colonies Australia, Canada, and South Africa. These three central blocks together reproduced much of the core position in Snyder and Kick's analysis of the 1960s data. The other seven positions were fairly homogeneous by region (e.g., South American, African, and Former Soviet blocks). Overall tie densities suggested "a structure for the global system that very roughly parallels world-system arguments," although the "gradual decline in ties moving from core to periphery in the system appears to support more 'continuous' interpretations of the world-system hierarchy, rather than purely 'discrete' interpretations that rely on dichotomous (core/periphery) or trichotomous (core/semiperiphery/periphery) articulations" (p. 316). The major change across three decades was the increasing centrality of the Asian core block relative to its earlier semiperipheral location. The world was almost completely connected, the center core stood out for its direct strong ties to other positions, and both Western European and Asian blocks were also broadly and intensively connected to many positions. In contrast, the peripheral South Pacific/Middle East and Africa blocks were isolated and weakly connected to few others, respectively. Most of the semiperipheral blocks (Southeast Asia/Middle East, South America, Former Soviet, and Eastern Europe) had direct, strong ties to the three central positions, but fewer to one another. The authors concluded, "There is rough parity of generic results using economic versus noneconomic ties but a fruitful direction for subsequent research would be a more theoretically driven project linking the position of nations in *each* network type to relevant domestic outcomes and antecedents" (p. 324).

Other researchers investigated different relational contents or applied alternative network methods to identify positions. Ronan Van Rossem (1996) analyzed both economic and noneconomic networks – imports, exports, arms trade, presence of foreign troops, diplomatic ties – for 163 nations in the 1980s. But, instead of structurally equivalent blockmodels, he applied regular equivalence analysis to identify similar roles based on observed triad patterns. In regular equivalence, actors are grouped into roles based on similarity of ties to equivalent alters, in contrast to structural equivalence based on their pattern of ties to the same alters. Van Rossem's results were generally consistent with the tripartite world-systems model, although he distinguished two peripheral positions, one with connections to both the core and semiperiphery, the second with ties only to the core. However, he found little impact of world-system roles on GDP growth in the 1980s: "The effects of world system role on dependency and economic performance are small and often not significant, while dependency has a moderate to strong effect on economic performance"

(p. 524). He concluded that nations are powerful in the world system primarily when they have large economies, which explains why China, India, and Brazil were prominent despite relatively low development. Other analysts confined their examinations to worldwide flows of specific commodities. For example, Matthew Mahutga and David Smith (2011) applied regular equivalence and hierarchical clustering methods to map jointly occupied roles in the international division of labor (IDL). Analyses of UN trade data on 55 commodities, aggregated into five broadly categorized networks for 94 nations in 1965, 1980, and 2000, identified six positions: core, core-contenders, upper-tier semiperiphery, strong periphery, weak periphery, and weakest periphery. The researchers tested a world systems hypothesis that core nations would experience the highest economic growth. Instead, countries occupying intermediate roles in the international division of labor – the five "core-contenders" China, Indonesia, South Korea, Thailand, and Spain and upper-tier semiperipheral nations like India and Brazil – experienced the highest GDP per capita growth during both periods, apparently "a function of the greater propensity for upward mobility enjoyed by countries in the middle of the IDL vis-à-vis their peripheral counterparts" (p. 270). These results offer hope that some countries might improve their positions within the world system, particularly the core-contender nations pursuing state-led export-oriented development strategies.

Supply and Commodity Chains

At the industry level of analysis, economists, sociologists, and geographers investigated networks variously described as *global supply chains*, *commodity chains*, or *value chains*. From a world-systems perspective, Terence Hopkins and Immanuel Wallerstein defined a commodity chain as "a network of labor and production processes whose end result is a finished commodity" (1986: 159). Chains involve sequentially linked organizations that design products, gather raw materials, assemble intermediate components, finish the goods, and transport them to retailers and dealers, who sell the final products to ultimate customers, which may be other businesses or individual consumers. Some economists constructed formal supply chain models and ran computer simulations to optimize network elements without regard to geographic features (e.g., Nagurney 2010). However, if the places of planning, extraction, production, transportation, and sales are located in different countries and regions, they comprise global paths suitable for analysis with network ideas and methods. Classical economists conceptualized commodity flows between pairs of nations as a function of comparative advantages. In David Ricardo's famous illustration, although Portugal produced both wine and cloth with less labor than England, their relative costs differed: England had greater difficulty making wine than cloth. Therefore, Portugal should produce excess wine and trade it for English cloth. Nations theoretically benefit from free trade by producing and trading those commodities in which they enjoy comparative advantages. Actual international trade chains are far more complex than simple bilateral transactions between producer and consumer countries.

Global commodity chain (GCC) theorists sought to capture the convolutions with network principles. "Such processes are better conceptualized as being highly complex network structures in which there are intricate links – horizontal, diagonal, as well as vertical – forming multi-dimensional, multi-layered lattices of economic activity. For that reason, an explicitly relational, network-focused approach promises to offer a better understanding of production systems" (Henderson et al. 2002: 442). GCC approaches shift the unit of analysis from nations to interconnected firms operating in global industries. Initial work by sociologists and geographers involved conceptual development, uncovering the full set of firms in a chain, and identifying the most powerful lead firms (chain-drivers) that organize and manage the activities of other network members. For Gary Gereffi, a key GCC issue was governance structure, the "authority and power relationships that determine how financial, material, and human resources are allocated and flow within a chain" (Gereffi 1994: 97). He distinguished two ideal types of chain-drivers: producer-driven and buyer-driven commodity chains (Gereffi 2001). In the former, a dominant manufacturer, such as General Motors or IBM, controls vertical layers of suppliers. The latter type is more common in light manufacturing industries, such as clothing, where the activities of a globally dispersed subcontracting network are coordinated by brand-label marketers. Analysts disputed whether these alternative network governance types generate distinct dynamics and outcomes. A preferred GCC research method was thickly described case studies of chains in specific industries, such as Japanese *maquiladoras* manufacturing electronics in Mexico (Kenney and Florida 1994) and African export agriculture (Daviron and Gibbon 2002). As the GCC perspective matured, it moved beyond its world-systems intellectual roots and confronted competition from a global value chain approach more closely tied to international business research than to sociology and geography (Bair 2005). The GCC emphasis on micro-level dynamics among firms complements the world-systems' macro-structural focus on stratified nations. GCC researchers examined distinctive activities by particular firms at specific locales, which constitute the mechanisms through which global capitalism accumulates the wealth of nations. The next section on world cities networks also looks at nascent efforts to integrate that approach with global commodity chain analysis.

World Cities Networks

The idea of global or world cities – urban areas commanding and controlling major global financial and trade transactions – spans three decades, although analyzing relations among them as a world cities network (WCN) was a relatively recent development. Drawing from central place theory in geography, John Friedmann (1986) generalized about the spatial division of labor in the world economy. Global capitalism requires key cities as "basing points" for organizing production and markets, for concentrating and accumulating international capital, and as destinations for domestic and transnational migration. World cities integrate regional, national, and international economies into the global economy.

They comprise a hierarchy in which the top-rank cities are power centers of global command and control that coordinate with lower-ranking cities servicing subordinate national and regional economies. Large portions of the world population fall outside the world city system into a "fragmented marginalized periphery" (Friedmann 1995: 41). The world city hierarchy is not static, because cities can attract or lose investment and rise or decline in the global command-and-control system, leading to a reordered urban landscape. Saskia Sassen (1991) theorized that, despite growing dispersion of production sites, "the more globalized the economy becomes, the higher the agglomeration of central functions in a relatively few sites, that is, in global cities" (1991: 5). World cities differ from traditional urban centers of trade and finance in four ways:

> [F]irst, as highly concentrated command points in the organization of the world economy; second, as key locations for finance and for specialized service firms, which have replaced manufacturing as the leading economic sectors; third, as sites of production, including the production of innovations, in these leading industries; and fourth, as markets for the products and innovations produced." (Sassen 1991: 4)

An increasing number of world cities provide management and services to geographically dispersed production sites, resulting in "the formation of new geographies of centrality that connect cities in a growing variety of cross-border networks" (Sassen 2002: 14). Empirical investigations of world cities, which began with Friedmann's ranked list based on his impressions of economic power, gravitated toward formal network analytic methods.

An early WCN analysis of intercity relations, by David Smith and Michael Timberlake (1995), examined the numbers of airline passengers flying between all pairs of 23 cities in 1991. Using regular equivalence methods, they found that London, New York, and Tokyo were the most central world cities, consistent with qualitative assessments of other scholars, but Paris also ranked in that top group. Clique and structural equivalence analyses of air passenger flights between 100 world cities from 1977 to 1997 disclosed great stability at the very top of the prominence hierarchy – London, Paris, Frankfurt, and New York were consistently in the top four – but Tokyo declined over time and was eventually surpassed within Asia by Hong Kong and Singapore (Shin and Timberlake 2000). Centrality analyses of intercity air travel for 1977, 1995, and 2005 revealed a gradual decoupling of the WCN from the world-system of nation-states due to the growing prominence of cities in the semi-periphery:

> Globalisation is raising the historical prominence of semi-peripheral and east Asian cities *vis-à-vis* earlier periods, but this rise in prominence follows a logic in which these cities remain subordinated to the global command-and-control centres. On the other hand, the prospects for upward mobility for peripheral cities are as distant as ever, with these places locked ever more firmly into lower-level roles in the world economy. This view suggests a qualitatively new pattern of a very old process of world system structuration. (Mahutga et al. 2010: 1940)

Criticisms of airline-based studies include the lack of origin/destination information about interconnecting flights, reliance on international rather than transnational data, and inability to differentiate trip purposes such as tourism and business travel (Derudder et al. 2008). While further research might resolve some of these drawbacks, other options arose for mapping the WCN.

In *The Global City: New York, London and Tokyo* (1991), Sassen highlighted the importance of "advanced producer service" organizations in those three metropolises that provided professional, financial, and creative services to far-flung business clients. Through their worldwide networks of branch offices located in the major cities of most regions, these firms generate the WCN. Geographers at Loughborough University in England ranked cities based on the presence of four types of producer services – accountancy, advertising, banking/finance, and corporate law. Initially they used the branch offices of 69 service firms among 263 cities to identify 55 world cities and sort them into three levels (Taylor 2000). Subsequent research conducted principal component analyses on a firm-by-city bipartite (two-mode) relational matrix whose cell entries indicated the office values for 100 global service firms across 123 cities (Taylor et al. 2002). The primary structure consisted of five clusters of Outer, US, Pacific Asian, Euro-German, and Old Commonwealth cities, but no simple hierarchy emerged in the WCN. Instead, regionalism appeared as important as hierarchy, indicating that "globalization processes simultaneously create more than one large scale of social activity" (Taylor 2004: 361). A similar taxonomy emerged from analyses of multiple networks (economic, cultural, political, social) for 100 global service firms operating offices in 315 cities (Taylor 2005). An investigation of WCN changes between 2000 and 2004 found overall structural stability, although cities in the US and sub-Saharan Africa were "generally losing global connectivity in relation to the rest of the world" (Taylor and Aranya 2008: 1). Between 2000 and 2008, the general increase in network connectivity was concentrated among South Asian, Chinese, and Eastern European cities (Derudder et al. 2010).

Using a more comprehensive dataset, Arthur Alderson and Jason Beckfield (2004) investigated the network of headquarter and branch locations of Fortune Global 500 corporations in 3,692 cities in 2000. The network was highly skewed, with Global 500 headquarters located in just 125 cities, less than four percent of the total. The researchers measured city power by three network centrality scores – outdegrees (number of branches sent to other cities), closeness (path distance to other cities), and betweenness (brokerage of shortest paths between pairs of cities) – and city prestige by indegree (number of branches received). A small number of cities monopolized power and prestige implying that "the world city system forms a fairly strong hierarchy" (p. 846). Four cities – London, New York, Paris, and Tokyo – scored highest on all four indicators because they each sent and received thousands of branches. Next, Alderson and Beckfield applied regular equivalence methods to blockmodel similar cities into positions and identify roles in the WCN. They found 34 blocks of two or more cities, with the four most powerful and prestigious cities jointly occupying a single *primary position*, defined as a clique with high levels of relations to outsiders. Using their binary image matrix (pp. 838–9), I plotted the locations of these

34 blocks based on the pattern of ties between them. In figure 5.1, the primary position London–New York–Paris–Tokyo (L-N-P-T) falls at the center and is surrounded by six other primary blocks (Amsterdam, Atlanta, Basel, Bristol, Caracas, Cologne). Further away are 10 cliquish blocks of cities connected mainly to members of the seven primary blocks (Aachen, Arnhem, Athens, Auckland, Bartlesville, Bochum, Brunswick, Evansville, Geel, Genoa), while 17 blocks located mostly at the periphery connect only to members of more powerful blocks but are unconnected among themselves. Alderson and Beckfield concluded that "the world city system comes close to approximating an idealized core/periphery structure" (p. 847). Further examination revealed an unsurprising covariation between city position in the WCN and the tripartite core-semiperiphery-periphery hierarchy of nations in the world system: "cities located in core countries will, on average, be more powerful and prestigious and occupy a more active position than cities located in noncore countries" (p. 847). Longitudinal network analyses of the power and prestige indicators, spanning 1981, 2000, and 2007 for 500 large corporations with branches located across 6,308 cities, revealed substantial restructuring of the world city hierarchy (Alderson et al. 2010). The system changed

> in such a way as to concentrate power in a small number of cities. However, in contrast to some accounts, we find no clear evidence for a new global geography of inequality. Rather, our results suggest just the opposite – the reproduction of the "old" geography in a starker form. At the level of the world city system at least, the world is not growing flatter. It is growing more uneven. (p. 1917)

In a recent issue of *Global Networks*, geographers discussed prospects for integrating the WCN and global commodity chains explanations of world economic change. Sassen (2010) proffered five analytic propositions about potential connections between the advanced producer services located in the WCN and commodity chains propagating with expanded global capitalism. For example, a possible connection arises because "cross-border operations nowadays require a whole series of organizational capabilities,

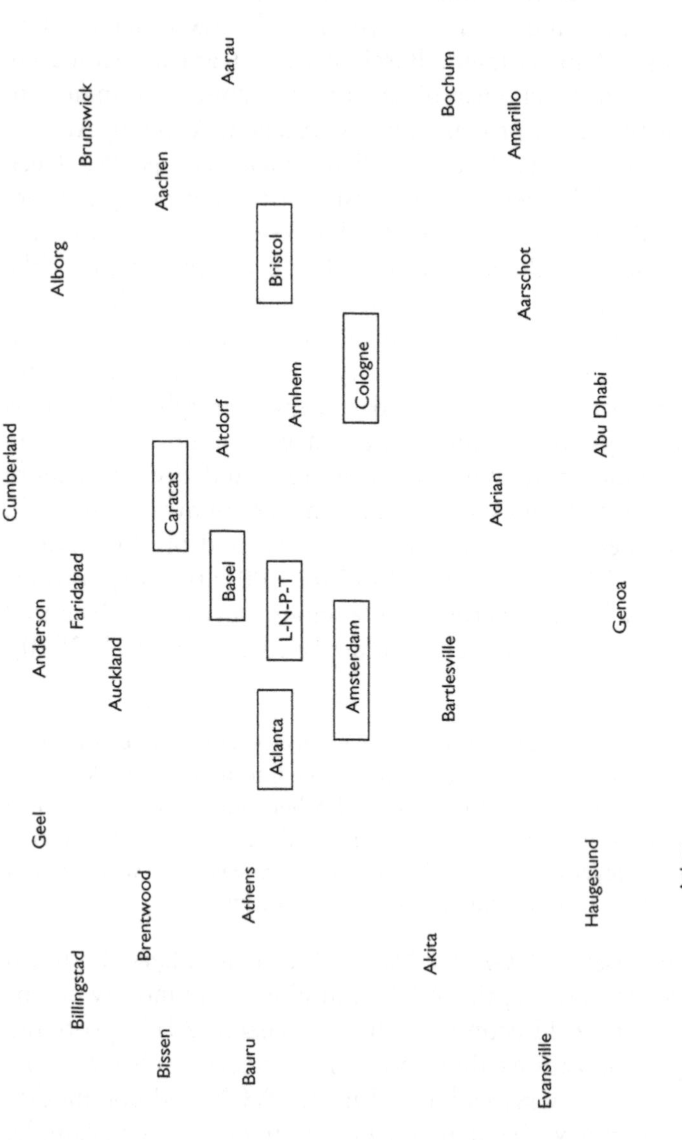

Source: Alderson and Beckfield (2004)

Figure 5.1 Block positions in the world city network 2000

and they are distributed across the [global commodity] chain in a far more evident way than is the case with WCNs" (p. 158). Other contributors reported empirical studies combining elements from both perspectives. Around Munich, Germany, a "mega-city region" emerged as high-tech and advanced producer services firms simultaneously established branches in other world cities and partnered with greater-Munich firms along individual value chains (Lüthi et al. 2010). Although global commodity chains frequently flow through seaports, ironically the branches of firms providing port-related advanced business services, such as maritime law and marine insurance, were located predominantly in non-port world cities. However, a few port cities, including Rotterdam, Houston, and Hamburg, stood out as sites where physical commodities and advanced services converged despite relatively low ranking in the WCN hierarchy (Jacobs et al. 2010). These initial efforts to map the spatial locations and explain the linkages between sites of global production and service provision raise analytical puzzles that ultimately will be solved with more robust theoretical and methodological tools.

A Transnational Capitalist Class?

Some theorists working in Marxist and other critical traditions speculated about the emergence of a transnational capitalist class whose ownership or control of the means of production would give it hegemony, that is, power to dominate the global economy. Leslie Sklair (1997: 514) argued that this class "is organized in four overlapping fractions: TNC [transnational corporation] executives, globalizing bureaucrats, politicians and professionals, consumerist elites (merchants and media)." Key persons in the transnational capitalist class belong to multiple fractions, either at the same time or through routine career moves among institutions. This conceptualization of a multi-institutional upper class transposed to the global level parallels some earlier theories and research on national power structures (Mills 1956) and ruling classes (Domhoff 1970). Sklair posited three attributes that render it truly transnational. First, its members are oriented toward global rather than national views on issues such as free trade and export-promotion strategies for development. Second, they "tend to be people from many countries, more and more of whom begin to consider themselves 'citizens of the world' as well as of their places of birth" (Sklair 1997: 522). Third, they share similar lifestyles of higher education, especially at business schools, and consumption of luxury goods and services. Shared interests in sustaining the accumulation of private profit and capitalist consumerism unify the four worldwide fractions despite much diversity of economic interests, politics, cultures, and ideologies (Sklair 2001). In contrast to this multiple-fraction class model, other theorists adhered to fundamental Marxist ideas about class formation, involving a historical materialist explanation of the worldwide division of labor, the globalization of the capitalist mode of production, and a spreading legal superstructure of property ownership that legitimates the private expropriation of surplus labor value in market exchanges. In this model, only the people directly engaged in global capital accumulation are members of the transnational capitalist class. State bureaucrats, politicians, media promoters, and other functionaries are subordinate elites whose primary roles are to help advance the interests of the dominant transnational capitalist class.

Major forces forming the transnational capitalist class include "the spread of transnational corporations, the sharp increase in foreign direct investment, the proliferation of mergers and acquisitions across national borders, the rise of a global financial system, and the increased interlocking of positions within the global corporate structure" (Robinson and Harris 2000: 11). Class membership may even transcend the conventional capitalism/socialism divide to encompass *statist globalizers* who operate state-controlled enterprises in authoritarian nations such as China, Russia, and the Gulf States (Harris 2009). Other analysts argued that the transnational capitalist class holds sway mainly in an English-speaking, Atlantic, liberal "heartland." Its aim of imposing "an imperialistic global governance and organization of production and finance on the planet at large" faces serious opposition by contenders developed under state auspices, China foremost among them (van der Pijl 2007: 626). One legal scholar detected within growing networks of international institutions – World Trade Organization, World Bank, International Monetary Fund, International Criminal Court, numerous nongovernmental organizations – the basis for a "nascent global state, whose current task is to realize the interests of an emerging transnational capitalist class" by undermining substantive democracy in developing countries (Chimni 2004: 1). Nonetheless, some scholars were skeptical whether global elites are really growing detached from their national identities and parochial interests embedded in various domestic capitalist economies (Macartney 2009). Others asked whether more nuanced reconceptualizations of class relations might improve knowledge about how the world political economy is evolving in relation to national and regional economies (Tabb 2009). The rest of this section examines network research addressing the emerging transnational capitalist class hypothesis.

One prevalent approach examined the interlocking directorate of persons who occupy seats on multiple boards of directors of transnational corporations and financial institutions. The underlying assumption is that identifying a transnational class requires mapping social connections among its members through their co-presence in the same dominant economic organizations. Similar to the national board interlocks discussed in chapter 4, global interlock analysts investigated structural relations in a firm-by-firm matrix created by multiplying a two-mode firm-by-person matrix with its transposed person-by-firm matrix. William Carroll and Meindert Fennema (2002) compared a stratified sample of the 176 leading international industrial corporations and financial companies in 1976 with a matched sample in 1996. Substantial turnover in industry composition occurred over the two decades, with fewer oil and metal companies and more trading, logistics, retail, and telecom firms. The interlock network grew less integrated by multiple-director ties between pairs of companies, but more integrated by single-director connections. Network density grew from 42 percent of possible ties in 1976 to 47 percent in 1996, while the size of the largest component (all dyads connected by one or more paths) grew slightly from 114 to 119 companies. The largest component's diameter (length of shortest path connecting the two most distant firms), dropped markedly from 11 in 1976 to 8 in 1996, an indication of improving communication efficiency. However, in both years about 75 percent of interlocks occurred among pairs of firms headquartered within the same country, a "clearly quite modest" increase in cross-border interlocking (p. 409). Most of the increase involved European-based firms, and no firms headquartered in the semiperiphery had seats with firms in North America, Europe, or Japan. In 1996, the 22 companies at the center of the network, connected by three or more transnational director interlocks, consisted of German, French, Swiss, British, and North American industrial and financial firms. None were from Japan or other Asian nations. The results gave "some support for the hypothesis that a transnational business community is in the making", but "equally striking is the extent to which this community remained in 1996 centered around the North Atlantic area" (p. 415). Or perhaps the network was still rooted in countries and regions of origin, and had not yet transformed into a truly transnational class. In a longitudinal analysis of 22,551 individuals on the boards of the world's 805 largest corporations, Carroll (2009) found that transnationalists (directors holding seats on companies headquartered in different nations) gained prominence relative to nationalists from 1996 to 2006. But, "national networkers, despite thinning ranks and sparser interlocks, continue to form the backbone of the global corporate elite, and remain on balance nationally cohesive" (p. 289). Finally, Carroll's research on Canadian corporations (Carroll 2007a), and on how the world cities hierarchy and interlocking directorates combine into a global network (Carroll 2007b), indicated that national business networks were persistent barriers to the formation of a fully fledged transnational capitalist class capable of defining and acting on its collective economic interests.

Large European corporations increasingly interlocked transnationally. Kees van Veen and Jan Kratzer (2011) examined 6,115 board seats of 362 corporations in 2006. More than 87 percent of directors held only one seat, but among a total of 1,128 interlocking directors, 39 percent spanned national boundaries. This proportion was much higher than values reported for previous decades, indicating greater cross-border integration. Based on degree centrality, "France is by far the most central European country within this network . . . followed by Germany, the Netherlands, Belgium, and the UK, and then other countries with quickly decreasing scores" (p. 17). Country centrality in the transnational network was strongly related to longevity in the European Union, with founding nations more connected than recent arrivals. Within-country interlock density and market institutions strongly covaried, with coordinated market economies (such as Germany and France) having much denser interlock networks than liberal market economies (e.g., UK and Ireland). Unfortunately, the authors did not speculate about cross-level dynamics: "To what extent and how the emerging transnational business elite is replacing national elites is an open question, linked with the consequences for the functioning of country-specific economic systems" (p. 21). Research on these mutual influences would require a longitudinal network design spanning many nations and years.

Other interlock researchers uncovered evidence consistent with an emergent transnational capitalist class. An analysis of the world's largest 500 firms from 1983 to 1998 by Jeffrey Kentor and Yong-Suk Jang (2004) observed a striking growth in the number of transnational interlocks concentrated among European Community firms – a consequence of EU policies expanding the internal common market for the free flow of goods, services, capital, and labor across state borders – as well as increased ties between European and US corporations. Notably absent were transnational linkages with Japanese and South Korean firms. "As the process of global integration among transnational corporations intensifies, these firms may become increasingly unified actors in the global economy, and the individuals who control these organizations may indeed emerge as a global capitalist class" (p. 366). For a reply and rebuttal in the debate, see Carroll and Fennema (2004) and Kentor and Jang (2006). Interlock analysis of the 80 largest transnational corporations found the proportion of boards with at least one cross-national director more than doubled, from 36 percent in 1993 to 75 percent in 2005 (Staples 2007). The merger and acquisition activities of the world's 148 largest transnational corporations and commercial banks identified one mechanism sustaining this growth: "cross-border acquisition almost always results in a more multinational board of directors, that multinational boards are more likely to do cross-border deals, and that once a board becomes multinational it stays that way" (Staples 2008: 31).

A less common approach investigated networks of elite affiliations with policy-planning organizations, also known as think tanks. These groups bring together leaders from business, government, academia, mass media, and the legal and scientific professions to discuss economic and social problems, reach consensus on public policy solutions, and devise strategies for action. Some organizations primarily conduct research while others engage in public-opinion influence and lobbying activities. Research on US policy planning organizations typically found a cohesive network, interlocked via multiple governing board positions held by corporate executives, and thus disposed to favor conservative policy solutions (Burris 2008). A crucial question at the international level is whether a comparable policy planning network expressed the policy interests of a transnational class? A case study of the European Round Table of Industrialists, consisting of 45 CEOs and chairs of the largest EU nonfinancial enterprises, concluded that it functions as "an elite platform for an emergent European transnational capitalist class from which it can formulate a common strategy and – on the basis of that strategy – seek to shape European socioeconomic governance through its privileged access to the European institutions" (van Apeldoorn 2000: 160). William Carroll and Colin Carson (2003) linked five prominent transnational policy planning groups (e.g., International Chamber of Commerce, Trilateral Commission, World Economic Forum) to 271 global corporations in 1996 through a few dozen mostly European and North American cosmopolitan persons holding multiple governance positions in both networks:

> The policy groups pull the directorates of the world's major corporations together, and collaterally integrate the lifeworld of the global corporate elite, but they do so selectively, reproducing regional differences in participation. These findings support the claim that a well-integrated global corporate elite has formed, and that global policy groups have contributed to its formation. (Carroll and Carson 2003: 66)

Although hesitant to conclude that this elite confirms the apotheosis of a transnational class, the authors argued that international policy planning groups provide political and cultural leadership integral to the formation of that class. An extension of the analysis in 2006 to 500 global corporations and 11 policy groups observed further network consolidation via policy boards, accompanied by increased European cohesion at both individual and organizational levels (Carroll and Sapinski 2010). A core-periphery structure emerged with Europeans playing key brokerage roles between Asia-Pacific and North Atlantic regional business councils. Suggestive as these findings are, the jury is still out about whether a cohesive transnational capitalist class has gained the capacity to act as a class-for-itself in global economic affairs.

Networks of the Global Financial Crisis

The severe impacts of the Global Financial Crisis of 2007–9 on real economies persisted through subsequent years of high unemployment, depressed housing markets, tottering growth, ballooning government deficits, and threats of budgetary default. This section examines scholarly efforts to understand how financial networks contributed to the crisis and its aftermaths. Contemporaneous accounts identified these major antecedents:

- Public policy shifts from business regulation toward free markets, beginning under Reagan in the US and Thatcher in the UK, curtailed governmental oversight of many economic activities, especially in the finance sector. The 1933 Glass-Steagall

Act, which had separated US commercial (depository) banking from investment banking, was repealed in 1999. The same financial institution could both lend and invest, thereby setting up potential conflicts of interest. The Tax Reform Act of 1986, by retaining tax deductions for mortgage interest on homes but not for consumer debt interest, helped to popularize cash-out refinancing of home mortgages as a cheaper form of borrowing than credit cards.

- A shadow banking system – comprising investment banks, hedge funds, money market funds, insurers – expanded rapidly to rival the traditional depository banking system. It was subject to looser oversight, less information disclosure, and fewer safety requirements than commercial banks; for example, maintaining lower ratios of debt-to-liquid assets.
- The Clinton Administration pressured Fannie Mae and Freddie Mac, government-sponsored underwriters in the secondary mortgage market, to boost home ownership of low- and middle-income families. Pressured as well by their stockholders to sustain profit growth, Fannie and Freddie assumed substantially higher risks by weakening their underwriting standards to compete against private mortgage companies in lending to borrowers unqualified for conventional loans.
- The US Federal Reserve, fearing a deflationary spiral after the dot.com stock market bubble burst in 2000, dropped interest rates to historically low levels. Easy credit conditions, fueled by inflows of foreign funds from China and Europe, encouraged consumers to take on record debts, often by cash-out refinancing their home mortgages.
- Starting in the 1990s, a worldwide housing bubble of steadily rising housing prices triggered construction booms in the US, UK, Ireland, Spain, and other economies, resulting in gluts of residential and commercial properties. To boost lending, predatory mortgage originators wrote increasing volumes of subprime mortgages targeted at people unlikely to meet repayment schedules, particularly for adjustable-rate loans that soon reset at higher interest. "Liar loans" simply asked borrowers to state their incomes without lenders attempting to verify them.

Sustaining the bubble were widely shared beliefs that housing prices could and would increase indefinitely.

- Financial institutions created innovative instruments – asset-based securities such as collateralized debt obligations (CDO) and mortgage-backed securities (MBS) – that derived their underlying value from steadily rising home prices and mortgage payments, but whose risks were difficult to price accurately. Investment banks bought up tens of billions in subprime loans from mortgage brokers, pooled them with other less risky loans, and aggressively resold the derivatives to insurers, pension funds, and other investors around the world. The financial sector grew steadily more leveraged.
- Credit-rating agencies, whose fees were paid by issuers of securities, failed to assign accurate risks to asset-backed securities, a fundamental conflict of interest that misled investors into over-confidence about their safety.
- American International Group (AIG) sold enormous quantities of underpriced credit default swaps (CDS), a derivative linked to MBSs which were akin to insurance protecting mortgage lending companies against loan defaults. CDS sellers receive regular premiums from buyers, who get payouts only if the debtors default. AIG failed to hedge sufficiently against possible decline in the values of the underlying assets. CDSs attracted speculators who sought to sell "short" the companies they believed were at risk of default.

By the middle of the 2000s, capital development around the globe had ominously grown to resemble the very "by-product of the activities of a casino" about which Keynes had warned. Meltdown of the unsustainable housing bubble commenced when US home prices began collapsing in 2007. With increasing numbers of subprime borrowers unable to meet mortgage payments, the snowballing defaults, evictions, and foreclosures left many mortgage holders "under water" (value of their property worth less than the loan). Banks, uncertain about which financial institutions had sufficient assets to cover their liabilities, grew wary of short-term lending. Credit markets dried up and the real economy tipped into recession, then accelerated toward depression as home and commercial construction ground to a halt while consumers cut back on purchases. An early casualty of the credit crunch was Northern Rock, which in September 2007 suffered the UK's first bank run in 140 years when depositors lined up outside branch offices to withdraw their savings. The US Federal Reserve and European Central Bank injected billions into the banking systems through securities purchases in 2008 and 2009, likely averting a second great depression. Financial institutions deeply involved in subprime securitization faced cascading heavy losses: Bear Stearns, Countrywide, Washington Mutual, IndyMac, Lehman Brothers, Merrill Lynch, Wachovia Bank, Fannie Mae and Freddie Mac in the US; Royal Bank of Scotland and Bradford & Bingley in the UK; Hypo Real Estate in Germany; the Dutch-Belgian Fortis group; Glitnir bank in Iceland. Many firms were forced into fire-sales to competitors, bankruptcy, or survival only through massive government bailouts and seizures. Unable to meet its CDS obligations, AIG was taken over by the Bush Administration in September 2008 as part of its Troubled Asset Relief Program (TARP) to bail out Wall Street firms by buying toxic mortgages. Stock markets tumbled worldwide, losing trillions in investor wealth, while unemployment stagnated long after the Great Recession from December 2007 to June 2009. Continuing lack of confidence by financial institutions in holding large amounts of property-backed debt and persistent huge government budget deficits threatened to slow economic recovery for years to come. A looming Greek sovereign debt default in 2012 threatened to become the proverbial iceberg tip that might capsize other Eurozone economies, including Portugal, Ireland, Italy, and Spain.

Network dynamics help to explain how small disturbances escalated into the Global Financial Crisis. Finance economists developed network models of financial systems that simulate how an initial bank failure, or "liquidity shock" occurring when a bank cannot meet its obligations, propagates through an interdependent banking system. Under some network structural conditions, a bank failure quickly dampens out, while in other circumstances it may trigger cascades of subsequent failures which threaten to bring down the entire system. (For an overview of models, see Haldane and May 2011.) Financial organizations routinely lend and borrow deposits from one another through interbank markets, enabling firms to cover short-term deficit positions. However, these interdependencies increase the risk that insolvency at one firm may quickly spread to others:

> But when some of these borrowers may be holders of so-called "toxic assets," the confidence in the ability of any potential borrower to pay back the loans comes into question. . . . At best, borrowers most likely to default could obtain funds at sky-high rates reflecting that default probability. At worst, the market could simply vanish almost overnight; it was this rapid vanishing that provides the best evidence that adverse selection was the root of the credit market meltdown. (Brennan 2009: 295)

Credit crunches diffuse through a financial network in a *contagion* process analogous to biological diseases or falling dominoes. Franklin Allen and Douglas Gale (2000) proposed a formal contagion model in which interbank linkages, formed through cross-holdings of demand deposits and derivative contracts, could be mobilized to halt a threat of contagion if healthy banks had sufficient incentives to help troubled banks by "holding interregional claims on other banks to provide insurance against liquidity preference shocks" (p. 1). Their model revealed that incomplete networks have higher risk of contagion than completely connected networks: "Better-connected networks are more resilient because the proportion of losses in one bank's portfolio is transferred to more banks through interbank agreements" (Allen and Babus 2009: 370). The drawback of a public policy to promote higher interbank network density as a hedge against system insolvency is weaker incentives to close inefficient banks.

In Yaron Leitner's (2005) model, network connections not only propagate liquidity shocks but induce solvent banks to bail out illiquid banks "even when they cannot precommit to do so" (p. 2946), because not contributing to a bailout dooms everyone if the system collapses. An infamous debacle occurred in the 1998 insolvency of Long-Term Capital Management (LTCM), a highly leverage hedge fund that applied complex mathematics to reap profits from price differentials across different bond markets. LTCM lost nearly $5 billion when the Russian government defaulted on its bonds. Fearing that contagion would multiply catastrophic losses across numerous financial markets, the Federal Reserve Fund of New York coordinated a voluntary bailout of LTCM by 14 private Wall Street creditors (notably excepting Bear Stearns, ironically an early casualty of the much bigger debacle of the next decade). Leitner's voluntary bailout model breaks down if funds are insufficient to rescue all struggling banks or if the available funds are sufficient but concentrated among a small group of banks: "The intuition is that the threat of losing future income may not be sufficient to induce an agent [bank] with a lot of cash to voluntarily hand over his entire endowment. In other words, the amount that an agent may be willing to contribute to a bailout cannot be more than what he loses by not participating" (p. 2927). Leitner's insights seemed prophetic just a few years later, when the cumulative losses in the Global Financial Crisis simply overwhelmed any possibility of a voluntary bailout.

A few empirical studies of global banking networks tested some implications of formal contagion models for understanding the 2007–9 crisis. Galina Hale (2011) used data on 15,089 international syndicated bank-to-bank loans to construct annual global banking networks between 1980 and 2009 among 7,938 bank and nonbank institutions in 141 countries. She calculated such network properties as size, density, clustering, and betweenness to observe network evolution across three decades. Hale found increased connectivity, beginning around the late 1990s, "suggesting a possibility that this increased density, if indeed associated with higher fragility and greater liquidity needs, could be partly responsible for the dramatic propagation of the global financial crisis" (p. 6). Clustering and asymmetry in lending increased substantially and may have contributed to network fragility and the rapid spread of the crisis. Network structure changed with the global business cycle: "network expansion slowed in recent years, especially during the 2007–9 crisis; during recessions in the United States, clusters tend to become less common in the network, while the span of the network tends to shrink." Although recessions seemed to encourage new loans, particularly from central to peripheral nations, banks were very cautious about lending during the 2007–9 Global Financial Crisis, making almost no new network connections in 2009. The global banking network appeared more sensitive to banking crises than to mundane recessions, while "during country-specific recessions or banking crises past relationships become more important as few new relationships are formed" (p. 7). Clearly, bank relationships in the global system are very susceptible and responsive to economic and financial shocks. A vicious structural dynamic transpires, with banking crises spreading faster in concentrated networks and crises accelerating network concentration. In contradiction to some formal network models discussed above, a policy implication of Hale's research is that systemic stability requires less interbank connectivity.

Two studies emphasized other financial network dimensions contributing to the crisis. A neoinstitutional critique by Pozner et al. (2010) remarked that "over-embeddedness of central actors within relatively closed networks and superstitious learning processes can exacerbate the biases to which decision makers are susceptible, leading to the institutionalization of a sub-optimal organizational practice" (p. 183). Competitive, normative, and mimetic pressures converged, "resulting in a dense, clique-like network of co-located institutions." These dense connections induced conformity to a single mind-set, rapid diffusion of highly profitable but ultimately maladaptive innovations such as subprime mortgages and securitized derivatives, and collective myopia in disregarding early warning signs. Increasing network cohesion and growing structural equivalence created an unquestioning consensus about the legitimacy and safety of risky financial innovations. Wall Street's small, closed network lacked structural holes across which diverse, discordant, and challenging information could travel. Going along with the crowd sustained everyone's fantasies of spectacular wealth. An extreme form of regulatory agency cooptation, the "privatization of legitimacy" (Pozner et al. 2010: 194), fatefully allowed the financial sector to self-regulate and diffuse responsibilities for actions contributing to the crisis. A network analysis of EU financial services regulation by Dimitrios Christopoulos and Lucia Quaglia (2009) mapped the flow of policy influence among 22 core organizations involved in negotiating the 2005 Capital Requirements Directive (CRD) regulations. The European Banking Federation and several German institutions played broker roles and occupied cohesive central positions, with French, Italian, and British organizations in relatively peripheral locations. Consequently, German banks and their regulators were successful in having many of their regulatory preferences incorporated into the CRD. Other organizations in brokerage structural positions were able to influence the CRD agenda at critical stages in the debate. This research is an important reminder that political networks are crucial in deciding the financial rules of the game which affect economic outcomes.

The Global Financial Crisis revealed weak and obsolete governance mechanisms for mobilizing and coordinating effective global responses. Ad hoc policies were cobbled together at national levels in desperate efforts to patch up an unraveling system. Katharina Pistor (2009) glimpsed a new global governance regime, arising like a phoenix from ashes of the old, comprising "the afflicted financial intermediaries and those that have come to their rescue. . . . They include private banks from the West, their home governments, and Sovereign Wealth Funds (hereafter referred to as SWFs) from the Middle and the Far East" (p. 553). A sovereign wealth fund is a state-owned investment fund, typically held by a central bank or savings accounts in other entities, that invests its assets globally to maximize long-term returns. Figure 5.2 shows the network of SWFs and governments taking minority equity stakes in a dozen of the largest US and European financial institutions between 2005 and 2008. For example, the US Federal Reserve invested in seven financial institutions as part of the TARP bailout (three of which were later severed, indicated by dashed lines). Singapore's Temasek invested in six institutions, while its sister organization, the Government of Singapore Investment Fund (GIC), invested in the Bank of America (BoA) and UBS, and made repeated investments in Citigroup. Three Middle East SWFs (Kuwait, Abu Dhabi,

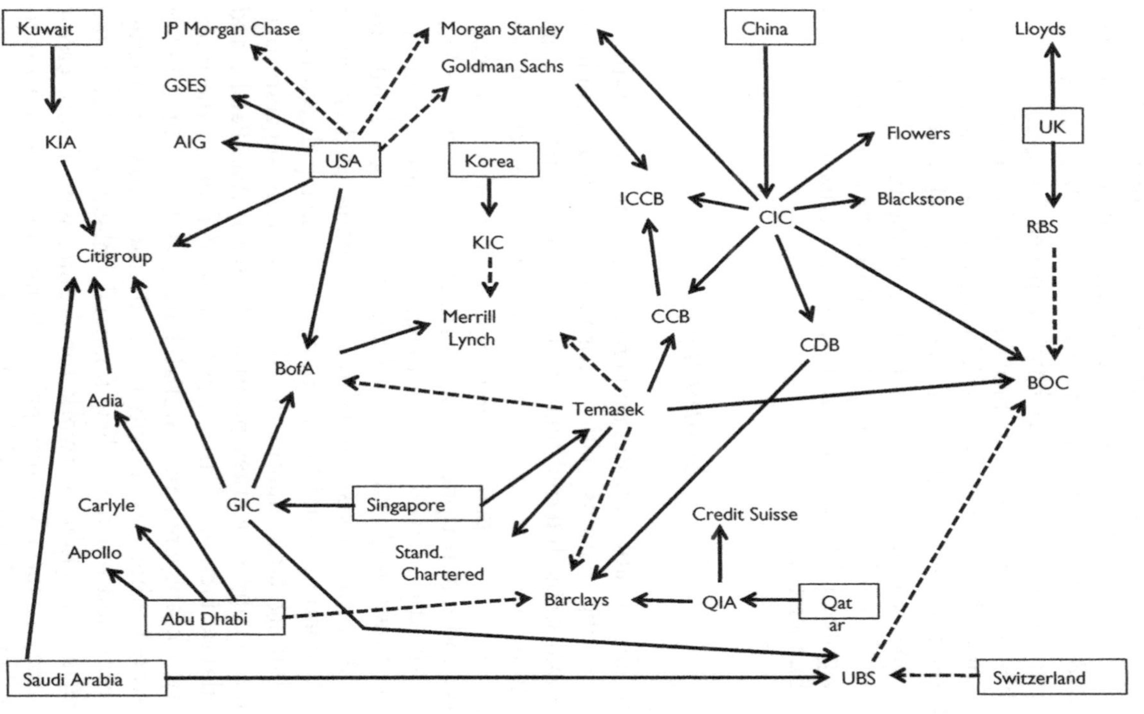

Source: Pistor (2009)

Figure 5.2 Global network of sovereign wealth investments

and Saudi Arabia) also invested in Citigroup. China's CIC directly invested in Morgan Stanley, Blackstone, and Flowers, and also channeled funds to Barclays through the China Development Bank (CDB). "While selected network ties have been either dissolved or trimmed down, others have deepened," suggesting that the new financial structure "has proven remarkably durable under the stress of global financial crisis. This raises the possibility that network relations – even if not a specific network configuration – will become a more permanent feature of the global financial marketplace" (p. 558). Pistor speculated about the evolving global network's potential to produce innovative governance responses in future financial crises.

Summary

Economic globalization creates numerous relations across national borders, linking nations, cities, corporations, and people in transnational webs. International trade of commodities and services integrates local, regional, and national economies into the global economy with great inequalities between nations in core, periphery, and semiperiphery. The world cities network is a hierarchical structure in which top-ranked urban centers plan and coordinate flows in global supply chains connecting subordinate locations. A transnational capitalist class capable of dominating the global economy could be emerging. An evolving directorship network linking large multinational corporations suggests that Europeans occupy brokerage positions between Asia-Pacific and North Atlantic factions. Cascading failures of firms in the interbank network triggered the Global Financial Crisis of 2007–9 when private institutions, heavily invested in securitized mortgage derivatives, could not meet their financial obligations. From the wreckage, a new global network for dealing with future credit crunches may connect Western private banks and governments to the sovereign wealth funds of East Asia and the Middle East.

6

Looking Forward

Starship Captain Jean-Luc Picard explains to a time traveler from twenty-first-century Earth, "the economics of the future are somewhat different. You see, money doesn't exist in the 24th century. . . . The acquisition of wealth is no longer the driving force in our lives. We work to better ourselves and the rest of humanity" (*Star Trek: First Contact* 1996). Material scarcity is eliminated by replicator machines that instantly produce all necessary commodities – food, clothing, equipment – by recycling and reassembling subatomic particles. Robots perform routine menial services, freeing humans from drudgery to pursue avocations, hobbies, and other self- and humanity-betterment activities. Specialized goods and services – vintage wines, transporters – are purchased using virtual "credits," replenished by working as little as five hours per week at indispensable tasks (Grinder 2011). Credits are nontransferable and balances are tracked by computerized accounts that eliminate possibilities for theft and fraud. With production facilities collectively owned, private corporations are unnecessary. Starfleet defends the United Federation of Planets against enemy civilizations, but its primary mission is galactic exploration – in the words of *USS Enterprise* Captain James T. Kirk, "to explore strange new worlds, to seek out new life and new civilizations, to boldly go where no man has gone before." Until the communistic utopia of Star Trek arrives, we remain mired in twenty-first-century economies where people, organizations, and governments face difficult, often painful, choices among alternatives under conditions of persistent resource scarcity. Likewise, network analysts must choose how best to allocate their efforts toward improving the quality of network theories and the tools to test them.

Theory Construction

As more economists become intrigued by network analysis, they are likely to invoke mainstream economics explanations grounded in the subjective expected utility maximization model of individual decision making. But, if every human choice is ultimately reducible to cost-benefit calculations, then nothing is explained because no research hypothesis is falsifiable. Economic sociologists should continue to promote alternative theoretical perspectives about the diverse social forces shaping the individual actions, formal organizations, and social institutions of economic life. The core principle is that economic activity is embedded among social, economic, cultural, political, religious, and other relationships. These interconnected subsystems exert such strong mutual influences that they cannot be isolated but must be taken jointly into account to develop comprehensive explanations. Social network analysis contributes distinctive concepts, propositions, and other theoretical tools for constructing rigorous theories of economic action. Hence, economic sociology in combination with network analysis promises to generate more accurate and insightful understandings of economic behavior than the simplified models of mainstream economics.

A social theory consists of an integrated set of propositions claiming to explain some phenomenon of interest at one or more levels of analysis. Propositions are statements connecting two or more concepts that are defined broadly but with sufficient precision to enable eventual operationalization and empirical testing. Theoretical propositions are integrated through shared concepts that permit the generation of novel and insightful predictions. Social network analysts often plunder other disciplines for theoretical inspiration; for example, psychological balance, organizational resource dependence, and transaction cost economics. For social network analysis to realize its full potential, it must create theories about relations among actors that are grounded in network principles. To prod analysts in that direction, Steven Borgatti and colleagues laid a foundation for network theory construction. They contrasted two fundamental models of network explanation: (a) the *flow model*, in which information and other resources travel "from node to node along paths consisting of ties interlocked through shared endpoints" (Borgatti and Lopez-Kidwell 2011: 43); and (b) the *bond model* of interdependencies, where "the network tie serves as a bond that aligns and coordinates action, enabling groups of nodes to act as a single node, often with greater capabilities" (Borgatti and Halgin 2011: 1174). They claimed that these two generic models underlie most network theorizing and can be jointly applied to uncover fundamental mechanisms to answer basic research questions about how network properties produce outcomes: Why are some actors and groups more similar to one another? Why do some actors and groups achieve more successful performance outcomes? Borgatti and Lopez-Kidwell (2011: 41–2) argued that the strength-of-weak-tie, structural hole, Coleman social capital, and small-world theories are all elaborations of the flow model. Superficial differences appear at the surface level "that ornaments the basic theory with variables drawn from the immediate empirical context and which serve as an interface to general social theory" (p. 43). An important implication for economic network theory construction is that mainstream economics concentrates on the flow model: price information flows between buyers and sellers in markets, followed by exchanges of money for goods and services. Importantly, the bond model is also crucial for understanding the social embeddedness of economic flows, especially the solidary ties and cohesive connections among families, friends, neighbors, coworkers, communities, firms, organizational fields, and industries. Combining mechanisms from both the flow and bond models could generate more comprehensive network theories that better explain economic actions.

Another major theoretical aspiration is to integrate multiple levels of economic networks by specifying relationships between micro-level actions of persons and macro-level structures of collectivities (groups, organizations, institutions). Almost three decades ago, James Coleman (1986: 1321) asserted that "the major theoretical obstacle to social theory built on a theory of action is not the proper refinement of the action theory itself, but the means by which purposive actions of individuals *combine* to produce a social outcome." In one illustration, he cited a configuration of "independent actors each with differing private interests or goals and each with resources that can aid others' realization of interests" (p. 1324). Economic markets for exchanges of private goods provided his most prominent example:

> The paradigmatic micro-to-macro theoretical work is in the economics of general equilibrium theory, which shows how individual holdings and preferences combine in a setting of competitive exchange to produce equilibrium prices and distribution of goods. Little work has been done toward examining the effects of the social and institutional structures within which markets operate . . . It may also be that work in network theory . . . will provide contributions in this field" (p. 1324).

Although economic sociologists subsequently investigated many social and institutional structures of markets, none developed a multi-level theory of economic networks. To sketch what such a project would involve, figure 6.1 adapts Coleman's macro-micro-macro schema to job searches in labor markets. As discussed in chapter 2, organizations seek to recruit qualified persons to fill vacant positions, while job candidates search for employers offering good positions. In the macro-to-micro link (1), organizational hiring practices affect individuals' strategies of looking for work. If employers recruit new workers primarily through impersonal means, such as advertising, job fairs, and employment agencies, then job candidates will concentrate their efforts on accessing those sources. However, if firms use personal recommendations and referrals, then candidates will cultivate their egocentric network alters for information, advice, and assistance. Over time, individual job-seeking actions may change, depending on whether weak or strong ties provide better channels for obtaining job information and getting hired (micro-to-micro link 2). For example,

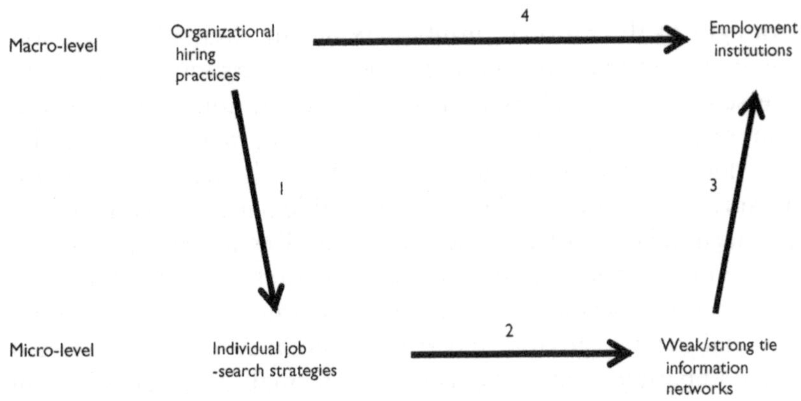

Figure 6.1 Macro-micro-macro relations in labor markets

chapter 2 contrasted American and Chinese labor market differences in job-seekers' dependence on weak or strong ties (*guanxi*), respectively, to find jobs. One likely consequence of China's transition to a competitive market economy is increasing worker reliance on weak ties to learn about and apply for job openings. Finally, structural transformations of employment institutions are influenced in part by macro-level factors, such as economic conditions and government policies (macro-to-macro link 4), but also by organizational responses to changes in the networking activities of job-seekers (micro-macro link 3).

Economic network analysts are not likely to converge on a single theoretical framework that unifies their disparate endeavors. However, serious efforts to identify fundamental mechanisms and to integrate them across levels of analysis could initiate a flourishing era of theory-guided research. The payoff from theory construction would be even greater if accompanied by improved measures, methods, and data on economic networks.

Empirical Tools

Social network analysis provides measures of economic relationships sufficiently rigorous to confront the mainstream economics paradigm of the rational, utility-maximizing, individual decision maker. Its strength and potential lie in the capacity to quantify diverse types of social connections, thus operationalizing the core economic sociology principle that economic activity is socially embedded. A major shortcoming is the wide array of network measures and datasets that render problematic the comparison and accumulation of empirical findings. Researchers proliferate unique questionnaire items to assess the presence, direction, and frequency of specific types of relations. Idiosyncratic indicators of social capital, advice, and trust abound. Alters are identified by incompatible name generators – even small differences in item wording can produce substantial variation in ego-actor responses. Few researchers use comparable procedures to bound the economic networks they investigate. Consequently, the literature is replete with case studies of nonprobability samples of consumers, employees, organizations, industries, and economies that impede generalization of results.

The situation will persist until network analysts can agree on some basic measurement and data collection procedures. One important step in that direction would be the creation of an online repository dedicated to network datasets. The Inter-University Consortium for Political and Social Research (ICPSR) has long served this important function for survey datasets, contributing immensely to consensus on standards. A social network archive could similarly help to systematize items, scales, and data collection methods. Project investigators would voluntarily deposit their codebooks and matrices in standardized formats for redistribution to other investigators, teachers, and students. Easy availability of well-documented specifications would enable network researchers to gain familiarity with prevalent practices in their specialties. Handbooks describing alternative network measures could be culled from original sources. Students would learn these protocols as part of their training in reanalyzing secondary data. Over time, best practices would diffuse and be replicated in new projects. The aim of this collective activity is not to impose orthodoxy, but to promote productive debates and ultimately foster greater compatibility and comparability across research designs.

The majority of social network studies are snapshots of social structure frozen in time. Yet, the assumption of activity observed at equilibrium is implausible. Economic network processes are most assuredly dynamic. Therefore, accurate representation of network evolution requires longitudinal datasets capable of accurately capturing changing relations. Cross-sectional network data are difficult and costly to produce, and longitudinal data even more so. But, the returns on the investment are huge in achieving greater realism and precision. Recent developments in statistical methods for analyzing longitudinal networks have greatly outrun data availability. Hence, economic networkers must advance their data collection designs to take advantage of the new analysis procedures. As commercial activity increasingly moves onto the Web, some longitudinal transaction data may become easier to obtain, at least in principle. In practice, privacy concerns and access to proprietary information will need to be negotiated with the data creators and owners.

Connecting Economy and Polity

Throughout this book, I have concentrated on networks of economic relations, broadly defined to encompass employment, production, financial, distribution, and consumption activities. Despite recurring remarks about the social embeddedness of economic life, I largely ignored the political contexts within which economic actions occur. Yet, in all "free" capitalist economies, the private sector is heavily intertwined with the government. Extensive government regulation and control of industries, and the reciprocal efforts by business to influence government decisions, makes them genuine *political* economies. Analyzing the networks connecting economy and polity would easily fill another book. Indeed, two decades ago I wrote one about political networks that touched only in passing on economic relations (Knoke 1990). Rather than undertaking here the formidable task of integrating both networks, I conclude with a brief discussion of the political money networks among businesses, labor unions, interest groups, and political parties seeking to influence public policymaking and the outcome of elections.

Swept into office in the 2008 elections, President Obama spent a big chunk of his political capital trying to reform the US health care system. Because unified corporate lobbying had defeated President Clinton's similar effort in the 1990s, Obama sought to win over key business interest groups. The Chamber of Commerce and large private insurance companies were adamantly opposed to any changes and spent millions of dollars on lobbyists and advertisements promoting their positions. The Obama Administration's "political remedy was to cut deals with medical providers and medical manufacturers that promised these groups millions of new patients and favorable terms of payment in exchange for their vocal support or silence" (Jacobs 2010: 621). The American Hospital Association, American Medical Association, and Pharmaceutical Research and Manufacturers of America supported many proposed changes. However, they opposed the public insurance ("single payer") option strongly advocated by labor unions, AARP, and liberal interest groups.

> As Democrat Senator Max Baucus took charge of negotiating the bill, he received more than $2.5 million from health insurance and health care companies, and five of his former staff went to work for 27 different lobbying organisations (Frontline 2010). According to Frontline's well-researched synopsis, Baucus made sure that single-payer and public insurer options were kept out. (Light 2011: 131)

In the end, the 2010 Patient Protection and Affordable Care Act passed without any votes from congressional Republicans. Among its provisions, the law expanded insurance coverage to 32 million Americans; mandated that most people obtain health insurance and most businesses offer employees coverage or pay a tax penalty; provided insurance subsidies to low-income people by raising taxes and fees on the rich; and regulated state health insurance markets where the uninsured and small businesses could purchase coverage. In the 2010 congressional elections, conservative voters rallying under the Tea Party banner helped return control of the House of Representatives to the Republican Party. The Supreme

Court agreed to rule on the constitutionality of "Obamacare" prior to the 2012 presidential election. Meanwhile, opposition lobbyists worked unrelentingly to weaken and dilute health care regulations written at the federal and state levels. An astute commentator remarked, "no one who follows the politics of US health care should think that the battle is over" (Skocpol 2010: 1291).

In 2010, a 5 to 4 Supreme Court ruling in *Citizens United v. Federal Election Commission* struck down restrictions on independent spending for political purposes by for-profit corporations and nonprofit groups, such as trade associations. Concluding that corporations have the same First Amendment rights of free speech and association as individuals, the ruling allowed organizations to spend unlimited funds from their treasuries to support or attack individual candidates. A major consequence of *Citizens United* and other federal court cases was the proliferation of "Super PACs," independent political action committees raising huge sums from corporations, unions, associations, and wealthy individuals. Their spending is unrestricted, provided they don't directly coordinate with candidates, which allows candidates to deny any responsibility for negative advertising. In the 2011–12 election cycle, Super PAC spending in the early Republican caucus and primary races greatly outpaced expenditures by the presidential candidates' campaigns (Eggen 2012). Newt Gingrich's campaign buckled in Iowa under millions of dollars of attack ads bought by Super PACs backing Mitt Romney. Yet, Gingrich's campaign slogged on, thanks to a timely $5 million donation from a billionaire casino owner to a pro-Gingrich Super PAC (Confessore and Lipton 2012). The eventual impacts of Super PACs and the political money network on the 2012 US elections, and their consequences for public policy decisions, are unresolved at the time of writing.

Despite prolonged high unemployment and sputtering economic recovery, the US political debate turned instead to fiscal austerity. Mushrooming deficits in Medicare, Medicaid, and Social Security funding assure continuing polarization and paralysis over the federal budget, deficit, and debt for years to come. The underlying questions are how large can and should the welfare state be, and who should pay for it? In Europe, deeply indebted governments imposed privatization, massive public services reductions, wage and pension cuts, and other budgetary contractions. Anti-austerity marches and riots erupting in Athens, Rome, Madrid, Dublin, and London may portend wider and more violent political unrest to come. Truly troubling times for the world, but also exciting opportunities ahead for economic network analysts.

Appendix: Network Resources

Many resources are available for people interested in learning more about network approaches to studying the economy. Some helpful social network books, software packages, and relational datasets are listed below.

Social Network Books

Barabási, Albert-László. 2002. *Linked: How Everything Is Connected to Everything Else and What It Means for Business, Science, and Everyday Life.* Cambridge, MA: Perseus.

Barabási, Albert-László. 2010. *Bursts: The Hidden Pattern Behind Everything We Do.* New York: Penguin.

Carrington, Peter and John Scott (eds.). 2011. *The SAGE Handbook of Social Network Analysis.* Thousand Oaks, CA: Sage Publications.

Carrington, Peter J., John Scott and Stanley Wasserman (eds.). 2005. *Models and Methods in Social Network Analysis.* New York: Cambridge University Press.

De Nooy, Wouter, Andrej Mrvar and Vladimir Batagelj. 2005. *Exploratory Social Network Analysis with Pajek.* New York: Cambridge University Press.

Easley, David and Jon Kleinberg. 2010. *Networks, Crowds, and Markets: Reasoning About a Highly Connected World.* New York: Cambridge University Press.

Freeman, Linton C. 2004. *The Development of Social Network Analysis; A Study in the Sociology of Science.* Vancouver: Empirical Press. <aris.ss.uci.edu/~lin/book.pdf >

Hanneman, Robert A. and Mark Riddle. 2005. *Introduction to Social Network Methods.* Riverside, CA: University of California, Riverside. <faculty.ucr.edu/~hanneman/nettext>

Hansen, Derek, Ben Shneiderman and Marc A. Smith. 2010. *Analyzing Social Media Networks with NodeXL: Insights from a Connected World.* Burlington, MA: Morgan Kaufmann.

Jackson, Matthew O. 2008. *Social and Economic Networks*. Princeton, NJ: Princeton University Press.

Knoke, David and Song Yang. 2008. *Social Network Analysis*, 2nd edn. Thousand Oaks, CA: Sage Publications.

Newman, Mark E.J. 2010. *Networks: An Introduction*. New York: Oxford University Press.

Newman, Mark E.J., Albert-László Barabási and Duncan J. Watts (eds.). 2006. *The Structure and Dynamics of Networks*. Princeton, NJ: Princeton University Press.

Russell, Matthew A. 2011. *Mining the Social Web: Analyzing Data from Facebook, Twitter, LinkedIn, and Other Social Media Sites*. Sebastopol, CA: O'Reilly.

Scott, John. 2000. *Social Network Analysis: A Handbook*, 2nd edn. London: Sage Publications.

Wasserman, Stanley and Katherine Faust. 1994. *Social Network Analysis: Methods and Applications*. New York: Cambridge University Press.

Watts, Duncan J. 1999. *Small Worlds: The Dynamics of Networks between Order and Randomness*. Princeton, NJ: Princeton University Press.

Watts, Duncan J. 2003. *Six Degrees: The Science of a Connected Age*. New York: W.W. Norton.

Software Packages

InFlow <orgnet.com/inflow3.html>
KrackPlot <www.andrew.cmu.edu/user/krack/krackplot.shtml>
MultiNet <www.sfu.ca/personal/archives/richards/Multinet/Pages/multinet.htm>
NetMiner <www.netminer.com/index.php >
Network Genie <secure.networkgenie.com>
ORA <www.casos.cs.cmu.edu/projects/ora/index.php>
Pajek <pajek.imfm.si/doku.php>
SIENA <www.stats.ox.ac.uk/~snijders/siena>
SoNIA <www.stanford.edu/group/sonia/index.html>
Statnet <www.statnet.org>
UCINET <www.analytictech.com/ucinet>
Visone <visone.info>

Network Datasets

Datamob <datamob.org>
Network Data <www-personal.umich.edu/~mejn/netdata>
Network Databases <www.nd.edu/~networks/resources.htm>

Appendix: Network Resources

Pajek Datasets <vlado.fmf.uni-lj.si/pub/networks/data/esna/default.htm>
Stanford Large Network Dataset Collection <snap.stanford.edu/data>
Trust Network Datasets <www.trustlet.org/wiki/Trust_network_datasets>

References

Agneessens, Filip and Rafael Wittek. 2008. "Social Capital and Employee Well-Being: Disentangling Intrapersonal and Interpersonal Selection and Influence Mechanisms." *Revue française de Sociologie* 49: 613–637.

Ahuja, Gautam. 2000. "Collaborative Networks, Structural Holes, and Innovation: A Longitudinal Study." *Administrative Science Quarterly* 45: 425–455.

Ahuja, Gautam, Francisco Polidoro Jr. and Will Mitchell. 2009. "Structural Homophily or Social Asymmetry? The Formation of Alliances by Poorly Embedded Firms." *Strategic Management Journal* 30: 941–958.

Akerlof, George A. and Robert J. Shiller. 2009. *Animal Spirits: How Human Psychology Drives the Economy, and Why It Matters for Global Capitalism.* Princeton, NJ: Princeton University Press.

Alderson, Arthur S. and Jason Beckfield. 2004. "Power and Position in the World City System." *American Journal of Sociology* 109: 811–851.

Alderson, Arthur S., Jason Beckfield and Jessica Sprague-Jones. 2010. "Intercity Relations and Globalisation: The Evolution of the Global Urban Hierarchy, 1981–2007." *Urban Studies* 47: 1899–1923.

Aldrich, Howard E. 1999. *Organizations Evolving*. Thousand Oaks, CA: Sage Publications.

Aldrich, Howard E. and Martin Ruef. 2006. *Organizations Evolving*, 2nd edn. Thousand Oaks, CA: Sage Publications.

Aldrich, Howard E. and Catherine Zimmer. 1986. "Entrepreneurship through Social Networks." In *The Art and Science of Entrepreneurship*, edited by David L. Sexton and Raymond W. Smiler. Cambridge, MA: Ballinger, pp. 3–23.

Al-Laham, Andreas and Terry L. Amburgey. 2010. "Who Makes You Central? Analyzing the Influence of International Alliance Experience on Network Centrality of Start-up Firms." *Management International Review* 50: 297–323.

Al-Laham, Andreas, Terry L. Amburgey and Kimberly Bates. 2008. "The

Dynamics of Research Alliances: Examining the Effect of Alliance Experience and Partner Characteristics on the Speed of Alliance Entry in the Biotech Industry." *British Journal of Management* 19: 343–364.

Al-Laham, Andreas, Terry L. Amburgey and Charles Baden-Fuller. 2010. "Who is My Partner and How Do We Dance? Technological Collaboration and Patenting Speed in US Biotechnology." *British Journal of Management* 21: 789–807.

Allen, Franklin and Ana Babus. 2009. "Networks in Finance." In *The Network Challenge: Strategy, Profit, and Risk in an Interlinked World*, edited by Paul R. Kleindorfer, Yoram (Jerry) Wind with Robert E. Gunther. Upper Saddle River, NJ: Prentice-Hall, pp. 367–382.

Allen, Franklin and Douglas Gale. 2000. "Financial Contagion." *Journal of Political Economy* 108: 1–33.

Almeida, Heitor V. and Daniel Wolfenzon. 2006. "A Theory of Pyramidal Ownership and Family Business Groups." *Journal of Finance* 61: 2637–2680.

Anderberg, Dan and Fredrik Andersson. 2007. "Stratification, Social Networks in the Labour Market, and Intergenerational Mobility." *Economic Journal* 117: 782–812.

Andre-Petersson, Lena, Gunnar Engstrom, Bo Hedblad, Lars Janzon and Maria Rosvall. 2007. "Social Support at Work and the Risk of Myocardial Infarction and Stroke in Women and Men." *Social Science & Medicine* 64: 830–841.

Arrow, Kenneth J. 2009. "Some Developments in Economic Theory Since 1940: An Eyewitness Account." *Annual Review of Economics* 1: 1–16.

Bae, Jonghoon and Martin Gargiulo. 2004. "Partner Substitutability, Alliance Network Structure, and Firm Profitability in the Telecommunications Industry." *Academy of Management Journal* 47: 843–859.

Bair, Jennifer. 2005. "Global Capitalism and Commodity Chains: Looking Back, Going Forward." *Competition and Change* 9(2): 153–180.

Baker, Wayne E. and Robert R. Faulkner. 2002. "Interorganizational Networks." In *Blackwell Companion to Organizations*, edited by Joel A. C. Baum. Oxford: Blackwell, pp. 520–540.

Balkundi, Prasad and David A. Harrison. 2006. "Ties, Leaders, and Time in Teams: Strong Inference about Network Structure's Effects on Team Viability and Performance." *Academy of Management Journal* 49: 9–68.

Balkundi, Prasad, Martin Kilduff, Zoe I. Barsness and Judd H. Michael. 2007. "Demographic Antecedents and Performance Consequences of Structural Holes in Work Teams." *Journal of Organizational Behavior* 28: 241–260.

Balkundi, Prasad, Zoe Barsness and Judd H. Michael. 2009. "Unlocking the Influence of Leadership Network Structures on Team Conflict and Viability." *Small Group Research* 40: 301–322.

Ballarino, Gabriele and Marino Regini. 2007. "Convergent Perspectives in Economic Sociology: An Italian View of Contemporary Developments in Western Europe and North America." *Socio-Economic Review* 6: 337–363.

References

Barabási, Albert-László and Réka Albert. 1999. "Emergence of Scaling in Random Networks." *Science* 286: 509–512.

Barnes, John. 1954. "Class and Committees in a Norwegian Island Parish." *Human Relations* 7: 39–58.

Barney, Jay B. 1985. "Dimensions of Informal Social Network Structure: Toward a Contingency Theory of Informal Relations in Organizations." *Social Networks* 7: 11–46.

Bass, Frank M. 1969. "A New Product Growth Model for Consumer Durables." *Management Science* 15: 215–227.

Batjargal, Bat. 2003. "Social Capital and Entrepreneurial Performance in Russia: A Longitudinal Study." *Organization Studies* 24: 535–556.

Bebchuk, Lucian Arye, Jesse M. Fried and David I. Walker. 2002. "Managerial Power and Rent Extraction in the Design of Executive Compensation." *University of Chicago Law Review* 69: 751–846.

Bello, Daniel C., Constantine S. Katsikeas and Matthew J. Robson. 2010. "Does Accommodating a Self-Serving Partner in an International Marketing Alliance Pay Off?" *Journal of Marketing* 74(6): 77–93.

Bian, Yanjie. 1997. "Bringing Strong Ties Back In: Indirect Ties, Network Bridges, and Job Searches in China." *American Sociological Review* 62: 366–385.

Bian, Yanjie and Soon Ang. 1997. "*Guanxi* Networks and Job Mobility in China and Singapore." *Social Forces* 75: 981–1005.

Biggart, Nicole Woolsey. 1989. *Charismatic Capitalism: Direct Selling Organizations in America*. Chicago, IL: University of Chicago Press.

Birke, Daniel. 2009. "The Economics of Networks: A Survey of the Empirical Literature." *Journal of Economic Surveys* 23: 762–793.

Bizjak, John, Michael Lemmon and Ryan Whitby. 2009. "Option Backdating and Board Interlocks. *Review of Financial Studies* 22(11): 4821–4847.

Blau, Peter M. and W. Richard Scott. 1962. *Formal Organizations: A Comparative Approach*. San Francisco, CA: Chandler.

Borgatti, Stephen P. and Rob Cross. 2003. "A Relational View of Information Seeking and Learning in Social Networks." *Management Science* 49: 432–445.

Borgatti, Stephen P. and Daniel S. Halgin. 2011. "On Network Theory." *Organization Science* 22: 1168–1181.

Borgatti, Stephen P. and Virginie Lopez-Kidwell. 2011. "Network Theory." In *The Sage Handbook of Social Network Analysis*, edited by John Scott and Peter J. Carrington. Thousand Oaks, CA: Sage, pp. 40–54.

Borgatti, Stephen P., Martin G. Everett and Linton C. Freeman. 2002. *UCINET 6 for Windows: Software for Social Network Analysis*. Cambridge, MA: Analytic Technologies.

Boswijk, H. Peter and Philip Hans Franses. 2005. "On the Econometrics of the Bass Diffusion Model." *Journal of Business & Economic Statistics* 23: 255–268.

References

Bourdieu, Pierre. 1979. *Algeria 1960*. Cambridge: Cambridge University Press.

Bourdieu, Pierre. 1986. "The Forms of Capital." In *Handbook of Theory and Research for the Sociology of Education*, edited by J. Richardson. Westport, CT: Greenwood Press, pp. 241–258.

Boyas, Javier and Leslie H. Wind. 2010. "Employment-Based Social Capital, Job Stress, and Employee Burnout: A Public Child Welfare Employee Structural Model." *Children and Youth Services Review* 32: 380–388.

Brass, Daniel J. 1985. "Men's and Women's Networks: A Study of Interaction Patterns and Influence in an Organization." *Academy of Management Journal* 28: 327–343.

Brennan, Timothy J. 2009. "Network Effects in Infrastructure Regulation: Principles and Paradoxes." *Review of Network Economics* 8: 279–301.

Bridges, William P. and Wayne J. Villemez. 1986. "Informal Hiring and Income in the Labor Market." *American Sociological Review* 51: 574–582.

Burris, Val. 2008. "The Interlock Structure of the Policy-Planning Network and the Right Turn in U.S. State Policy." *Research in Political Sociology* 17: 3–42.

Burt, Ronald S. 1980. "Autonomy in a Social Topology." *American Journal of Sociology* 85: 892–925.

Burt, Ronald S. 1988. "The Stability of American Markets." *American Journal of Sociology* 94: 356–395.

Burt, Ronald S. 1992. *Structural Holes: The Social Structure of Competition*. Cambridge, MA: Harvard University Press.

Burt, Ronald S. 1999. "The Social Capital of Opinion Leaders." *Annals of the American Academy of Political and Social Science* 566: 37–54.

Burt, Ronald S. 2004. "Structural Holes and Good Ideas." *American Journal of Sociology* 110: 349–399.

Burt, Ronald S. 2005. *Brokerage & Closure: An Introduction to Social Capital*. Oxford: Oxford University Press.

Burt, Ronald S. 2010. *Neighbor Networks: Competitive Advantage Local and Personal*. New York: Oxford University Press.

Burt, Ronald S. and Debbie S. Carlton. 1989. "Another Look at the Network Boundaries of American Markets." *American Journal of Sociology* 95: 723–753.

Calvó-Armengol, Antoni and Matthew O. Jackson. 2007. "Networks in Labor Markets: Wage and Employment Dynamics and Inequality." *Journal of Economic Theory* 132: 27–46.

Campbell, John P. 1990. "Modeling the Performance Prediction Problem in Industrial and Organizational Psychology." In *Handbook of Industrial and Organizational Psychology*, edited by M. D. Dunnette and L. M. Hough. Palo Alto, CA: Consulting Psychologists Press, pp. 687–732.

Cao, Xun. 2010. "Networks as Channels of Policy Diffusion: Explaining Worldwide Changes in Capital Taxation, 1998–2006." *International Studies Quarterly* 54: 823–854.

References

Carland, James W., Frank Hoy, William R. Boulton and Jo Ann C. Carland. 1984. "Differentiating Entrepreneurs from Small Business Owners: A Conceptualization." *Academy of Management Journal* 9: 354–359.

Carroll, William K. 2007a. "From Canadian Corporate Elite to Transnational Capitalist Class: Transitions in the Organization of Corporate Power." *The Canadian Review of Sociology and Anthropology* 44(3): 265–288.

Carroll, William K. 2007b. "Global Cities in the Global Corporate Network." *Environment and Planning A* 39: 2297–2323.

Carroll, William K. 2009. "Transnationalists and National Networkers in the Global Corporate Elite." *Global Networks* 9: 289–314.

Carroll, William K. and Colin Carson. 2003. "Forging a New Hegemony? The Role of Transnational Policy Groups in the Network and Discourses of Global Corporate Governance." *Journal of World-Systems Research* 9: 66–102.

Carroll, William K. and Meindert Fennema. 2002. "Is There a Transnational Business Community?" *International Sociology* 17: 393–419.

Carroll, William K. and Meindert Fennema. 2004. "Problems in the Study of the Transnational Business Community: A Reply to Kentor and Jang." *International Sociology* 19: 369–378.

Carroll, William K. and Jean Philippe Sapinski. 2010. "The Global Corporate Elite and the Transnational Policy-Planning Network, 1996–2006: A Structural Analysis." *International Sociology* 25: 501–538.

Carter, Nancy M. and Christine Silva. 2010. *Pipeline's Broken Promise*. New York: Catalyst. <www.catalyst.org/file/340/pipeline's_broken_promise_final_021710.pdf> (accessed February 14, 2011).

Case, Donald O., J. David Johnson, James E. Andrews, Suzanne L. Allard and Kimberly M. Kelly. 2004. "From Two-Step Flow to the Internet: The Changing Array of Sources for Genetics Information Seeking." *Journal of the American Society for Information Science & Technology* 55: 660–669.

Castellani, Davide and Antonello Zanfei. 2004. "Choosing International Linkage Strategies in the Electronics Industry: The Role of Multinational Experience." *Journal of Economic Behavior & Organization* 53: 447–475.

Chang, Sea-Jin. 2006. "Business Groups in East Asia: Post-crisis Restructuring and New Growth." *Asia Pacific Journal of Management* 23: 407–417.

Chang, Sea-Jin and Jaebum Hong. 2000. "Economic Performance of Group-Affiliated Companies in Korea: Intragroup Resource Sharing and Internal Business Transactions." *Academy of Management Journal* 43: 429–448.

Chang, Sea-Jin and Jaebum Hong. 2002. "How Much Does the Business Group Matter in Korea?" *Strategic Management Journal* 23: 265–274.

Chen, Xinxiang. 2010. "Modes of State Intervention and Business Group Performance in China's Transitional Economy." *Journal of Socio-Economics* 39: 619–630.

Child, John and David Faulkner. 1998. *Strategies of Co-operation: Managing Alliances, Networks, and Joint Ventures*. New York: Oxford University Press.

Chimni, B.S. 2004. "International Institutions Today: An Imperial Global State in the Making." *European Journal of International Law* 15: 1–37.

Choi, Hanool, Sang-Hoon Kim and Jeho Lee. 2010. "Role of Network Structure and Network Effects in Diffusion of Innovations." *Industrial Marketing Management* 39: 170–177.

Christopoulos, Dimitrios and Lucia Quaglia. 2009. Network Constraints in EU Banking Regulation: The Capital Requirements Directive." *Journal of Public Policy* 29: 179–200.

Chung, Seungwha (Andy), Harbir Singh, and Kyungmook Lee. 2000. "Complementarity, Status Similarity and Social Capital as Drivers of Alliance Formation." *Strategic Management Journal* 21: 1–22.

Clark, Amy S. 2006. "Employers Look at Facebook, Too." CBS Evening News <www.cbsnews.com/stories/2006/06/20/eveningnews/main1734920.shtml> (accessed May 23, 2010).

Cloodt, Myriam, John Hagedoorn and Nadine Roijakkers. 2006. "Trends and Patterns in Interfirm R&D Networks in the Global Computer Industry: An Analysis of Major Developments, 1970–1999." *Business History Review* 80: 725–746.

Colander, David, Richard P. F. Holt and J. Barkley Rosser, Jr. 2004. "The Changing Face of Mainstream Economics." *Review of Political Economy* 16: 485–499.

Coleman, James S. 1986. "Social Theory, Social Research, and a Theory of Action." *American Journal of Sociology* 91: 1309–1335.

Coleman, James S. 1988a. "Social Capital in the Creation of Human Capital." *American Journal of Sociology* 94: S95–S121.

Coleman, James S. 1988b. "The Creation and Destruction of Social Capital: Implications for the Law." *Notre Dame Journal of Law, Ethics & Public Policy* 3(3): 375–404.

Coleman, James S. 1990. "Social Capital." In *Foundations of Social Theory*. Cambridge, MA: Harvard University Press, pp. 300–321.

Coleman, James S., Elihu Katz and Herbert Menzel. 1957. "The Diffusion of an Innovation among Physicians." *Sociometry* 20: 253–270.

Coleman, James S., Elihu Katz and Herbert Menzel. 1966. *Medical Innovation: Diffusion of a Medical Drug among Doctors*. Indianapolis, MN: Bobbs-Merrill.

Confessore, Nicholas and Eric Lipton. 2012. "A Big Check, and Gingrich Gets a Big Lift." *New York Times*, January 9, 2012. <www.nytimes.com> (accessed January 15, 2012).

Convert, Bernard and Johan Heilbron. 2007. "Where Did the New Economic Sociology Come From?" *Theory and Society* 36: 31–54.

Corneo, Giacomo and Olivier Jeanne. 1997. "Snobs, Bandwagons, and the Origin of Social Customs in Consumer Behavior." *Journal of Economic Behavior and Organization* 32: 333–347.

Corrado, Raffaele and Maurizio Zollo. 2006. "Small Worlds Evolving:

Governance Reforms, Privatizations, and Ownership Networks in Italy. *Industrial and Corporate Change* 15: 319–352.

Cross, Rob and Jonathon N. Cummings. 2004. "Tie and Network Correlates of Individual Performance in Knowledge-Intensive Work." *Academy of Management Journal* 47: 928–937.

Cross, Rob and Robert J. Thomas. 2008. "How Top Talent Uses Networks and Where Rising Stars Get Trapped." *Organizational Dynamics* 37: 165–180.

Cross, Rob, Ronald E. Rice and Andrew Parker. 2001. "Information Seeking in Social Context: Structural Influences and Receipt of Information Benefits." *IEEE Transactions on Systems, Man & Cybernetics: Part C – Applications & Reviews* 31: 438–448.

Cyert, Richard and James G. March. 1963. *A Behavioral Theory of the Firm.* Oxford: Blackwell.

Daviron, Benoit and Peter Gibbon 2002. "Global Commodity Chains and African Export Agriculture." *Journal of Agrarian Change* 2: 137–161.

Davis, Gerald F., Mina Yoo and Wayne E. Baker. 2003. "The Small World of the American Corporate Elite, 1982–2001." *Strategic Organization* 1: 301–326.

Delre, Sebastiano A., Wander Jager, Tammo H. A. Bijmolt and Marco A. Janssen. 2010. "Will It Spread or Not? The Effects of Social Influences and Network Topology on Innovation Diffusion." *Journal of Product Innovation Management* 27: 267–282.

Derudder, Ben, Frank Witlox, James Faulconbridge and Jon Beaverstock. 2008. "Airline Data for Global City Network Research: Reviewing and Refining Existing Approaches." *GeoJournal* 71: 5–18.

Derudder, Ben, Peter Taylor, Pengfei Ni, Anneleen De Vos, Michael Hoyler, Heidi Hanssens, David Bassens, Jin Huang, Frank Witlox, Wei Shen and Xiaolan Yang. 2010. "Pathways of Change: Shifting Connectivities in the World City Network, 2000–08." *Urban Studies* 47(9): 1861–1877.

Devos, Erik, Andrew Prevost and John Puthenpurackal. 2009. "Are Interlocked Directors Effective Monitors?" *Financial Management* 38(4): 861–887.

Dholakia, Utpal M., Richard P. Bagozzi and Lisa Klein Pearo. 2004. "A Social Influence Model of Consumer Participation in Network- and Small-Group-Based Virtual Communities." *International Journal of Research in Marketing* 21: 241–263.

Dicken, Peter, Philip F. Kelly, Kris Olds and Henry Wai-Chung Yeung. 2001. "Chains and Networks, Territories and Scales: Towards a Relational Framework for Analysing the Global Economy." *Global Networks* 1: 89–112.

Dickinson, Tim. 2010. "The Spill, the Scandal and the President." *Rolling Stone*, June 28. <www.rollingstone.com/politics/news/the-spill-the-scandal-and-the-president-20100608> (accessed May 27, 2010).

DiMaggio, Paul and Joseph Nathan Cohen. 2005. "Information Inequality and Network Externalities: A Comparative Study of the Diffusion of Television and the Internet." In *The Economic Sociology of Capitalism*, edited by Victor

Nee and Richard Swedberg. Princeton, NJ: Princeton University Press, pp. 227–267.

DiMaggio, Paul and Hugh Louch. 1998. "Socially Embedded Consumer Transactions: For What Kinds of Purchases do People Most Often Use Networks?" *American Sociological Review* 63: 619–637.

DiMaggio, Paul J. and Walter W. Powell. 1991. "Introduction." In *The New Institutionalism in Organizational Analysis*, edited by Paul J. DiMaggio and Walter W. Powell. Chicago, IL: University of Chicago Press, pp. 1–38.

Dirks, Kurt T. and Donald L. Ferrin. 2001. "The Role of Trust in Organizational Settings." *Organization Science* 12: 450–467.

Dobrow, Shoshana R. and Monica C. Higgins. 2005. "Developmental Networks and Professional Identity: A Longitudinal Study." *Career Development International* 10: 567–583.

Domhoff, G. William. 1970. *The Higher Circles: The Governing Class in America*. New York: Vintage Books.

Drago, Carlos, Francesco Millo, Roberto Ricciuti and Paolo Santella. 2011. "Corporate Governance Reforms, Interlocking Directorship Networks and Company Value in Italy (1998–2007)." CESifo Group Munich, CESifo Working Paper Series.

Dubini, Paola and Howard E. Aldrich. 1991. "Personal and Extended Networks Are Central to the Entrepreneurial Process." *Journal of Business Venturing* 6: 305–313.

Ducharme, Lori J. and Jack K. Martin 2000. "Unrewarding Work, Coworker Support, and Job Satisfaction: A Test of the Buffering Hypothesis." *Work and Occupations* 27: 223–243.

Duesenberry, James S. 1949. *Income, Saving and the Theory of Consumer Behavior*. Cambridge, MA: Harvard University Press.

Duesenberry, James. 1960. "Comment on Gary S. Becker's 'An Economic Analysis of Fertility.'" In *Demographic and Economic Change in Developed Countries*, edited by University-National Bureau Committee for Economic Research. Princeton, NJ: Princeton University Press, pp. 231–234.

Duffy, Michelle K., Daniel C. Ganster, Jason D. Shaw, Jonathan L. Johnson and Milan Pagon. 2006. "The Social Context of Undermining Behavior at Work." *Organizational Behavior & Human Decision Processes* 101: 105–126.

Durkheim, Emile. 1984 [1893]. *The Division of Labor in Society*. New York: Free Press.

Durrington, Vance A., Judi Repman and Thomas W. Valente. 2000. "Using Social Network Analysis to Examine the Time of Adoption of Computer-Related Services among University Faculty." *Journal of Research on Computing in Education* 33: 16–27.

Duysters, Geert and Boris Lokshin. 2011. "Determinants of Alliance Portfolio Complexity and Its Effect on Innovative Performance of Companies." *Journal of Product Innovation Management* 28: 570–585.

Dyer, Jeffrey H., Harbir Singh and Prashant Kale. 2008. "Splitting the Pie: Rent Distribution in Alliances and Networks." *Managerial & Decision Economics* 29(2/3): 137–148.

Eggen, Dan. 2012. "Are Iowa Caucuses Harbinger of the Super-PAC Era?" *Washington Post*, January 3. <www.washingtonpost.com> (accessed January 16, 2012).

Elfring, Tom and Willem Hulsink. 2007. "Networking by Entrepreneurs: Patterns of Tie-Formation in Emerging Organizations." *Organization Studies* 28: 1849–1872.

Elmuti, Dean and Yunus Kathawala. 2001. "An Overview of Strategic Alliances." *Management Decision* 39(3): 205–17.

Emirbayer, Mustafa. 1997. "Manifesto for a Relational Sociology." *American Journal of Sociology* 103: 281–317.

Etzioni, Amitai. 1988. *The Moral Dimension: Toward a New Economics*. New York: Free Press.

Fan, Ying. 2002. "*Guanxi*'s Consequences: Personal Gains at Social Cost." *Journal of Business Ethics* 38: 371–380.

Feenstra, Robert C. and Gary G. Hamilton. 2006. *Emergent Economies, Divergent Paths: Economic Organization and International Trade in South Korea and Taiwan*. New York: Cambridge University Press.

Feenstra, Robert C., Gary G. Hamilton and Eun Mie Lim. 2002. "Chaebol and Catastrophe: A New View of the Korean Business Groups and Their Role in the Financial Crisis." *Asian Economic Papers* 1: 1–45.

Fernandez, Roberto M. and Nancy Weinberg. 1997. "Sifting and Sorting: Personal Contacts and Hiring in a Retail Bank." *American Sociological Review* 62: 883–902.

Fernandez, Roberto M., Emilio J. Castilla and Paul Moore. 2000. "Social Capital at Work: Networks and Employment at a Phone Center." *American Journal of Sociology* 105: 1288–1356.

Fich, Eliezer M. and Lawrence J. White. 2003. "CEO Compensation and Turnover: The Effects of Mutually Interlocked Boards." *Wake Forest Law Review* 38: 935–959.

Fich, Eliezer M. and Lawrence J. White. 2005. "Why Do CEOs Reciprocally Sit on Each Other's Boards?" *Journal of Corporate Finance* 11: 175–195.

Finch, John H. 2007. "Economic Sociology as a Strange Other to Both Sociology and Economics." *History of the Human Sciences* 20: 123–140.

Finlay, William and James E. Coverdill. 2000. "Risk, Opportunism, and Structural Holes." *Work & Occupations* 27: 377–405.

Flap, Henk D. and Ed Boxman. 2001. "Getting Started: The Influence of Social Capital on the Start of the Occupational Career." In *Social Capital: Theory and Research*, edited by Nan Lin, Karen S. Cook and Ronald S. Burt. Chicago, IL: Aldine de Gruyter, pp. 159–184.

Flap, Henk D. and Beate Völker. 2001. "Goal Specific Social Capital and Job

Satisfaction: Effects of Different Types of Networks on Instrumental and Social Aspects of Work." *Social Networks* 23: 297–320.

Fourcade, Marion. 2007. "Theories of Markets and Theories of Society." *American Behavioral Scientist* 50: 1015–1034.

Frank, Andre Gunder. 1966. "The Development of Underdevelopment." *Monthly Review* 18: 17–31.

French, Cecil. 1963. "Some Structural Aspects of a Retail Sales Group." *Human Organization* 22: 146–151.

Friedman, Milton. 1970. "The Methodology of Positive Economics." In *Essays in Positive Economics*. Chicago, IL: University of Chicago Press, pp. 3–43.

Friedman, Thomas, 2005. *The World Is Flat*. New York: Farrar, Straus and Giroux.

Friedmann, John. 1986. "The World City Hypothesis." *Development and Change* 17: 69–84.

Friedmann, John. 1995. "Where We Stand: A Decade of World City Research." In *World Cities in a World-System*, edited by Paul L. Knox and Peter J. Taylor. New York: Cambridge University Press, pp. 21–47.

Frontline. 2010. *Obama's Deal: Chronology*. New York: Frontline.

Gargiulo, Martin and Mario Benassi. 2000. "Trapped in Your Own Net? Network Cohesion, Structural Holes, and the Adaptation of Social Capital." *Organization Science* 11: 183–196.

Gargiulo, Martin, Gokhan Ertug and Charles Galunic. 2009. "The Two Faces of Control: Network Closure and Individual Performance among Knowledge Workers." *Administrative Science Quarterly* 54: 299–333.

Gay, Brigitte and Bernard Dousset. 2005. "Innovation and Network Structural Dynamics: Study of the Alliance Network of a Major Sector of the Biotechnology Industry." *Research Policy* 34: 1457–1475.

Gereffi, Gary. 1994. "The Organization of Buyer-Driven Global Commodity Chains: How U.S. Retailers Shape Overseas Production Networks." In *Commodity Chains and Global Capitalism*, edited by Gary Gereffi and Miguel Korzeniewicz. Westport, CT: Praeger, pp. 5–122.

Gereffi, Gary. 2001. "Beyond the Producer-Driven/Buyer-Driven Dichotomy: The Evolution of Global Value Chains in the Internet Era." *IDS Bulletin*, 32(3): 30–40.

Gerlach, Michael L. 1992. "The Japanese Corporate Network: A Blockmodel Analysis." *Administrative Science Quarterly* 37: 105–139.

Gillespie, Nicole and Graham Dietz. 2009. "Trust Repair after an Organization-Level Failure." *Academy of Management Review* 34: 127–145.

Gilsing, Victor, Bart Nooteboom, Wim Vanhaverbeke, Geert Duysters and Ad van den Oorda. 2008. "Network Embeddedness and the Exploration of Novel Technologies: Technological Distance, Betweenness Centrality and Density." *Research Policy* 37: 1717–1731.

Gloria-Palermo, Sandye and Giulio Palermo. 2005. "Austrian Economics and

Value Judgments: A Critical Comparison with Neoclassical Economics." *Review of Political Economy* 17: 63–78.

Goerzen, Anthony. 2007. "Alliance Networks and Firm Performance: The Impact of Repeated Partnerships." *Strategic Management Journal* 28: 487–509.

Goerzen, Anthony and Paul W. Beamish. 2005. "The Effect of Alliance Network Diversity on Multinational Enterprise Performance." *Strategic Management Journal* 26: 333–354.

Goldberg, Stephanie. 2010. "Young Job-Seekers Hiding Their Facebook Pages." *CNN* <www.cnn.com/2010/TECH/03/29/facebook.job-seekers/index.html> (accessed May 23, 2010).

Gould, Roger V. and Roberto M. Fernandez. 1989. "Structures of Mediation: A Formal Approach to Brokerage in Transaction Networks." *Sociological Methodology* 19: 89–126.

Granovetter, Mark S. 1973. "The Strength of Weak Ties." *American Journal of Sociology* 78: 1360–1380.

Granovetter, Mark S. 1974. *Getting a Job: A Study of Contacts and Careers.* Chicago, IL: University of Chicago Press.

Granovetter, Mark S. 1982. "The Strength of Weak Ties Revisited: A Network Theory Revisited." In *Social Structure and Network Analysis*, edited by P. Marsden and N. Lin. Beverly Hills, CA: Sage Publications, pp. 105–130.

Granovetter, Mark S. 1983. "The Strength of Weak Ties: A Network Theory Revisited." *Sociological Theory* 1: 201–233.

Granovetter, Mark S. 1985. "Economic Action and Social Structure: The Problem of Embeddedness." *American Journal of Sociology* 91: 481–510.

Granovetter, Mark S. 1992. "Economic Institutions as Social Constructions: A Framework for Analysis." *Acta Sociologica* 35: 3–11.

Granovetter, Mark S. 2002. "A Theoretical Agenda for Economic Sociology." In *The New Economic Sociology: Developments in an Emerging Field*, edited by Mauro Guillén, Randall Collins, Paula England and Marshall Meyer. New York: Russell Sage Foundation, pp. 35–60.

Granovetter, Mark. 2005a. "The Impact of Social Structure on Economic Outcomes." *Journal of Economic Perspectives* 19: 33–50.

Granovetter, Mark. 2005b. "Business Groups." In T*he Handbook of Economic Sociology*, edited by N. J. Smelser and R. Swedberg. Princeton, NJ: Princeton University Press, pp. 429–450.

Granovetter, Mark and Roland Soong. 1983. "Threshold Models of Diffusion and Collective Behavior." *Journal of Mathematical Sociology* 9(3): 165–179.

Granovetter, Mark and Roland Soong. 1986. "Threshold Models of Interpersonal Effects in Consumer Demand." *Journal of Economic Behavior and Organization* 7: 83–99.

Greve, Henrich R., Joel A. C. Baum, Hitoshi Mitsuhashi and Timothy J. Rowley. 2010. "Built to Last but Falling Apart: Cohesion, Friction, and Withdrawal from Interfirm Alliances." *Academy of Management Journal* 53: 302–322.

Grinder, Matt. 2011. "Unofficial Economics of Star Trek." <vanparecon.resist.ca/StarTrekEcon> (accessed August 6, 2011).

Groenewegen, John. 1997. "Institutions of Capitalism: American, European and Japanese Systems Compared." *Journal of Economic Issues* 31: 333–347.

Guillén, Mauro F. 1994. *Models of Management: Work, Authority, and Organization in Comparative Perspective*. Chicago, IL: University of Chicago Press.

Gulati, Ranjay. 1995a. "Does Familiarity Breed Trust? The Implications of Repeated Ties for Contractual Choices in Alliances." *Academy of Management Journal* 38: 85–112.

Gulati, Ranjay. 1995b. "Social Structure and Alliance Formation Patterns: A Longitudinal Analysis." *Administrative Science Quarterly* 40: 619–652.

Gulati, Ranjay. 2007. "Silo Busting: How to Execute on the Promise of Customer Focus." *Harvard Business Review* 85(5): 98–108.

Gulati, Ranjay and Martin Gargiulo. 1999. "Where Do Networks Come From?" *American Journal of Sociology* 104: 1439–1493.

Gulati, Ranjay and Harbir Singh. 1998. "The Architecture of Cooperation: Managing Coordination Costs and Appropriation Concerns in Strategic Alliances." *Administrative Science Quarterly* 43: 781–814.

Gulati, Ranjay and Maxim Sytch. 2008. "Does Familiarity Breed Trust? Revisiting the Antecedents of Trust." *Managerial & Decision Economics* 29(2/3): 165–190.

Gulati, Ranjay, Nitin Nohria and Akbar Zaheer. 2000. "Strategic Networks." *Strategic Management Journal* 21: 203–215.

Gulati, Ranjay, Dovev Lavie and Harbir Singh. 2009. "The Nature of Partnering Experience and the Gains from Alliances." *Strategic Management Journal* 30: 1213–1233.

Guler, Isin, Mauro Guillén and John Muir Macpherson. 2002. "Global Competition, Institutions, and Organizational Change: The International Diffusion of the ISO 9000 Quality Standards." *Administrative Science Quarterly* 47: 207–232.

Hagedoorn, John. 1993. "Understanding the Rationale of Strategic Technology Partnering: Interorganizational Modes of Cooperation and Sectoral Differences." *Strategic Management Journal* 14: 371–385.

Hagedoorn, John. 2002. "Inter-Firm R&D Partnerships: An Overview of Major Trends and Patterns Since 1960." *Research Policy* 31: 477–492.

Haldane, Andrew G. and Robert M. May. 2011. "Systemic Risk in Banking Ecosystems." *Nature* 469: 351–355.

Hale, Galina. 2011. "Bank Relationships, Business Cycles, and Financial Crisis." Working Paper 2011–14. San Francisco: Federal Reserve Bank of San Francisco. <www.frbsf.org/publications/economics/papers/2011/wp11-14bk.pdf> (accessed June 22, 2011).

Hardcastle, David A. and Patricia R. Powers with Stanley Wenocur. 2004.

Community Practice: Theories and Skills for Social Workers, 2nd edn. New York: Oxford University Press.

Hardy, Thomas. 1886. *The Mayor of Casterbridge*. The Literature Network <www.online-literature.com/hardy/casterbridge/23> (accessed August 1, 2011).

Harris, Jeffrey. 2006. *The Dialectics of Globalization: Economic and Political Conflict in a Transnational World*. Newcastle: Cambridge Scholars Press.

Harris, Jerry. 2009. "Statist Globalization in China, Russia and the Gulf States." *Perspectives on Global Development and Technology* 8(2–3): 139–163.

Healy, Kieran. 2006. *Last Best Gifts: Altruism and the Market for Human Blood and Organs*. Chicago, IL: University of Chicago Press.

Henderson, Jeffrey, Peter Dicken, Martin Hess, Neil M. Coe and Henry Wai-Chung Yeung. 2002. "Global Production Networks and the Analysis of Economic Development." *Review of International Political Economy* 9: 436–464.

Henisz, Witold J., Bennet A. Zelner and Mauro Guillén. 2005. "The Worldwide Diffusion of Market-Oriented Infrastructure Reform, 1977–1999." *American Sociological Review* 70: 871–897.

Henttonen, Kaisa, Minna Janhonen, Jan-Erik Johanson, and Kaisu Puumalainen. 2010. "The Demographic Antecedents and Performance Consequences of the Social-Network Structure in Work Teams." *Team Performance Management* 16: 388–412.

Higgins, Monica C. and Kathy E. Kram. 2001. "Reconceptualizing Mentoring at Work: A Developmental Network Perspective." *Academy of Management Review* 26: 264–288.

Hite, Julie M. and William S. Hesterly. 2001. "The Evolution of Firm Networks: From Emergence to Early Growth of the Firm." *Strategic Management Journal* 22: 275–286.

Hoang, Ha and Bostjan Antoncic. 2003. "Network-Based Research in Entrepreneurship: A Critical Review." *Journal of Business Venturing* 18: 165–187.

Hodgson, Geoffrey M. 1992. "The Reconstruction of Economics: Is There Still a Place for Neoclassical Theory?" *Journal of Economic Issues* 26: 749–767.

Hodgson, Geoffrey M. 2007. "Evolutionary and Institutional Economics as the New Mainstream." *Evolutionary and Institutional Economics Review* 4: 7–25.

Holzer, Harry J. 1988. "Search Methods Used by Unemployed Youth." *Journal of Labor Economics* 6: 1–20.

Hopkins, Terence and Immanuel Wallerstein. 1986. "Commodity Chains in the World Economy Prior to 1800." *Review* 10: 157–170.

Hoshi, Takeo. 2006. "Economics of the Living Dead." *Japanese Economic Review* 57: 30–49.

Hsu, Carolyn L. 2005. "Capitalism without Contracts versus Capitalists without

Capitalism: Comparing the Influence of Chinese *guanxi* and Russian *blat* on Marketization." *Communist and Post-Communist Studies* 38: 309–327.

Huang, Xianbi. 2008a. "*Guanxi* Networks and Job Searches in China's Emerging Labour Market: A Qualitative Investigation." *Work, Employment and Society* 22: 467–484.

Huang, Xianbi. 2008b. "Boundaries of *Guanxi* Networks: Empirical Evidence from the Emerging Labor Market in China." *Shehui/Society: Chinese Journal of Sociology* 28(6): 39–59.

Hurlbert, Jeanne S. 1991. "Social Networks, Social Circles, and Job Satisfaction." *Work and Occupations* 18: 415–430.

Hyder, Akmal S. and Lars Torsten Ericksson. 2005. "Success is Not Enough: The Spectacular Rise and Fall of a Strategic Alliance between Two Multinationals." *Industrial Marketing Management* 34: 783–796.

Ibarra, Herminia. 1992. "Homophily and Differential Returns: Sex Differences in Network Structure and Access in an Advertising Firm." *Administrative Science Quarterly* 37: 422–447.

Ibarra, Herminia. 1993. "Personal Networks of Women and Minorities in Management: A Conceptual Framework." *Academy of Management Review* 18: 56–87.

Ibarra, Herminia. 1995. "Race, Opportunity, and Diversity of Social Circles in Managerial Networks." *Academy of Management Journal* 38: 673–701.

Ibarra, Herminia. 1997. "Paving an Alternative Route: Gender Differences in Managerial Networks." *Social Psychology Quarterly* 60: 91–102.

Ibarra, Herminia, Nancy M. Carter and Christine Silva. 2010. "Why Men Still Get More Promotions Than Women." *Harvard Business Review* 88: 80–126.

Inkpen, Andrew C. and Eric W. K. Tsang. 2005. "Social Capital, Networks, and Knowledge Transfer." *Academy of Management Review* 30: 146–165.

Jack, Sarah L. 2005. "The Role, Use and Activation of Strong and Weak Network Ties: A Qualitative Analysis." *Journal of Management Studies* 42: 1233–1259.

Jackson, Matthew O. 2008. *Social and Economic Networks*. Princeton, NJ: Princeton University Press.

Jackson, Matthew O. and Alison Watts. 2002. "The Evolution of Social and Economic Networks." *Journal of Economic Theory* 106: 299–321.

Jackson, Matthew O. and Asher Wolinsky. 1996. "A Strategic Model of Social and Economic Networks." *Journal of Economic Theory* 71: 44–74.

Jacobs, David and Benjamin Cornwell. 2007. "Labor Markets and Organizations: A Screening Theory of Hiring Networks and Racially Homogeneous Employment." *Research in Social Stratification and Mobility* 25: 39–55.

Jacobs, Lawrence. 2010. "What Health Reform Teaches Us about American Politics." *PS: Political Science & Politics* 43: 619–623.

Jacobs, Wouter, Cesar Ducruet and Peter De Langen. 2010. "Integrating World Cities into Production Networks: The Case of Port Cities." *Global Networks* 10: 92–113.

Jevons, William Stanley. 1965 [1879]. "Preface to the Second Edition." In *The Theory of Political Economy*, 5th edn. New York: Augustus Kelly, pp. xi–liii.

Jiang, Chunyan and Shuming Zhao. 2009. "Does Stage Matter? The Roles of Organizational Learning, Social Network, and Corporate Entrepreneurship in Chinese New Ventures." *Frontiers of Business Research in China* 3: 362–392.

Jiang, Ruihua Joy, Qingjiu Tom Tao and Michael D. Santoro. 2010. "Alliance Portfolio Diversity and Firm Performance." *Strategic Management Journal* 31: 1136–1144.

Jiang, Xu and Yuan Li. 2009. "An Empirical Investigation of Knowledge Management and Innovative Performance: The Case of Alliances." *Research Policy* 38: 358–368.

Johnson, LuAnne R. and David Knoke. 2004. "'Skonk Works Here': Activating Network Social Capital in Complex Collaborations." *Advances in Interdisciplinary Studies of Work Teams* 10: 243–262.

Johnson-Cramer, Michael, Salvatore Parise and Rob Cross. 2007. "Managing Change through Networks and Values." *California Management Review* 49: 85–109.

Johnston, Michael F. and Rodolfo Alvarez. 2008. "Social Networks and Stratification in the Urban Chinese Labor Market: The Case of Laid-Off Textile Workers and their Officials in the Tianjin Municipality." *Sociological Inquiry* 78: 490–512.

Kahneman, Daniel and Amos Tversky 1979. "Prospect Theory: An Analysis of Decision under Risk." *Econometrica* 47: 263–291.

Kalaignanam, Kartik, Venkatesh Shankar and Rajan Varadarjan. 2007. "Asymmetric New Product Development Alliances: Win-Win or Win-Lose Partnerships?" *Management Science* 53: 357–374.

Kale, Prashant, Harbir Singh and Howard Perlmutter. 2000. "Learning and Protection of Proprietary Assets in Strategic Alliances: Building Relational Capital." *Strategic Management Journal* 21: 217–237.

Kanter, Rosabeth. 1977. *Men and Women of the Corporation*. New York: Basic Books.

Katz, Elihu and Paul F. Lazarsfeld. 1955. *Personal Influence: The Part Played by People in the Flow of Mass Communications*. Glencoe, IL: Free Press.

Katz, Michael L. and Carl Shapiro. 1985. "Network Externalities, Competition, and Compatibility." *American Economic Review* 75: 424–440.

Kaufman, Bruce E. 2007. "The Institutional Economics of John R. Commons: Complement and Substitute for Neoclassical Economic Theory." *Socio-Economic Review* 5: 3–45.

Keen, Steve. 2001. *Debunking Economics: The Naked Emperor of the Social Sciences*. Sydney, Australia: Pluto Press.

Keen, Steve and Russell Standish. 2006. "Profit Maximization, Industry Structure, and Competition: A Critique of Neoclassical Theory." *Physica* 370: 81–85.

Keister, Lisa A. 1998a. "Social Ties and the Formation of Chinese Business Groups." *Sociological Analysis*, 2: 99–118.

Keister, Lisa A. 1998b. "Engineering Growth: Business Group Structure and Firm Performance in China's Transition Economy." *American Journal of Sociology* 104: 404–440.

Keister, Lisa A. 2009. "Interfirm Relations in China: Group Structures and Firm Performance in Business Groups." *American Behavioral Scientist* 52: 1709–1730.

Kenis, Patrick and David Knoke. 2002. "How Organizational Field Networks Shape Interorganizational Tie-Formation Rates." *Academy of Management Review* 27: 275–293.

Kenney, Martin and Richard Florida. 1994. "Japanese Maquiladoras: Production Organization and Global Commodity Chains." *World Development* 22: 27–44.

Kentor, Jeffrey and Yong-Suk Jang. 2004. "Yes, There is a (Growing) Transnational Business Community: A Study of Global Interlocking Directorates 1983–98." *International Sociology* 19: 355–368.

Kentor, Jeffrey and Yong-Suk Jang. 2006. "Different Questions, Different Answers: A Rejoinder to Carroll and Fennema." *International Sociology* 21: 602–606.

Keynes, John Maynard. 1936. *The General Theory of Employment, Interest and Money*. London: Macmillan.

Khanna, Tarun and Krishna Palepu. 1999. "Policy Shocks, Market Intermediaries, and Corporate Strategy: The Evolution of Business Groups in Chile and India." *Journal of Economics and Management Strategy* 8: 271–310.

Khanna, Tarun and Jan W. Rivkin. 2001. "Estimating the Performance Effects of Business Groups in Emerging Markets." *Strategic Management Journal* 22: 45–74.

Khanna, Tarun and Yishay Yafeh. 2005. "Business Groups and Risk Sharing around the World." *Journal of Business* 78: 301–340.

Khanna, Tarun and Yishay Yafeh. 2007. "Business Groups in Emerging Markets: Paragons or Parasites?" *Journal of Economic Literature* 45: 331–372.

Khanna, Tarun, Ranjay Gulati and Nitin Nohria. 1998 "The Dynamics of Learning Alliances: Competition, Cooperation, and Relative Scope." *Strategic Management Journal* 19: 193–210.

Kick, Edward L. and Byron L. Davis. 2001. "World-System Structure and Change: An Analysis of Global Networks and Economic Growth across Two Time Periods." *American Behavioral Scientist* 44: 1561–1578.

Kick, Edward L., Laura A. McKinney, Steve McDonald and Andrew Jorgenson. 2011. "A Multiple-Network Analysis of the World System of Nations, 1995–1999." In *The Sage Handbook of Social Network Analysis*, edited by John Scott and Peter J. Carrington. Thousand Oaks, CA: Sage, pp. 311–327.

Kilduff, Martín and Hongseok Oh. 2006. "Deconstructing Diffusion: An

Ethnostatistical Examination of Medical Innovation Network Data Reanalyses." *Organizational Research Methods* 9: 432–455.

Kilduff, Martin, Craig Crossland, Wenpin Tsai and David Krackhardt. 2008. "Organizational Network Perceptions versus Reality: A Small World After All?" *Organizational Behavior & Human Decision Processes* 107: 15–28.

Kim, Hicheon, Heechun Kim and Robert E. Hoskisson. 2010. "Does Market-Oriented Institutional Change in an Emerging Economy Make Business-Group-Affiliated Multinationals Perform Better? An Institution-Based View." *Journal of International Business Studies* 41: 1141–1160.

Kirzner, Israel. 1973. *Competition and Entrepreneurship*. Chicago, IL: University of Chicago Press.

Kliman, Andrew. 2007. *Reclaiming Marx's Capital: A Refutation of the Myth of Inconsistency*. Lanham, MD: Lexington Books.

Kmec, Julie A. 2007. "Ties That Bind? Race and Networks in Job Turnover." *Social Problems* 54: 483–503.

Kmec, Julie A. and Lindsey B. Trimble. 2009. "Does It Pay to Have a Network Contact? Social Network Ties, Workplace Racial Context, and Pay Outcomes." *Social Science Research* 38: 266–278.

Knight, Frank. 1985 [1921]. *Risk, Uncertainty, and Profit*. Chicago, IL: University of Chicago Press.

Knittel, Christopher R. and Victor Stango. 2010. "Shareholder Value Destruction following the Tiger Woods Scandal." University of California Davis working paper <www.econ.ucdavis.edu/faculty/knittel/papers/Tiger_latest.pdf> (accessed June 19, 2010).

Knoke, David. 1990. *Political Networks: The Structural Perspective*. New York: Cambridge University Press.

Knoke, David. 2001. *Changing Organizations: Business Networks in the New Political Economy*. Boulder, CO: Westview.

Knoke, David. 2009. "Playing Well Together: Creating Corporate Social Capital in Strategic Alliance Networks." *American Behavioral Scientist* 52: 1690–1708.

Knoke, David and Song Yang. 2008. *Social Network Analysis*, 2nd edn. Thousand Oaks, CA: Sage.

Knorr Cetina, Karin. 2004. "Capturing Markets? A Review Essay on Harrison White on Producer Markets." *Socio-Economic Review* 2: 137–147.

Kogut, Bruce and Gordon Walker. 2001. "The Small World of German Corporate Networks in the Global Economy." *American Sociological Review* 66: 317–335.

Krauth, Brian V. 2004. "A Dynamic Model of Job Networking and Social Influences on Employment." *Journal of Economic Dynamics and Control* 28: 1185–1204.

Krippner, Greta R. and Anthony S. Alvarez. 2007. "Embeddedness and the

Intellectual Projects of Economic Sociology." *Annual Review of Sociology* 33: 219–240.

Krugman, Paul. 2009. "How Did Economists Get It So Wrong?" *New York Times Magazine*, September 6.

Kuipers, Kathy J. 2009. "Formal and Informal Network Coupling and its Relationship to Workplace Attachment." *Sociological Perspectives* 52: 455–479.

Kumar, M. V. Shyam. 2010. "Differential Gains Between Partners in Joint Ventures: Role of Resource Appropriation and Private Benefits." *Organization Science* 21: 232–248.

Kunst, Laurien and Jan Kratzer. 2007. "Diffusion of Innovations through Social Networks of Children." *Young Consumers* 8: 36–51.

La Porta, Rafael, Florencio Lopez-de-Silanes, and Andrei Shleifer. 1999. "Corporate Ownership around the World." *Journal of Finance* 54: 471–517.

Labianca, Giuseppe and Daniel J. Brass. 2006. "Exploring the Social Ledger: Negative Relationships and Negative Asymmetry in Social Networks in Organizations." *Academy of Management Review* 31: 596–614.

Lai, Gina, Nan Lin and Shu-Yin Leung. 1998. "Network Resources, Contact Resources, and Status Attainment." *Social Networks* 20: 159–178.

Lan, Pei-Chia. 2002. "Networking Capitalism: Network Construction and Control Effects in Direct Selling." *Sociological Quarterly* 43: 165–184.

Lavie, Dovev. 2008. "Alliance Portfolios and Firm Performance: A Study of Value Creation and Appropriation in the U.S. Software Industry." *Strategic Management Journal* 28: 1187–1212.

Lavie, Dovev and Stewart R. Miller. 2008. "Alliance Portfolio Internationalization and Firm Performance." *Organization Science* 19: 623–646.

Lavie, Dovev and Lori Rosenkopf. 2006. "Balancing Exploration and Exploitation in Alliance Formation." *Academy of Management Journal* 49: 797–818.

Lazarsfeld, Paul F., Bernard Berelson and Hazel Gaudet. 1948. *The People's Choice*. New York: Columbia University Press.

Lechner, Christian, Michael Dowling, and Isabell Welpe. 2006. "Firm Networks and Firm Development: The Role of the Relational Mix." *Journal of Business Venturing* 21: 514–540.

Ledeneva, Alena. 2008. "*Blat* and *Guanxi*: Informal Practices in Russia and China." *Comparative Studies in Society and History* 50: 118–144.

Lee, Keonbeom, Mike W. Peng and Keun Lee. 2008. "From Diversification Premium to Diversification Discount during Institutional Transitions." *Journal of World Business* 43: 47–65.

Lee, Seung Hwan (Mark), June Cotte and Theodore J. Noseworthy. 2010. "The Role of Network Centrality in the Flow of Consumer Influence." *Journal of Consumer Psychology* 20: 66–77.

Leff, Nathaniel H. 1978. "Industrial Organization and Entrepreneurship in the Developing Countries: The Economic Groups." *Economic Development and Cultural Change* 26: 661–675.

Leibenstein, Harvey. 1950. "Bandwagon, Snob and Veblen Effects in the Theory of Consumers' Demand." *Quarterly Journal of Economics* 64: 183–207.

Leitner, Yaron. 2005. "Financial Networks: Contagion, Commitment, and Private Sector Bailouts." *Journal of Finance* 60: 2925–2953.

Levin, Daniel Z. and Rob Cross. 2004. "The Strength of Weak Ties You Can Trust: The Mediating Role of Trust in Effective Knowledge Transfer." *Management Science* 50: 1477–1490.

Levin, Peter. 2008. "Culture and Markets: How Economic Sociology Conceptualizes Culture." *Annals of the American Academy of Political and Social Science* 619: 114–129.

Levine, Michael E. and Jennifer L. Florence. 1990. "Regulatory Capture, Public Interest, and the Public Agenda: Toward a Synthesis." *The Journal of Law, Economics, & Organization* 6: 167–198.

Li, Jing, Changhui Zhou and Edward J. Zajac. 2009. "Control, Collaboration, and Productivity in International Joint Ventures: Theory and Evidence." *Strategic Management Journal* 30: 865–884.

Lievrouw, Leah A. 2009. "New Media, Mediation, and Communication Study." *Information, Communication & Society* 12: 303–325.

Light, Donald W. 2011. "Historical and Comparative Reflections on the U.S. National Health Insurance Reforms." *Social Science & Medicine* 72(2): 129–132.

Lin, Nan. 2001. *Social Capital: A Theory of Social Structure and Action*. New York: Cambridge University Press.

Lin, Nan, Walter M. Ensel and John C. Vaughn. 1981. "Social Resources, Strength of Ties and Occupational Status Attainment." *American Sociological Review* 46: 393–405.

Lin, Zhiang (John), Haibin Yang and Bindu Arya. 2009. "Alliance Partners and Firm Performance: Resource Complementarity and Status Association." *Strategic Management Journal* 30: 921–940.

Lincoln, James R. and Michael Gerlach. 2004. *Japan's Network Economy: Structure, Persistence, and Change*. New York: Cambridge University Press.

Lincoln, James R. and Jon Miller. 1979. "Work and Friendship Ties in Organizations: A Comparative Analysis of Relational Networks." *Administrative Science Quarterly* 24: 181–199.

Lincoln, James R., Michael L. Gerlach, and Christina L. Ahmadjian. 1996. "Keiretsu Networks and Corporate Performance in Japan." *American Sociological Review* 61: 67–88.

Lindsay, Colin, Malcolm Grieg and Ronald W. McQuaid. 2005. "Alternative Job Search Strategies in Remote Rural and Peri-Urban Labour Markets: The Role of Social Networks." *Sociologia Ruralis* 45: 53–70.

Liukkonen, Virpi, Pekka Virtanen, Mika Kivimaki, Jaana Pentti and Jussi Vahtera. 2004. "Social Capital in Working Life and the Health of Employees." *Social Science & Medicine* 59: 2447–2458.

Lonien, Claude. 2007. "Chapter 1. The Old Japanese Keiretsu Model." *The Japanese Economy* 34(3): 5–36.

Lorrain, François and Harrison C. White. 1971. "Structural Equivalence of Individuals in Social Networks." *Journal of Mathematical Sociology* 1: 49–80.

Loscocco, Karyn, Shannon M. Monnat, Gwen Moore and Kirsten B. Lauber. 2009. "Enterprising Women: A Comparison of Women's and Men's Small Business Networks." *Gender & Society* 23: 388–411.

Lunnan, Randi and Sven A. Haugland. 2008. "Predicting and Measuring Alliance Performance: A Multidimensional Analysis." *Strategic Management Journal* 29: 545–556.

Luo, Yadong. 2008. "Structuring Interorganizational Cooperation: The Role of Economic Integration in Strategic Alliances." *Strategic Management Journal* 29: 617–637.

Lüthi, Stefan, Alain Thierstein and Viktor Goebel. 2010. "Intra-Firm and Extra-Firm Linkages in the Knowledge Economy: The Case of the Emerging Mega-City Region of Munich." *Global Networks* 10: 114–137.

M'Chirgui, Zouhaïer. 2010. "Small World Characteristics of Innovative Smart Card Networks." *International Journal of Innovation Management* 14: 221–252.

Macartney, Huw. 2009. "Variegated Neo-Liberalism: Transnationally Oriented Fractions of Capital in EU Financial Market Integration." *Review of International Studies* 35(2): 451–480.

Mahutga, Matthew C. and David A. Smith. 2011. "Globalization, the Structure of the World Economy and Economic Development. *Social Science Research* 40: 257–272.

Mahutga, Matthew C., Xiulian Ma, David A. Smith and Michael F. Timberlake. 2010. "Economic Globalisation and the Structure of the World City System: The Case of Airline Passenger Data." *Urban Studies* 47: 1925–1947.

Mani, Dalhia and David Knoke. 2011. "On Intersecting Ground: The Changing Structure of US Corporate Networks." *Social Network Analysis and Mining* 1: 43–58.

Marsden, Peter V. 1996. "The Staffing Process: Recruitment and Selection Methods." In *Organizations in America: Analyzing Their Structures and Human Resource Practices*, edited by Arne L. Kalleberg, David Knoke, Peter V. Marsden, and Joe L. Spaeth. Newbury Park, CA: Sage Publications, pp. 133–156.

Marsden, Peter V. and Jeanne S. Hurlbert. 1988. "Social Resources and Mobility Outcomes: A Replication and Extension." *Social Forces* 66: 1038–1059.

Marx, Karl. 1981. *Capital*, Vol. 3. London: Penguin.

Marx, Karl. 1989 [1859]. "Preface to A Contribution to the Critique of Political

Economy." In *Karl Marx and Friedrich Engels Selected Works*. Moscow: Progress Publishers.

Mason, Roger. 1995. "Interpersonal Effects on Consumer Demand in Economic Theory and Marketing Thought, 1890–1950." *Journal of Economic Issues* 29: 871–881.

Mason, Roger. 2000. "The Social Significance of Consumption: James Duesenberry's Contribution to Consumer Theory." *Journal of Economic Issues* 34: 553–572.

Matthews, Ralph, Ravi Pendakur and Nathan Young. 2009. "Social Capital, Labour Markets, and Job-Finding in Urban and Rural Regions: Comparing Paths to Employment in Prosperous Cities and Stressed Rural Communities in Canada." *The Sociological Review* 57: 306–330.

Mayer, Adalbert. 2009. "Online Social Networks in Economics." *Decision Support Systems* 47(3): 169–184.

Mayer, Roger C., James H. Davis and F. David Schoorman. 1995. "An Integrative Model of Organizational Trust." *Academy of Management Review* 20: 709–734.

McEvily, Bill, Vincenzo Perrone and Akbar Zaheer. 2003. "Trust as an Organizing Principle." *Organization Science* 14: 91–103.

McGuire, Gail M. 2000. "Gender, Race, Ethnicity, and Networks: The Factors Affecting Status of Employees' Network Members." *Work and Occupations* 27: 500–523.

McGuire, Gail M. 2002. "Gender, Race, and the Shadow Structure: A Study of Informal Networks and Inequality in a Work Organization." *Gender & Society* 16: 303–322.

McGuire, Gail M. 2007. "Intimate Work: A Typology of the Social Support that Workers Provide to their Network Members." *Work and Occupations* 34: 125–147.

McGuire, Jean and Sandra Dow. 2009. "Japanese *Keiretsu*: Past, Present, Future." *Asia Pacific Journal of Management* 26(2): 333–351.

Mesmer-Magnus, Jessica R. and Leslie A. DeChurch. 2009. "Information Sharing and Team Performance: A Meta-Analysis." *Journal of Applied Psychology* 94: 535–546.

Meyer, John W. and Brian Rowan. 1977. "Institutionalized Organizations: Formal Structure as Myth and Ceremony." *American Journal of Sociology* 83: 340–363.

Mikl-Horke, Gertraude. 2008. "Austrian Economics and Economic Sociology: Past Relations and Future Possibilities for a Socio-Economic Perspective." *Socio-Economic Review* 6: 201–226.

Mills, C. Wright. 1956. *The Power Elite*. New York: Oxford University Press.

Mintz, Beth and Michael Schwartz. 1981. "Interlocking Directorates and Interest Group Formation." *American Sociological Review* 46: 851–869.

Mitsuhashi, Hitoshi and Henrich R. Greve. 2009. "A Matching Theory of

Alliance Formation and Organizational Success: Complementarity and Compatibility." *Academy of Management Journal* 52: 975–995.

Mizruchi, Mark S. 1996. "What Do Interlocks Do? An Analysis, Critique, and Assessment of Research on Interlocking Directorates." *Annual Review of Sociology* 22: 271–298.

Mizruchi, Mark S. and Linda Brewster Stearns. 2001. "Getting Deals Done: The Use of Social Networks in Bank Decision-Making." *American Sociological Review* 66: 647–671.

Montgomery, James D. 1992. "Job Search and Network Composition: Implications of the Strength-of-Weak-Ties Hypothesis." *American Sociological Review* 57: 586–596.

Moody, James and Douglas R. White. 2003. "Structural Cohesion and Embeddedness: A Hierarchical Concept of Social Groups."*American Sociological Review* 68: 103–127.

Moreno, Jacob L. 1934. *Who Shall Survive?* Washington, DC: Nervous & Mental Disease Publishing Co.

Morrissey, Brian. 2010. "Apple Dominates Social Brand Ranking." *Adweek* 51(1): 5.

Mouw, Ted. 2006. "Estimating the Causal Effect of Social Capital: A Review of Recent Research." *Annual Review of Sociology* 32: 79–102.

Nagurney, Anna. 2010. "Optimal Supply Chain Network Design and Redesign at Minimal Total Cost and with Demand Satisfaction." *International Journal of Production Economics* 128: 200–208.

Nelson, Richard and Sidney Winter. 1982. *An Evolutionary Theory of Economic Change.* Cambridge, MA: Harvard University Press.

Nooteboom, Bart. 2006. "Simmel's Treatise on the Triad (1908)." *Journal of Institutional Economics* 2: 365–383.

Obstfeld, David. 2005. "Social Networks, the *Tertius Iungens* Orientation, and Involvement in Innovation." *Administrative Science Quarterly* 50: 100–130.

Office of Inspector General. 2010. *Investigative Report – Island Operating Company, et al.* May 24. Washington, DC: US Department of the Interior <abcnews.go.com/images/Politics/MMS_inspector_general_report_pdf.pdf> (accessed May 27, 2010).

Okazaki, Shintaro. 2009. "The Tactical Use of Mobile Marketing: How Adolescents' Social Networking Can Best Shape Brand Extensions." *Journal of Advertising Research* 49: 12–26.

Oksanen, Tuula, Anne Kouvonen, Mika Kivimaki, Jaana Pentti, Marianna Virtanen, Anne Linna and Jussi Vahtera. 2008. "Social Capital at Work as a Predictor of Employee Health: Multilevel Evidence from Work Units in Finland." *Social Science & Medicine* 66: 637–649.

Ozcan, Pinar and Kathleen M. Eisenhardt. 2009. "Origin of Alliance Portfolios: Entrepreneurs, Network Strategies, and Firm Performance."*Academy of Management Journal* 52: 246–279.

Parsons, Stephen D. 2006. "Max Weber and Economic Sociology." *American Journal of Economic and Sociology* 65: 1111–1124.

Parsons, Talcott. 1951. *The Social System*. Glencoe, IL: Free Press.

Parsons, Talcott and Neil J. Smelser. 1956. *Economy and Society: A Study in the Integration of Economics and Social Theory*. London: Routledge & Kegan Paul.

Peluchette, Joy and Katherine Karl. 2010. "Examining Students' Intended Image on Facebook: 'What Were They Thinking?!'" *Journal of Education for Business* 85: 30–37.

Peng, Yusheng. 2004. "Kinship Networks and Entrepreneurs in China's Transitional Economy." *American Journal of Sociology* 109: 1045–1074.

Petersen, Trond, Ishak Saporta and Marc-David L. Seidel. 2000. "Offering a Job: Meritocracy and Social Networks." *American Journal of Sociology* 106: 763–816.

Peukert, Helge. 2004. "Max Weber: Precursor of Economic Sociology and Heterodox Economics?" *American Journal of Economics and Sociology* 63: 987–1020.

Pistor, Katharina. 2009. "Global Network Finance: Institutional Innovation in the Global Financial Market Place." *Journal of Comparative Economics* 37: 552–567.

Podolny, Joel M. 2005. *Status Signals: A Sociological Study of Market Competition*. Princeton, NJ: Princeton University Press.

Podolny, Joel M. and James N. Baron. 1997. "Relationships and Resources: Social Networks and Mobility in the Workplace." *American Sociological Review* 62: 673–693.

Polanyi, Karl. 1957 [1944]. *The Great Transformation*. Boston, MA: Beacon Press.

Polidoro, Francisco, Gautam Ahuja and Will Mitchell. 2011. "When the Social Structure Overshadows Competitive Incentives: The Effects of Network Embeddedness on Joint Venture Dissolution." *Academy of Management Journal* 54: 203–223.

Pollilo, Simone and Mauro Guillén. 2005. "Globalization Pressures and the State: The Global Spread of Central Bank Independence." *American Journal of Sociology* 110: 1764–1802.

Post, Thierry, Martijn J. van den Assem, Guido Baltussen and Richard H. Thaler. 2008. "Deal or No Deal? Decision Making under Risk in a Large-Payoff Game Show." *American Economic Review* 98: 38–71.

Powell, Walter W., Kenneth W. Koput and Laurel Smith-Doerr. 1996. "Interorganizational Collaboration and the Locus of Innovation: Networks of Learning in Biotechnology." *Administrative Science Quarterly* 41: 116–145.

Powell, Walter W., Douglas R. White, Kenneth W. Koput and Jason Owen-Smith. 2005. "Network Dynamics and Field Evolution: The Growth of

Interorganizational Collaboration in the Life Sciences." *American Journal of Sociology* 110: 1132–1205.

Pozner, Jo-Ellen, Mary K. Stimmler and Paul M. Hirsch. 2010. "Terminal Isomorphism and the Self-Destructive Potential of Success: Lessons from Subprime Mortgage Origination and Securitization." *Research in the Sociology of Organizations* 30: 183–216.

Preston, Lee E. 2004. "Reputation as a Source of Corporate Social Capital." *Journal of General Management* 30(2): 43–49.

PRNewswire. 2009. "Perot Systems Announces Strategic Alliance with China Telecom." <www.prnewswire.com/news-releases/perot-systems-announces-strategic-alliance-with-china-telecom-65986717.html> (accessed May 18, 2011).

Provan, Keith G., Amy Fish and Joerg Sydow. 2007. "Interorganizational Networks at the Network Level: A Review of the Empirical Literature on Whole Networks." *Journal of Management* 33: 479–516.

Rappaport, Steven. 1996. "Abstraction and Unrealistic Assumptions in Economics," *Journal of Economic Methodology* 3(2): 215–236.

Reagans, Ray E. and Bill McEvily. 2003. "Network Structure and Knowledge Transfer: The Effects of Cohesion and Range." *Administrative Science Quarterly* 48: 240–267.

Reagans, Ray and Ezra W. Zuckerman. 2001. "Networks, Diversity, and Productivity: The Social Capital of Corporate R&D Teams." *Organization Science* 12: 502–517.

Reagans, Ray, Ezra Zuckerman and Bill McEvily. 2004. "How to Make the Team: Social Networks vs. Demography as Criteria for Designing Effective Teams." *Administrative Science Quarterly* 49: 101–133.

Ren, Bing, Kevin Y. Au and Thomas A. Birtch. 2009. "China's Business Network Structure during Institutional Transitions." *Asia Pacific Journal of Management* 26: 219–240.

Ren, Hong and Barbara Gray. 2009. "Repairing Relationship Conflict: How Violation Types and Culture Influence the Effectiveness of Restoration Rituals." *Academy of Management Review* 34: 105–126.

Renzulli, Linda A. and Howard E. Aldrich. 2005. "Who Can You Turn To? Tie Activation within Core Business Discussion Networks." *Social Forces* 84: 323–341.

Renzulli, Linda A., Howard E. Aldrich and James Moody. 2000. "Family Matters: Gender, Networks, and Entrepreneurial Outcomes." *Social Forces* 79: 523–546.

Reuer, Jeffrey J. and Maurizio Zollo. 2005. "Termination Outcomes of Research Alliances." *Research Policy* 34: 101–115.

Reuer, Jeffrey J., Maurizio Zollo and Harbir Singh. 2002. "Post-Formation Dynamics in Strategic Alliances." *Strategic Management Journal* 23: 135–151.

Robinson, John P. 1976. "Interpersonal Influence in Election Campaigns: Two Step-flow Hypothesis." *Public Opinion Quarterly* 40: 304–319.

Robinson, William I. and Jerry Harris. 2000. "Towards a Global Ruling Class? Globalization and the Transnational Capitalist Class." *Science & Society* 64: 11–54.

Rodan, Simon. 2010. "Structural Holes and Managerial Performance: Identifying the Underlying Mechanisms." *Social Networks* 32: 168–179.

Roethlisberger, Fritz J. and William J. Dickson. 1939. *Management and the Worker*. Cambridge, MA: Harvard University Press.

Rogers, Everett M. 1962. *The Diffusion of Innovations*. New York: Free Press.

Rogers, Everett M. and Floyd F. Shoemaker. 1971. *Communication of Innovations: A Cross-Cultural Approach*. New York: Free Press.

Romanelli, Elaine. 1991. "The Evolution of New Organizational Forms." *Annual Review of Sociology* 17: 79–103.

Rosenkopf, Lori and Giovanna Padula. 2008. "The Microstructure of Network Evolution: An Empirical Investigation of Alliance Formation in the Mobile Communications Industry." *Organization Science* 19: 669–687.

Rousseau, Denise M., S.B. Sitkin, Ronald S. Burt and C. Camerer. 1998. "Not So Different After All: A Cross-Disciplinary View of Trust." *Academy of Management Review* 23: 393–404.

Rowley, Timothy J., Henrich R. Greve, Hayagreeva Rao, Joel A.C. Baum and Andrew V. Shipilov. 2005. "Time to Break Up: Social and Instrumental Antecedents of Firm Exits from Exchange Cliques." *Academy of Management Journal* 48: 499–520.

Ryan, Bryce and Neal C. Gross. 1943. "The Diffusion of Hybrid Seed Corn in Two Iowa Communities." *Rural Sociology* 8: 15–24.

Salk, Jane E. and Mary Yoko Brannen. 2000. "National Culture, Networks, and Individual Influence in a Multinational Management Team." *Academy of Management Journal* 43: 191–202.

Sassen, Saskia. 1991. *The Global City: New York, London and Tokyo*. Princeton, NJ: Princeton University Press.

Sassen, Saskia. 2002. "Locating Cities on Global Circuits." *Environment & Urbanization* 14: 13–30.

Sassen, Saskia. 2010. "Global Inter-City Networks and Commodity Chains: Any Intersections?" *Global Networks* 10: 150–163.

Schilling, Melissa A. and Corey C. Phelps. 2007. "Interfirm Collaboration Networks: The Impact of Large-Scale Network Structure on Firm Innovation." *Management Science* 53: 1113–1126.

Schmidt, Klaus-Helmut. 2007. "Organizational Commitment: A Further Moderator in the Relationship between Work Stress and Strain?" *International Journal of Stress Management* 14: 26–40.

Schumpeter, Joseph A. 1934 [1912]. *The Theory of Economic Development*. Cambridge, MA: Harvard University Press.

Schumpeter, Joseph A. 1942. *Capitalism, Socialism and Democracy*. New York: Harper.

Schweitzer, Frank, Giorgio Fagiolo, Didier Sornette, Fernando Vega-Redondo, Alessandro Vespignani and Douglas R. White. 2009. "Economic Networks: The New Challenges." *Science* 325(July 24): 422–425.

Scott, John. 2000. *Social Network Analysis: A Handbook*, 2nd edn. London: Sage.

Scott, W. Richard. 2001. *Institutions and Organizations*, 2nd edn. Thousand Oaks, CA: Sage.

Shah, Reshma H. and Vanitha Swaminathan. 2008. "Factors Influencing Partner Selection in Strategic Alliances: The Moderating Role of Alliance Context." *Strategic Management Journal* 29: 471–494.

Shi, Weilei (Stone), Livia Markoczy and Gregory G. Dess. 2009. "The Role of Middle Management in the Strategy Process: Group Affiliation, Structural Holes, and Tertius Iungens." *Journal of Management* 35: 1453–1480.

Shin, Kyoung-Ho and Michael F. Timberlake. 2000. "World Cities in Asia: Cliques, Centrality and Connectedness." *Urban Studies* 37: 2257–2285.

Shropshire, Christine. 2010. "The Role of the Interlocking Director and Board Receptivity in the Diffusion of Practices." *Academy of Management Review* 35: 246–264.

Simmel, Georg. 1955 [1922]. *Conflict and The Web of Group Affiliations*, translated and edited by Kurt Wolff and Reinhard Bendix. Glencoe, IL: Free Press.

Simmel, Georg. 1950. *The Sociology of Georg Simmel*, compiled and translated by Kurt H. Wolff. Glencoe, IL: Free Press.

Simon, Herbert A. 1957. *Models of Man: Social and Rational*. New York: Wiley.

Singh, Deeksha S. and Ajai S. Gaur. 2009. "Business Group Affiliation, Firm Governance, and Firm Performance: Evidence from China and India." *Corporate Governance: An International Review* 17: 411–425.

Sirmon, David G. and Peter J. Lane. 2004. "A Model of Cultural Differences and International Alliance Performance." *Journal of International Business Studies* 35: 306–319.

Sklair, Leslie. 1997. "Social Movements for Global Capitalism: The Transnational Capitalist Class in Action." *Review of International Political Economy* 4: 514–538.

Sklair, Leslie. 2001. *The Transnational Capitalist Class*. Oxford: Blackwell.

Skocpol, Theda. 2010. "The Political Challenges that May Undermine Health Reform." *Health Affairs* 29: 1288–1292.

Slotte-Kock, Susanna and Nicole Coviello. 2010. "Entrepreneurship Research on Network Processes: A Review and Ways Forward." *Entrepreneurship: Theory & Practice* 34: 31–57.

Smångs, Mattias. 2006. "The Nature of the Business Group: A Social Network Perspective." *Organization* 13: 889–909.

Smelser, Neil J. and Richard Swedberg. 2005. "Introducing Economic Sociology." In *The Handbook of Economic Sociology*, 2nd edn. Princeton, NJ: Princeton University Press, pp. 2–25.

Smith, Adam. 1937 [1776]. *An Inquiry into the Nature and Causes of the Wealth of Nations*. New York: Modern Library.

Smith, David A. and Michael F. Timberlake. 1995. "Conceptualising and Mapping the Structure of the World System's City System." *Urban Studies* 32: 287–302.

Smith, Ted, James R. Coyle, Elizabeth Lightfoot and Amy Scott. 2007. "Reconsidering Models of Influence: The Relationship between Consumer Social Networks and Word-of-Mouth Effectiveness." *Journal of Advertising Research* 47: 387–397.

Snyder, David and Edward L. Kick. 1979. "Structural Position in the World System and Economic Growth 1955–1970: A Multiple-Network Analysis of Transnational Interactions." *American Journal of Sociology* 84: 1096–1126.

Snyder, Peter J., Richard L. Priem and Edward Levitas. 2009. "The Diffusion of Illegal Innovations among Management Elites." *Academy of Management Annual Meeting Proceedings*, pp. 1–6.

Sorenson, Olav and Toby E. Stuart. 2001. "Syndication Networks and the Spatial Distribution of Venture Capital Investments." *American Journal of Sociology* 106: 1546–1588.

Stafsudd, Anna. 2009. "Corporate Networks as Informal Governance Mechanisms: A Small Worlds Approach to Sweden." *Corporate Governance: An International Review* 17: 62–76.

Staples, Clifford L. 2007. "Board Globalization in the World's Largest TNCs 1993–2005." *Corporate Governance: An International Review* 15: 311–21.

Staples, Clifford L. 2008. "Cross-Border Acquisitions and Board Globalization in the World's Largest TNCS, 1995–2005." *Sociological Quarterly* 49: 31–51.

Stark, David and Balázs Vedres. 2006. "Social Times of Network Spaces: Network Sequences and Foreign Investment in Hungary." *American Journal of Sociology* 111: 1367–1411.

Street, Christopher T. and Ann-Frances Cameron. 2007. "External Relationships and the Small Business: A Review of Small Business Alliance and Network Research." *Journal of Small Business Management* 45: 239–266.

Stuart, Toby E. 1998. "Network Positions and Propensity to Collaborate: An Investigation of Strategic Alliance Formation in High-Technology Industry." *Administrative Science Quarterly* 43: 668–698.

Stuart, Toby E. 2000. "Interorganizational Alliances and the Performance of Firms: A Study of Growth and Innovation Rates in a High-Technology Industry." *Strategic Management Journal* 21: 791–811.

Stuart, Toby E. and Soojin Yim. 2010. "Board Interlocks and the Propensity to be Targeted in Private Equity Transactions." *Journal of Financial Economics* 97: 174–189.

Swaminathan, Vanitha and Christine Moorman. 2009. "Marketing Alliances,

Firm Networks, and Firm Value Creation." *Journal of Marketing* 73(5): 52–69.

Swedberg, Richard. 1998. *Max Weber and the Idea of Economic Sociology*. Princeton, NJ: Princeton University Press.

Swedberg, Richard. 2003. *Principles of Economic Sociology*. Princeton, NJ: Princeton University Press.

Tabb, William K. 2009. "Globalization Today: At the Borders of Class and State Theory." *Science & Society* 73: 34–53.

Tarde, Gabriel. 1969. *On Communication and Social Influence. Selected Papers*, edited by Terry N. Clark. Chicago, IL: University of Chicago Press.

Taylor, Peter J. 2000. "World Cities and Territorial States under Conditions of Contemporary Globalization." *Political Geography* 19(1): 5–32.

Taylor, Peter J. 2004. "Regionality in the World City Network." *International Social Science Journal* 56: 361–372.

Taylor, Peter J. 2005. "Leading World Cities: Empirical Evaluations of Urban Nodes in Multiple Networks." *Urban Studies* 42(9): 1593–1608.

Taylor, Peter J. and Rolee Aranya. 2008. "A Global 'Urban Roller Coaster'? Connectivity Changes in the World City Network, 2000–2004." *Regional Studies* 42: 1–16.

Taylor, Peter J., G. Catalano and D.R.F. Walker. 2002. "Exploratory Analysis of the World City Network." *Urban Studies* 39: 2377–2394.

Teichert, Thorsten A. and Katja Schöntag. 2010. "Exploring Consumer Knowledge Structures Using Associative Network Analysis." *Psychology & Marketing* 27: 369–398.

Thornton, Patricia H. 1998. "The Sociology of Entrepreneurship." *Annual Review of Sociology* 25: 19–46.

Tichy, Noel M. and Charles J. Fombrun. 1979. "Network Analysis in Organizational Settings." *Human Relations* 32: 923–965.

Tichy, Noel M., Michael Tushman and Charles J. Fombrun. 1979. "Social Network Analysis for Organizations." *Academy of Management Review* 4: 507–519.

Todeva, Emanuela and David Knoke. 2002. "Strategische Allianzen und Sozialkapital von Unternehmen." ("Strategic Alliances and Corporate Social Capital") *Kölner Zeitschrift für Sociologie und Sozialpsychologie*. Sonderheft 42: 345–380.

Todeva, Emanuela and David Knoke. 2005. "Strategic Alliances and Models of Collaboration." *Management Decision* 43: 123–148.

Tsai, Wenpin. 2001. "Knowledge Transfer in Intraorganizational Networks: Effects of Network Position and Absorptive Capacity on Business Unit Innovation and Performance." *Academy of Management Journal* 44: 996–104.

US Census Bureau. 2006. "Half of U.S. Businesses Are Home-Based, Majority of Firms Self-Financed, Census Bureau Reports." Press Release, September 27.

<www.census.gov/newsroom/releases/archives/business_ownership/cb06-148.html> (accessed October 24, 2010).

Ulset, Svein. 2008. "The Rise and Fall of Global Network Alliances." *Industrial and Corporate Change* 17: 267–300.

Urbina, Ian. 2010. "Inspector General's Inquiry Faults Regulators." *New York Times*, May 24. <www.nytimes.com> (accessed May 27, 2010).

Uzzi, Brian. 1996. "The Sources and Consequences of Embeddedness for the Economic Performance of Organizations: The Network Effect." *American Sociological Review* 61: 674–698.

Uzzi, Brian and Ryan Lancaster. 2004. "Embeddedness and Price Formation in the Corporate Law Market." *American Sociological Review* 69: 319–344.

Uzzi, Brian and Jarrett Spiro. 2005. "Collaboration and Creativity: The Small World Problem." *American Journal of Sociology* 111: 447–504.

Valente, Thomas W. 1995. *Network Models of the Diffusion of Innovations.* Cresskill, NJ: Hampton Press.

Valente, Thomas W. 1996. "Social Network Thresholds in the Diffusion of Innovations." *Social Networks* 18: 69–89.

Valente, Thomas W. and Patchareeya Pumpuang. 2007. "Identifying Opinion Leaders to Promote Behavior Change." *Health Education & Behavior* 34: 881–896.

van Apeldoorn, Bastiaan. 2000. "Transnational Class Agency and European Governance: The Case of the European Round Table of Industrialists." *New Political Economy* 5: 157–181.

van der Pijl, Kees. 2007. "Capital and the State System: A Class Act." *Cambridge Review of International Affairs* 20: 619–637.

van Emmerik, I.J. Hetty and Veerle Brenninkmeijer. 2009. "Deep-Level Similarity and Group Social Capital: Associations with Team Functioning." *Small Group Research* 40: 650–669.

Van Rossem, Ronan. 1996. "The World-System Paradigm as General Theory of Development: A Cross-National Test." *American Sociological Review* 61: 508–527.

van Veen, Kees and Jan Kratzer. 2011. "National and International Interlocking Directorates within Europe: Corporate Networks within and among Fifteen European Countries." *Economy and Society* 40: 1–25.

Vanhaverbeke, Wim, Victor Gilsing, Bonnie Beerkens and Geert Duysters. 2009. "The Role of Alliance Network Redundancy in the Creation of Core and Non-core Technologies." *Journal of Management Studies* 46: 215–244.

Vanhonacker, Wilfried R. 2004. "*Guanxi* Networks in China: How to be the Spider, Not the Fly." *China Business Review* 31(3): 48–53.

Veblen, Thorstein. 1899. *The Theory of the Leisure Class: An Economic Study of the Evolution of Institutions*. New York: Macmillan.

Vedres, Balázs and David Stark. 2010. "Structural Folds: Generative Disruption in Overlapping Groups." *American Journal of Sociology* 115: 1150–1190.

Velthuis, Olav. 2005. *Talking Prices: Symbolic Meanings of Prices on the Market for Contemporary Art*. Princeton, NJ: Princeton University Press.

Verspagen, Bart and Geert Duysters. 2004. "The Small Worlds of Strategic Technology Alliances." *Technovation* 23: 563–571.

Wallerstein, Immanuel. 1974. *The Modern World-System*. New York: Academic Press.

Wallerstein, Immanuel. 1979. *The Capitalist World-Economy*. Cambridge: Cambridge University Press.

Wank, David L. 1996. "Institutional Process of Market Clientelism: *Guanxi* and Private Business in a South China City." *The China Quarterly* 147: 820–838.

Wasserman, Stanley and Katherine Faust. 1994. *Social Network Analysis: Methods and Applications*. New York: Cambridge University Press.

Wassmer, Ulrich. 2008. "Alliance Portfolios: A Review and Research Agenda." *Journal of Management* 36: 141–171.

Watts, Duncan J. 1999. "Networks, Dynamics, and the Small-World Phenomenon." *American Journal of Sociology* 105: 493–528.

Watts, Duncan J. and Steven H. Strogatz. 1998. "Collective Dynamics of 'Small-World' Networks." *Nature* 393: 440–442.

Weber, Max. 1930 [1904]. *The Protestant Ethic and the Spirit of Capitalism*. New York: Scribners.

Weber, Max. 1946 [1922a]. "Bureaucracy." In *From Max Weber: Essays in Sociology*, edited by H.H. Gerth and C. Wright Mills. New York: Oxford University Press, pp. 196–244.

Weber, Max. 1947 [1922b]. *Economy and Society* Vol. 1. Citations from *The Theory of Social and Economic Organization*, edited and translated by Talcott Parsons. New York: Oxford University Press.

Weber, Max. 1978 [1922c]. "The Nature of Social Action." In *Weber: Selections in Translation*, edited by Walter G. Runciman, translated by Eric Matthews. Cambridge: Cambridge University Press, pp. 1–32.

Wegge, Jürgen, Klaus-Helmut Schmidt, Carole Parkes and Rolf van Dick. 2007. "Taking a Sickie: Job Satisfaction and Job Involvement as Interactive Predictors of Absenteeism in a Public Organization." *Journal of Occupational and Organizational Psychology* 80: 77–89.

Weimann, Gabriel. 1982. "On the Importance of Marginality: One More Step into the Two-Step Flow of Communication." *American Sociological Review* 47: 764–773.

Weimann, Gabriel. 1983. "The Strength of Weak Conversational Ties in the Flow of Information and Influence." *Social Networks* 5: 245–267.

Westphal, James D., Steven Boivie and Daniel Han Ming Chng. 2006. "The Strategic Impetus for Social Network Ties: Reconstituting Broken CEO Friendship Ties." *Strategic Management Journal* 27: 425–445.

White, Douglas R., Jason Owen-Smith, James Moody, and Walter W.

Powell. 2004. "Networks, Fields and Organizations." *Computational and Mathematical Organization Theory* 10: 95–117.

White, Harrison C. 1981. "Where Do Markets Come From?" *American Journal of Sociology* 87: 517–547.

White, Harrison C. 1993. "Markets in Production Networks." In *Explorations in Economic Sociology*, edited by R. Swedberg. New York: Russell Sage Foundation, pp. 161–175.

White, Harrison C. 2002a. *Markets from Networks: Socioeconomic Models of Production*. Princeton, NJ: Princeton University Press.

White, Harrison C. 2002b. "Markets and Firms: Notes Toward the Future of Economic Sociology." In *The New Economic Sociology: Developments in An Emerging Field*, edited by Mauro Guillén, Randall Collins, Paula England and Marshall Meyer. New York: Russell Sage Foundation, pp. 129–147.

White, Harrison C. 2003. "Autonomy vs. Equivalence within Market Network Structure?" In *Dynamic Social Network Modeling and Analysis*, edited by Ronald Breiger, Kathleen Carley and Philippa Pattison. Washington, DC: National Research Council, pp. 78–88.

White, Harrison C., Scott A. Boorman and Ronald L. Breiger. 1976. "Social Structure from Multiple Networks. I. Blockmodels of Roles and Positions." *American Journal of Sociology* 81: 730–779.

Williamson, Oliver E. 1975. *Markets and Hierarchies, Analysis and Antitrust Implications: A Study in the Economics of Internal Organization*. New York: Free Press.

Wittek, Rafael. 2001. "Mimetic Trust and Intra-Organizational Network Dynamics." *Journal of Mathematical Sociology* 25: 109–138.

Wortham, Jenna. 2009. More Employers Use Social Networks to Check Out Applicants. *New York Times*, August 20. <bits.blogs.nytimes.com/2009/08/20/more-employers-use-social-networks-to-check-out-applicants> (accessed May 23, 2010).

Xiao, Zhixing and Anne S. Tsui. 2007. "When Brokers May Not Work: The Cultural Contingency of Social Capital in Chinese High-tech Firms." *Administrative Science Quarterly* 52: 1–31.

Yakubovich, Valery. 2005. "Weak Ties, Information, and Influence: How Workers Find Jobs in a Local Russian Labor Market." *American Sociological Review* 70: 408–421.

Yi, Lee Mei and Paul Ellis. 2000. "Insider-Outsider Perspectives of *Guanxi*." *Business Horizons* (January–February): 25–30.

Yoshino, Michael Y. and U. Srinivasa Rangan. 1995. *Strategic Alliances: An Entrepreneurial Approach to Globalization*. Cambridge, MA: Harvard University Press.

Zaheer, Akbar and Giuseppe Soda. 2009. "Network Evolution: The Origins of Structural Holes." *Administrative Science Quarterly* 54: 1–31.

Zaheer, Akbar, Remzi Gözübüyük and Hana Milanov. 2010. "It's the

Connections: The Network Perspective in Interorganizational Research." *Academy of Management Perspectives* 24: 62–77.
Zelizer, Viviana A. 1994. *Pricing the Priceless Child*. Princeton, NJ: Princeton University Press.
Zelizer, Viviana A. 2005. *The Purchase of Intimacy*. Princeton, NJ: Princeton University Press.

Index

Index

Index